En la vida todo es verdad y todo mentira
Sueños hay que verdad son

European Masterpieces
Cervantes & Co. Spanish Classics Nº 78

Founding Editor: Tom Lathrop
Cervantes Society of America

General Editor: Matthew Wyszynski
University of Akron

Pedro Calderón de la Barca

En la vida todo es verdad y todo mentira

Sueños hay que verdad son

Edited by

John Slater
University of California, Davis

and

Harrison Meadows
University of Tennessee, Knoxville

NEWARK ✤ DELAWARE

Cover photograph by Mar Rey Bueno.

Cervantes & Co. Spanish Classics #78

European Masterpieces
An imprint of LinguaText, LLC.
103 Walker Way
Newark, Delaware 19711-6119 USA
(302) 453-8695
Fax: (302) 453-8601

MANUFACTURED IN THE UNITED STATES OF AMERICA

ISBN: 978-1-58977-119-2

*For our teachers at Earlham College
and Furman University*

Acknowledgements

WE STARTED THINKING ABOUT *En la vida todo es verdad y todo mentira*, a play about people living high in the mountains, in Boulder, Colorado. The faculty and students of the University of Colorado had a great hand in shaping the final outcome of this book and we are grateful to them, especially to Julio Baena, Andrés Prieto, and Núria Silleras Fernández. The University of Colorado's Center for the Humanities and the Arts provided fellowship funds. Inspiring views of the high places have had a hand here, too.

This edition of *Sueños hay que verdad son* began as a transcription of Pedro Pando y Mier's *Autos sacramentales, alegóricos y historiales* (1717) undertaken by John Slater. Many University of Colorado students helped standardize and modernize spelling and punctuation by checking against Ángel Valbuena Prat's edition of Calderón's *Obras completas*. A great debt is owed to Michael McGaha, who kindly allowed us to follow the corrections and emendations he made in his critical edition of *Sueños hay que verdad son*. We have also made a number of additions to follow his line numbering. Anyone who is serious about knowing this play better should consult McGaha's edition of the play and his other works on the representation of Joseph in medieval and early modern Spanish literature.

We began our edition of *En la vida...* by transcribing the published edition of 1665. Many patient students helped us with corrections and suggestions, especially Diana López-Ferretti, John Giblin, Rebeca Rubio and Evan Brown. We also consulted Don William Cruickshank's marvelous edition of the play, as our notes below indicate.

Students, friends, and colleagues have been generous with their time and suggestions throughout the preparation of these plays. This edition is a testament to that generosity and their enthusiasm. To all of you, we say, thank you. We hope that you have as much fun reading these plays as we have had preparing them for you.

Table of Contents

Introduction to Students

About This Book

THE BOOK YOU ARE holding contains two plays by Pedro Calderón de la Barca: *En la vida todo es verdad y todo mentira* and *Sueños hay que verdad son*. There are three reasons we published these plays and published them together. First, and most basic, our hope is that this book will help undergraduate students enjoy two marvelous plays—one a *comedia* and the other an *auto sacramental*—by Calderón. Secondly, we hope that this book will help students understand more about a number of motifs that many readers associate with Calderón's plays: dreaming, the limitations of the senses, and human beings' ability to distinguish between what is real and what is not. Third, students interested in writing research papers or learning more about the sources of Calderón's works will find these plays are an excellent point of departure. Both plays in this edition have fascinating things to say about how literature represents the passage of time; Calderón drew inspiration for both plays, at least to some degree, from the works of a previous playwright named Antonio Mira de Amescua. *En la vida todo es verdad y todo mentira* seems to draw on Mira de Amescua's *La rueda de la Fortuna*; Michael McGaha shows in his edition that *Sueños hay que verdad son* owes a significant debt to Mira de Amescua's *El más feliz cautiverio*. There is more research to be done on the relationships between Calderón's plays and those of his contemporaries and there is no reason that this work shouldn't be done by students like you. Throughout the text, we point out a number of instances in which Calderón alludes to earlier works of literature. You may recognize some of these references, or none of them. The important thing to know is that Calderón takes a preexisting framework for his plots, and then fleshes out those plots with bits and pieces of works by other authors, tales and legends, as well as with many original ideas and sublimely beautiful language. This synthesis allows Calderón's plays to comment broadly on Spanish literature.

Some students who read this book will already be familiar with one of Calderón's most famous plays, *La vida es sueño*, and what it says about dreams. The two plays in this edition help give a fuller picture of Calderón's ideas about dreaming and how human beings are able to acquire knowledge. What writers meant by "dreaming" during the seventeenth century was quite complicated. For many authors and philosophers, dreaming was a way to learn about the world that did not depend on the five senses. Dreams could be false, or they could be true. So sometimes "dreaming" means almost the same thing as "being deceived." At other times dreams are one of the ways that we learn about things that cannot be seen with the naked eye.

One contemporary of Calderón's named Pedro Rodríguez de Monforte wrote an entire book about dreams entitled *Sueños misteriosos de la escritura*. Rodríguez de Monforte believed that when we dream our powers of understanding are active, but they are not limited by the rules of reason; Rodríguez de Monforte called this "a restriction of the senses that leaves the superior powers of the soul unrestrained" (5).[1] You might almost say that for Rodríguez de Monforte, dreaming is like thinking with the soul.

Many authors were interested in how dreaming might offer a model of understanding in a world of uncertainty. Reading these two plays by Calderón together helps readers understand the playwright's nuanced understanding of dreaming, reason, illusion, and the operations of the mind.

THEATER IN SEVENTEENTH-CENTURY SPAIN

The seventeenth century was a wonderful time for theater in Spain. The year was divided into seasons, which roughly followed the reli-

---

[1] "aunque tal vez en sueños parece que actúa el entendimiento, es sin aquellas reglas que dispone la razón... [es] un embargo de los sentidos exteriores dejando las potencias de la porción superior del Alma" (Rodríguez de Monforte 5).

gious calendar of the Roman Catholic Church. Each season had its own kind of dramatic spectacle. The season for commercial theaters in a city like Madrid started in Easter. Commercial theaters offered playgoers long afternoons of entertainment that included music, drama, and dancing. People went to the theater to see more than just a play; they went for a show, a production, and an hours-long spectacle. The centerpiece of such an afternoon would be a *comedia*, a play that could be serious or humorous. *Comedias* were written in verse, were generally about 3000 verses long, and were divided into three acts or *jornadas*. Before, after, and between the acts of the *comedia*, there were short skits called *entremeses* (often very funny), spirited dances, and songs.

The show started with music, perhaps sung or played on the guitar; next there would be a *loa*, a poem recited to warm up the crowd or a brief skit (Arellano 62). The *comedia* would start after the *loa*. After each act, there might be dancing or an *entremés*, and after the third (final) act, there would be a *mojiganga* or "fin de fiesta." *Mojigangas* and *entremeses* were usually silly and very often erotic. *Comedias* are sometimes about honor; *entremeses* are generally about dishonesty (and very often about marital infidelity). You can think of this afternoon of theater (including the *comedia*, *entremeses*, dancing, music and so on) as forming a complete dramatic spectacle. The meaning of this spectacle could be modulated by adding or substituting parts. (Was the *comedia* too heavy or dark? It could be punched up with an especially funny *entremés* between the acts.) So for spectators, the meaning of the dramatic spectacle would be shaped by the interplay of the *comedia* and the *entremés*, the music and the dancing.[2]

Philip III (Felipe III), the king who ruled Spain from 1598-1621, loved plays and went to the theater himself. His son, King Philip IV (Felipe IV), had his own palace theater that showed complicated *comedias* with marvelous stage designs and effects. Some of the set designs included mountains that opened up to reveal enchanted palaces

---

2 *En la vida...* inspired at least one *loa* and an *entremés*. María-Luisa Lobato points out that Calderón poked fun at his own play, parodying *En la vida...* in an *entremés* entitled *El triunfo de Juan Rana* (Calderón, *Teatro cómico* 554-55). Sor Juana Inés de la Cruz wrote a *loa* or introduction to the play that includes phrases from Calderón's original (523).

inside them (Ruano de la Haza and Allen 419-426). A similar set design might have been used for one of the plays in this book—*En la vida, todo es verdad y todo mentira*—which was originally written for the private entertainment of Philip IV and his guests. Opportunities to see a *comedia* alongside the king were highly prized by noblemen and officials.

Kings may have loved plays, but at times commercial theaters were closed by law for months or even years at a time. Theaters might be shut down to show respect for a death in the royal family, as when the son of Philip IV, Prince Baltasar Carlos, died in 1646. But the fact that the theaters were closed does not mean there were no dramatic spectacles to be seen. During these somber occasions, large temporary monuments called *túmulos* were built in churches or in city squares. Commemorative events organized around the *túmulo* would be another kind of dramatic spectacle. Theaters were also closed for the seasons of Advent and Lent. At these times, important churches and cathedrals would invite religious leaders to preach sermons; these preachers were often quite famous and renowned for their skills at oratory. Sermons may have marked the holiest occasions in the life of the Church, but they could also be highly theatrical. So throughout the year, the residents of Spain's cities had access to dramatic spectacles in the street, in churches, and in theaters.

One of the most important seasons for religious plays followed the feast day or holiday called Corpus Christi. It is a springtime festival, falling 60 days after Easter, always on a Thursday and either in late May or June. "Corpus Christi" means "the body of Christ" and the festival was a time to contemplate how the body of Jesus Christ became present in the bread and wine of Communion. In other words, it is a festival in honor of the Eucharist. As Charles Davis and John E. Varey explain, Corpus Christi was "the supreme dramatic occasion in the year" (291). One of the most anticipated parts of the Corpus Christi celebrations was the staging of two *autos sacramentales,* such as *Sueños hay que verdad son* (the second play in this book). An *auto sacramental,* sometimes called simply an *auto,* was a one-act allegorical play, written in verse about the Eucharist; Calderón was the undisputed master of the genre. Marcel Bataillon points out that May and June were wonderful times to be outdoors in Madrid, people were ready for a celebration, and *autos* were performed on movable carts or *carros* in the open air (460).

The word "cart" hardly does justice to the plays' elaborate staging; towers and scenery were constructed on top of the carts, and a number of carts would be combined to make a temporary, but lavish stage. John E. Varey describes the carts concisely:

> The center cart was flat and provided the main playing area. Two other carts were attached to the ends of the central cart, and these bore a box-like structure on two levels. The upper of these two levels contained machinery for stage effects, and the lower level served both as a *vestuario* for the actors not on stage, and as the location of part of the action… The dramatist shaped his material in such a way that it could be performed in the manner described in an open street or square, with the audience clustered round on two sides, approximating the conditions of theatre in the round. ("The Staging," 299-300)[3]

The actors (both men and women) wore sumptuous costumes. After performing the *auto* in Madrid for Corpus Christi, theatrical troupes would take their shows on the road, slowly drawing their carts to the villages and towns surrounding Madrid to perform *autos* and *comedias* during local festivals (Davis and Varey). This meant that people from all walks of life, whether in the capital of Madrid or in outlying villages, were able to see works by Calderón.

Theater's popularity did not insulate it from controversy. Some religious leaders believed that plays were an unseemly, distasteful, and even sinful entertainment. The thought that actors of dubious character played the roles of saints and the Virgin Mary horrified some. García de Loaisa y Girón complained in 1598 that most sins involved only one of the five senses at a time, but plays tricked all the senses into

---

3 *Sueños hay que verdad son* was staged on four carts. McGaha's diagram for the 1670 staging of the play indicates that the arrangement of the carts was somewhat different than in Varey's description ("Introducción" 58). Varey describes the staging for *Sueños hay que verdad son* in *Cosmovisión y escenografía* (346-348).

sinning; he said that "en las comedias" the ears are soiled "con lo que oyen," the eyes are tainted "con lo que ven" and the very soul burns with "el mal deseo" (Cotarelo 394). Some people complained that university students spent all of their time going to the theater: "con [las comedias] se distraen los estudiantes y se perturban los estudios" (Cotarelo 163). Other religious figures believed that theater and university studies made a good combination. Luis Pueyo y Abadía, late in the seventeenth century, wrote that "…venir a la universidad es bueno, ir a la comedia no lo tengo por malo, pero la junta de Universidad y Teatro" makes students reasonable people (14). These controversies suggest that theater was on the minds of many in Spain during the life of Calderón.

Pedro Calderón de la Barca

Calderón's life was extraordinary. He was, of course, a successful playwright. But his pursuits were not limited to literature. Calderón was wounded in wartime, studied at the best schools, was caught up in intrigue, and later in life became a priest. He was at home in the rarified world of the royal court, and also wrote plays—such as *La plazuela de Santa Cruz*—about life in the streets of Madrid (Calderón, *Teatro cómico breve*).

He was born in 1600. Like many members of the intellectual elite during his day, Calderón was educated at the Jesuit *Colegio Imperial*, beginning in 1608. He studied theology at the university in Alcalá de Henares and later learned canon law (the law of the Church) at the university in Salamanca. By 1619 he had finished his studies; he was nineteen years old, which was not uncommon at the time. His life would seem to be building up to a career in the Church as a priest, but Calderón had other plans first.

Calderón's early years were a fairly tumultuous time for the city of Madrid. One of King Philip III's advisors convinced the king to move the capital north to Valladolid; when the king and his court left Madrid, important sources of income left with them. Madrid suffered. The court moved back to Madrid a few years later and never left again. By the time that Calderón began writing plays in the early 1620s, Madrid was the established capital; the city was growing and theater was flourishing. One of his earliest plays (*Amor, honor y poder*) was staged in 1623. By 1629 Calderón had mastered his craft and was writing wonderful plays, such as *La dama duende*. Just a few years later, in 1635, he would write two of his masterpieces: *La vida es sueño* and *El médico de su honra*. Calderón's works began to be published in 1636 and his *autos sacramentales* won him praise and even more recognition at the Corpus Christi celebrations. Along with his fame as a playwright, Calderón began to accumulate honors; in 1637 he was made a knight of the Order of Santiago. The first four decades of his life were a remarkable success.

In 1640, however, unrest and war broke out in Portugal (which had been part of Spain since 1580) and Cataluña. Calderón fought in Cataluña until 1642 and was injured. Only two years later, in 1644, the queen of Spain, Isabel of Bourbon, died and the theaters were closed. They were still closed in 1646, when Prince Baltasar Carlos passed away, and remained closed until 1649. Between fighting in Cataluña and the closure of the theaters, Calderón lost almost an entire decade when he was at the height of his dramatic career. In 1651 Calderón was ordained a priest and gave up writing for commercial theaters; for the next thirty years, Calderón would write plays for the court and religious *autos sacramentales*. (Calderón wrote both plays in this book during this new period of his life.)

The fact that he gave up writing for commercial theaters does not mean that Calderón stopped innovating. He was a pioneer of musical theater, for example. The king showed favor to Calderón; the playwright became the personal chaplain to Philip IV in 1663. By 1677, five volumes of Calderón's plays had been printed. He was still writing as his eightieth birthday approached. In 1680, he wrote his last *comedia* and he was working on his last *auto sacramental* when he passed away in Madrid on May 25, 1681.

READING SEVENTEENTH-CENTURY PLAYS

In one sense, a play such as *En la vida todo es verdad y todo mentira* or *Sueños hay que verdad son* is a work of literature, to be read and enjoyed. In another sense, however, a play is simply one element needed to create a performance. Reading a play and seeing a play performed are obviously very different experiences, just as reading song lyrics is very different than listening to a song. So reading a play demands a special kind of imagination. As you read, think about the following:

-which characters are on stage? Having a lot of characters on stage at the same time can create a sense of importance; having one character on stage alone can create a sense of isolation, privacy, or intimacy.

-where might the characters be on stage? The positions of actors on the stage may create a visual impression of symmetry or disorder. You should also think about how close together the actors are: close enough to touch one another or do they have to speak loudly to hear each other?

-what do we know that the characters do not? It is often the case that the audience knows things that a particular character does not. Keep track of what the characters know and do not know.

-how are characters speaking and to whom? Sometimes a character is nearly at a loss for words; this means the actor may deliver the lines hesitatingly or very slowly. At other times, the character does not know he is being overheard and says things he shouldn't; another character may know she is being overheard and speak accordingly.

-are there pauses or silences? Calderón's plays do not indicate when the actors should pause. (When you look at a page of his plays you may just see a long stream of words!) But if you can imagine what is happening or imagine the emotional state of the character, you can sometimes figure out how silence might produce a big effect. Characters do not always answer one another right away.

-do the characters mean what they say? Characters lie to each other and say things they don't mean. They can also misunderstand one another or fail to catch the tone of a particular statement. So ask yourself whether characters say things sincerely or sarcastically or with the intent to deceive.

One way to accomplish these tasks is to think like an actor or a director. If a tyrant were ordering you around or if you found out that someone had spread lies about you, how would you react? What do you speak like when you are confused or hurt or in love? Could you speak that way right now if you wanted to? If you can figure out what the characters are feeling, the nature of the interactions among characters, and the tone of a particular scene, you will have a much easier time understanding the words of the play. To do this, however, you will probably have to read at least twice: once to figure out what the words mean and a second time to imagine the action.

You may find the following vocabulary helpful when you discuss the play with others:

acotación stage direction

accesorios props

actor/farsante/comediante actor ("farsante" was more common during the seventeenth century)

aparte an aside, words heard only by the audience, not by other characters; an aside generally expresses the true thoughts of a character

acto/jornada an act of a play; *comedias* have three acts, *autos sacramentales* have only one

autor the leader of a troupe of actors, responsible for directing and staging a play

dramaturgo the playwright, also called simply a *poeta de comedias*

irse/salir The verb *salir* is used when the actor takes the stage or goes out on stage. The verb *irse* is used when the actor exits the stage (or enters the backstage area); the text usually says *vase* (an archaic way of saying *se va*) when one character exits or *vanse* when multiple characters exit the stage

escenario/tablado stage

escenografía set design

espectadores/público audience

parlamento a long speech or series of lines delivered to another character

personaje character

puesta en escena the actual staging or representing of a play
soliloquio soliloquy
verso a verse or line of the play

Versification and Metrification

One of the most interesting things about *comedias* and *autos sacramentales* is that playwrights use different poetic "meters" according to the mood or tone they want to create. "Poetic meter" refers to how the rhythm of a verse is organized. Different rhythms establish different tones in the poems and therefore different meanings. This is obviously true in music: the way a song sounds is a big part of what a song means. It is also true of theater; the rhythm of the words and the meter of the verses contribute to the way a scene sounds. A playwright like Calderón carefully adjusts the meter of his verses according to the mood he wants to create. In the same way, you probably wouldn't write a limerick if you wanted to express sincerely how much you loved your mother.

Because a single play can contain many different meters, we say that Spanish plays from the seventeenth century are "polymetric" or *polimétricos* (literally, "having many meters"). In Spanish, as in English, it is usually the case that longer lines of verse sound more grand or important. A typical long verse has 11 syllables; the term for "11-syllable verse" is "hendecasyllabic" or *endecasílabo*. Shorter verse forms lend themselves to comic situations or more natural-sounding speech. A typical short verse has 8 syllables; the term for "8-syllable verse" is "octosyllabic" or *octosílabo*. Still other verse forms, such as the *silva*, mix short (7 syllable) and long (11 syllable) lines, oftentimes to convey strong emotions. The main verse forms that appear in the two plays in this book are:

décima – Ten lines of 8-syllable verses, rhymed *abbaa-ccddc*. Rhyme is consonant.

quintilla – Five lines of 8-syllable verses, that have a number of possible rhyme schemes: *ababa, abbab, abaab, aabab, aabba*. Rhyme is consonant.

redondilla – Four lines of 8-syllable verses, rhymed *abba, cddc*, etc. Rhyme is consonant.

romance – A series of 8-syllable verses with no fixed number of verses. Rhyme is assonant.

silva – A flexible verse form made up of 7- and 11-syllable verses. There is no fixed number of verses and rhyme schemes vary. Rhyme is consonant.

soneto – Fourteen lines of 11-syllable verses. Sonnets have 4 stanzas; first, 2 *cuartetos* of 4 lines each, and then 2 *tercetos* of 3 lines each. The *cuartetos* are rhymed *ABBA-ABBA*. The rhyme in the *tercetos* varies; Calderón uses *CDE-CDE* in *Sueños hay que verdad son* (649-662).

Counting syllables can be challenging because of synalepha or *sinalefa* (when multiple vowel sounds run together, forming a single syllable). But as you look at a page of a dramatic text, one of the most important things to know is that a single verse can be divided up among characters. An example of three octosyllabic verses will show what we mean:

1788	LEÓNIDO	¡Astolfo!
1788	ERACLIO	¡Astolfo!
1788	LEÓNIDO	Aun el eco
1789		no me responde.
1789	ERACLIO	Aun le faltan
1790		suspiros para mí al viento.

As you can see on the left of the quote, each of the verses in the play is numbered. The first octosyllabic verse in the passage above is number 1788 and is made up of the words "Astolfo Astolfo Aun el eco," even though these words are spoken by different characters. That is why some of the words are indented: the indentations show that the eight-syllable verse has not ended yet. The new octosyllabic verse (1789) begins with "no me responde" and is completed with "Aun le faltan." The third octosyllabic verse (1790) is all on one line: "suspiros para mi aliento." When two characters share a verse, it stitches together the dialogue; it sometimes sounds as if one character were completing the thought of the other. Traditionally, only complete verses are numbered (and stage directions are not counted). An example of what we mean is found in verses 1309-1315 of *En la vida....* The following *looks* like a lot of lines, but the numbers on the left indicate completed verses:

	LUQUETE	¡Que andaluvio!
1310	SABAÑÓN	¡Que antuvión!
	FOCAS	¡Libia!
	LIBIA	¡Focas!
	FOCAS	¡Cintia!
1311	CINTIA	¡Ismenia!
	UNOS	¡Al monte!
1312	OTROS	¡A la población!
	OTROS	¡A la choza!
	OTROS	¡Al risco!
1313	OTROS	¡Al llano!
1314	LIBIA	Pues en tanta confusión,
1315		embarazando las iras...

This means that verse 1311, for example, is an octosyllabic verse made up of the words "Libia / Focas / Cintia / Ismenia." Due to synalepha, the "a" in Cintia shares a syllable with the initial "i" in "Ismenia." In other words, when Focas cries out "¡Cintia!" the final vowel sound bleeds into the beginning of Cintia's "¡Ismenia!" Sharing a syllable can be quite an intimate act, a way of breathing together (and "breathing together" is the etymology of "conspire").

EN LA VIDA, TODO ES VERDAD Y TODO MENTIRA: INTRODUCTION

En la vida... is very loosely based on historical events that were well known during Calderón's lifetime. Some of the characters (such as Focas) lived during the seventh century, a chaotic period of late Roman antiquity. Many of the events of the play, however, are invented.[4] As in the case of *La vida es sueño*, the setting of *En la vida...* is a place that

---

4   An eighteenth-century commenter on this play, Ignacio de Luzán, complained that although Focas truly was taken from the pages of history, other characters, notably Cintia, were not (Armona 265).

might have seemed rather exotic to courtly audiences in seventeer century Madrid: the kingdom of Trinacria (what we now call the island of Sicily).[5] As we learn in Act One, this kingdom is part of a larger empire, roughly equivalent to the Byzantine Empire, stretching across the Mediterranean (and referred to in the play as "el Imperio de Constantinopla"). Mauricio, who dies before the play begins, was emperor of this empire until his death. The relationship between Trinacria (a small kingdom) and Constantinopla (an empire that contains Trinacria) is fairly straightforward: Trinacria must pay tribute to Constantinopla or be punished. As you can imagine, this does not always sit well with the king of Trinacria, despite the fact that Mauricio is widely recognized to be the legitimate emperor.[6] About 30 years before the beginning of the play, the king of Trinacria decided he no longer wanted to pay tribute. In retribution for this, Mauricio attacked him. And that is when all the trouble started.

As Focas tells the story in Act One, the king of Trinacria was desperate because he was on the verge of losing the war to the emperor Mauricio. So, the king called on Focas for help. Focas was an arrogant, conniving, and ruthless bandit who lived in the mountains of Trinacria. Focas *was* able to help the king and Focas did defend Trinacria, but he did not stop there: he killed the emperor of Constantinopla, and then he turned around and killed the king of Trinacria, too. Focas ultimately subdued the rest of the Byzantine Empire and established himself as emperor. Focas is seen by other characters as an illegitimate usurper. At the beginning of the play, Focas returns to Trinacria, having been the emperor of Constantinopla for 30 years.

Other events related to the war between Trinacria and Constantinopla 30 years before the start of the play are crucial, too. When Mauricio attacked Trinacria, he was accompanied by his pregnant wife Audocia. As Mauricio was falling into the hands of Focas, Audocia gave birth to a son. Terrified that Focas would kill her child, Audocia gave the newborn to a trusted advisor named Astolfo. Audocia died in childbirth and Astolfo escaped with the baby and made his way to

---

5 During Calderón's lifetime, Sicily was part of the Spanish Empire. In the play, however, Trinacria is a wild place, full of unmapped forests and mystery.

6 The former king of Trinacria is not named in this play; his daughter is Cintia.

Mount Etna, a volcano, where he hid in the mountain's caves. Meanwhile, Focas' lover—a beautiful village girl named Irífile who was pregnant with Focas' child—was traveling to see Focas at the battlefront. But, on the way, she got lost near Mount Etna and herself was dying in childbirth when the very same Astolfo came upon her. Irífile, like Audocia, gave her newborn to Astolfo to raise and protect.

Over the next three decades, Astolfo raised both boys—one the son of the legitimate emperor Mauricio, the other the son of the usurper Focas—in the caves of Mount Etna, dressing them in animal skins and hiding from them the identities of their fathers. They live in complete isolation and have no idea that they may be heirs to an empire. One of the boys is Mauricio's heir and the other is Focas' heir, but only Astolfo knows which is which. Even the audience is kept in the dark.

The action of the play involves two questions about inheritance. First, which of the wild, mountain boys is really Focas' son? Second, which of the two young men is the rightful heir to the throne of Constantinopla? The play begins with Focas returning to Trinacria in search of his son. Trinacria is now overseen by Cintia, the daughter of the king that Focas overthrew 30 years ago.

CHARACTERS

Focas: The aging emperor of Constantinopla. He was raised by wolves on the hillsides of Mount Etna (a volcano). Focas was a bandit who rose to become emperor.

Cintia: The princess of Trinacria. Her father, the former king of Trinacria, was overthrown by Focas. Cintia now rules Trinacria, but owes obedience to Focas.

Libia: Lisipo's daughter. She hunts to procure food for her father.

Astolfo: In the past, he was the advisor and ambassador to Mauricio (the former emperor of Constantinopla). Astolfo raises Leónido and Eraclio in secrecy.

Leónido and **Eraclio**: Both young men were raised by Astolfo in total isolation in the mountains of Sicily. One is the son of Focas and the other is the son of Mauricio, but when the play begins they do not know their true identities.

Sabañón and **Luquete**: Two *graciosos* or humorous characters who are responsible for the comic relief in the play.

Lisipo: A powerful sorcerer who, during the course of the play, comes to be in the service of Focas. He lives in the mountain wilderness with his daughter, Libia.

Federico: the duke of Calabria (a region on the mainland of Italy near Sicily). His mother, Casandra, was Mauricio's sister. This makes Federico the nephew of Mauricio.

Characters who are mentioned but do not appear:

Mauricio: He was once the emperor of Constantinopla but was killed by Focas 30 years before the start of the play.

Audocia: Mauricio's wife; she died in childbirth, giving her son to Astolfo.

Irífile: The lover of Focas. She died in childbirth 30 years ago, and as in the case of Audocia, her son comes to be raised by Astolfo.

Casandra: Mauricio's sister and Federico's mother.

HISTORICAL BACKGROUND: THE WORLD OF 1659

1659, when Calderón wrote *En la vida...*, was one of the most difficult years in a disastrous century. Spain had been at war with France and other European countries almost continuously since 1618. In 1659, Spain signed a peace treaty with France—called the "Peace of the Pyrenees" or the "Treaty of the Pyrenees"—that forced the Spanish Crown to surrender control of lands in strategic locations. In the opinion of many, the Peace of the Pyrenees marked one of the low points in the dynasty.

The grave state of Spain's foreign relations was compounded by problems at home. In 1659, King Philip IV of Spain was growing older—he was 54 years old—and the male heir to throne was a sickly toddler born two years before named Felipe Próspero. Felipe Próspero would die at age 3, and some may already have guessed how close the prince was to death.[7] King Philip had long had difficulty producing a male heir, and this difficulty was a source of global concern. Spain had recently suffered economic crises and internal unrest, in addition to

---

7 At the time *En la vida...* was first performed in 1659, Felipe Próspero actually had a younger brother, Fernando Tomás, who would die later in 1659.

military defeats, but it was still a massive empire. It was not clear what would happen if Philip IV died without a capable, male heir. Philip had daughters, but some countries strongly opposed female succession. Without a male heir, France might invade or Spain might break apart throwing the colonies and all of Europe into further violent conflict. Another complicating factor was that Philip IV had an illegitimate son, named Juan José de Austria, who was charismatic, healthy, and by 1659 already trusted with important diplomatic and military missions.[8] Many recognized that the illegitimate Juan José might have made a better king than his legitimate half-brothers, who after generations of inbreeding were either physically or mentally challenged. The question of succession, of who would be the next king, was on many people's minds.

People had learned the hard way not to trust too much in the longevity of Philip IV's legitimate sons. There had been another prince, named Baltasar Carlos (1629-1646), whose birth had been greeted with jubilation and relief. Antonio Lorea, writing during the seventeenth century, called Baltasar Carlos Spain's "only hope" or "única esperanza" (150-51). When the prince died after a brief illness in 1646, the news was met with shock and confusion. Between the death of Baltasar Carlos and the birth of Felipe Próspero, Spain went over a decade without a male heir to the throne. After Felipe Próspero died in 1661, the world would have to wait four long years for the future king, Carlos, to be born. When the new prince did arrive, he was intellectually limited and unable to have children of his own. So 1659, in the middle of all of these worries and problems, was a profoundly uncomfortable time for Spain and for the King.

Calderón tackles these anxieties and concerns head on. One of the most important themes in the play has to do with succession. In one sense, it is a story about fathers and sons, or how parents see themselves reflected in their children. In another sense, *En la vida...* asks us to think about what makes a legitimate leader. Is it having the right

---

8 Coincidentally, Juan José was the child of an extra-marital affair between the King and María Inés Calderón, a famous actor. Greer explains how Calderón may have represented the controversies surrounding royal succession and Juan José de Austria (169-170).

bloodlines or connections? Is it being a good person? Or is a true leader one who will do anything in order to lead?

Part of what *En la vida...* stages is a means by which people arrive at a politically acceptable consensus. In the play, there is a problem of paternity and succession; there are two fathers (one dead, one alive) and two sons, but only one person knows whose son is whose. Both of the fathers claimed the same throne, so the political stakes are high; in biological terms, the problem of paternity implies one father's chance to ensure that his own genes are passed on *and* that his rival's lineage is blotted out. An elaborate experiment is staged to determine which of the two men is the emperor's son; from the beginning, the premises of this experiment are scrutinized and criticized.

SUEÑOS HAY QUE VERDAD SON: INTRODUCTION

In *Sueños hay que verdad son*, Calderón takes the Old Testament story of Joseph from the book of Genesis and joins it to the New Testament logic of an *auto sacramental*. Although everyone agrees that *Sueños hay que verdad son* is an *auto sacramental*, not everyone agrees on what an *auto sacramental* is. Bruce Wardropper remarked that definitions of the *auto sacramental* are often imperfect (29). The "definitions of the genre," explained Alexander A. Parker, "are widely divergent and even contradictory" (58). Domingo Ynduráin's definition is perhaps the most pragmatic: an *auto* contains a Eucharistic theme and is represented for Corpus Christi (3). For the purposes of understanding *Sueños hay que verdad son,* we can add two more aspects to Ynduráin's definition: it is a one-act play and it is an allegory. Of these four parts, two are straightforward. A one-act play is fairly short and not divided into multiple acts. As we mentioned earlier, Corpus Christi was the feast day that took place on the Thursday 60 days after Easter. The other two elements of the definition—concerning the Eucharist and allegory—demand closer inspection.

The word "Eucharist" is sometimes a synonym for "Holy Communion," but it also means the consecrated bread and wine of Holy Communion. Protestants generally believe that Communion is a symbolic act that helps believers focus on the events that led up to the crucifixion of Christ. So for Protestants, the bread and wine of Communion are just that: bread and wine. For Roman Catholics, on the other hand, the consecrated bread and wine are the physical body and blood of Jesus Christ. The Eucharist only appears to be a wafer of bread or a portion of wine. This is crucial: it looks like one thing (bread and wine) but everything—excluding its appearance—has become something else (the body and blood of Christ). As you can imagine, there was a lot of theological debate about how something that looked like bread could really be flesh. Some people argued that the bread and the body actually occupied the same space. Other people argued that only the appearance of bread was left behind so that believers would still have to have faith. Still others wondered how, if God was everywhere, he could be especially present in the Eucharist. There were centuries of arguments about these subjects for a very good reason: the Eucharist forms the center of a life of religious devotion for many Roman Catholics.

Why do you need to know all of this? Because a few decades before Calderón was born, the Roman Catholic Church hammered out its teachings about the Eucharist definitively. This happened at a series of meetings in Italy attended by representatives from many parts of the Roman Catholic world known as the Council of Trent. They met and prayed and disputed for decades. Partly, all of this meeting and deciding was in response to the challenge created by Martin Luther and the Protestant Reformation. Roman Catholics wanted to have better answers to the questions that many people were asking about religion. The Council of Trent was where those answers were agreed upon; the movement that Church leaders started subsequently is often called the Counterreformation. A key part of the Counterreformation was the idea that religion should be experienced more intensely, often on an emotional level, and that there should be more teaching about what Roman Catholics actually believed. This is where *autos sacramentales* would play a role. In part, the plays are *didactic*, meaning that their purpose is to teach people, as well as entertain. The focus of that teaching is the Eucharist. After you read the play, you'll want to ask yourself how well the play works as a form of educational media. Did the play convince you of anything?

ALLEGORY, THE EUCHARIST, AND INVISIBILITY

Sueños hay que verdad son is an allegory. Allegory simply means that the characters make sense on two levels. The first level is literal. The second is the level of concepts or ideas. For example, in *Sueños hay que verdad son* there are characters named "El Sueño" and "La Fe." On the literal level, these are characters that walk and speak and fight and deceive. At the same time, they are embodiments of concepts; their walking and speaking and fighting and deceiving tell us something about the concepts they embody. They obviously are not believable or verisimilar as characters. No one sees La Fe and asks, "Wow, is that what religious faith really looks like in person?" At the same time, you might see what La Fe does and say, "Yes, religious faith is just like that."

Allegory points to a reality beyond itself. You are going to read a play that is partly about a character named La Castidad (chastity). A character like that suggests the existence of *something* beyond itself—the beliefs about when to have sex and when not to—just as La Fe suggests the existence of faith far beyond the confines of this play. At times, characters can straddle a line between allegory and realism. You might see a movie in which the bad guy is the embodiment or personification of all evil and, at the same time, a particular person named Count Dracula. In this play, some of the characters personify concepts very clearly: El Sueño, La Fe, and La Castidad. Other characters are human figures drawn from the Bible that may or may not personify particular qualities: José, Benjamín, Rubén, and so on. Still other characters, such as El Copero and El Panadero, have the kind of double existence (historical and allegorical) we often find in parables and fables. As you will see, El Copero, a cupbearer who serves wine, and El Panadero, a baker, have literal and what is sometimes called typological meaning. Their literal meaning has to do with events of the Old Testament, but their secondary or typological meaning (bread and wine) foreshadows the events of the New Testament.

Allegory, Eucharist, and *auto sacramental* are all related in a very specific way for Calderón. The Eucharist for Roman Catholics has a surface appearance (bread and wine) and an imperceptible reality (body and blood). Similar to this, allegory has a literal meaning (a character we can see named La Fe) and a conceptual significance that we can know but perhaps not see (the faith personified by La Fe). You can imagine the double phenomenon of appearance and reality in the Eucharist as parallel to the double phenomenon of literal and conceptual meanings in allegory.

So, allegory is a way of visualizing something invisible. Calderón's *autos sacramentales* use allegory's power to talk about what is visible and what is not, what is present and what is not, in order to create a context in which Roman Catholic teaching about the Eucharist makes more sense. Luckily, Calderón is not just interested in teaching; he is also a fantastic playwright who knows how to entertain. So he joins theological questions to an exciting plot: the Old Testament story of Joseph and his brothers. As is the case with a lot of juicy Old Testament stories, this one has jealousy, betrayal, deception, suffering, and redemption.

The Biblical Story of Joseph

Joseph (or José) is, perhaps above all, a dreamer. He has extraordinary and prophetic dreams and he knows how to interpret the dreams of others. The Old Testament story of Joseph (Genesis 37-45) has inspired many works, such as the Broadway musical, *Joseph and the Technicolor Dreamcoat*. (The Old Testament Joseph is *not* the same person we find in the story of Joseph, Mary, and Jesus in the New Testament.) Knowing his story will make *Sueños hay que verdad son* easier to understand.

Joseph first appears in the biblical narrative of Genesis in Chapter 37 as "the son of [Jacob's] old age"; this made him Jacob's favorite son because Joseph was born when Jacob had nearly lost hope of having children by his wife Rachel. However, his father's favoritism brings upon Joseph the hatred of his brothers (who were born to Jacob's other wife Leah, and Jacob's servants Bilhah and Zilpah).

This hatred increases when Joseph tells his brothers he has had a dream in which they all bow down to him. Infuriated, the brothers sell Joseph into slavery, dip his coat in blood, and tell Jacob that a wild animal mauled Joseph. Joseph is taken as a slave to Egypt, where false accusations of lasciviousness land him in jail. It is here that Calderón picks up the events of Joseph's life in *Sueños hay que verdad son*. In jail,

Joseph meets two other prisoners: Pharaoh's chief cupbearer and chief baker. Both have had disturbing dreams, and Joseph offers to interpret them.

The cupbearer dreams of a grapevine with three branches; in the dream, the cupbearer squeezes grapes from the vine into Pharaoh's cup. Joseph interprets the dream to mean that in three days Pharaoh will give the cupbearer his old job back. The baker dreams that he had three baskets of baked goods, but birds ate the bread. Joseph interprets the dream to mean that Pharaoh will condemn the baker to death in three days. Joseph's interpretations prove true. The cupbearer is restored to his position and the baker is hanged.

Two years later, Pharaoh himself has two dreams that no one can interpret. The cupbearer remembers how Joseph accurately interpreted dreams in the past, and Joseph is brought to Pharaoh. Pharaoh recounts his dreams to Joseph; in the first, seven thin cows devour seven fat cows; in the second dream, seven skinny ears of grain swallow up seven healthy ears. Joseph tells Pharaoh that Egypt will first experience seven years of plenty followed by seven years of famine. Joseph advises that they begin to store up supplies in preparation for the famine years.

After having successfully stored up grain during the years of plenty, "all the world came to Joseph in Egypt to buy grain" (41:57). Among those who traveled to Egypt to procure grain are the very brothers that betrayed Joseph and sold him into slavery. (Although they travel without their youngest brother, Benjamin.) The brothers arrive in Egypt and attempt to buy grain from Joseph, who recognizes them but treats "them like strangers" (42:7). He also accuses them of being spies and makes them prove their honesty by giving them a test: Joseph holds one of his brothers hostage and tells the rest to return home. Joseph explains that he will release the captive brother when the rest return with Benjamin (the brother who had stayed home). The brothers return home, laden with grain and money. Joseph's plan is set in motion.

Jacob reluctantly permits his sons to take Benjamin with them back to Egypt. When the brothers arrive, they are taken directly to Joseph's house and dine with him. Joseph appears satisfied and sends them on their way with sacks filled with grain. However, he has his servant place a silver cup in Benjamin's sack. Joseph then accuses Benjamin of stealing and threatens to make him a slave. The brothers ask to be taken as slaves in Benjamin's stead. Moved by their plea, Joseph reveals his true identity to his brothers. Joseph sends his brothers back to Canaan in Pharaoh's wagons to retrieve Jacob and they all settle in Egypt to live in the "best of all the land" (45:20).

One of the things you will notice about the way the biblical story is portrayed in the play is that the *words* of the play often refer directly to the Old Testament, while the *actions* of the characters produce visual images Christians associate with the New Testament. The interplay of word and movement in Calderón's play binds together all of Biblical history. You don't have to know Biblical history to enjoy *Sueños hay que verdad son*. You only need to read carefully and imagine how the play might be staged. Dale Pratt pointed out in an important article about *autos sacramentales* that narrow theological or Biblical interpretations never exhaust the interpretative possibilities of an *auto*; the pleasure readers find in literature is part of what literature means. That part, the pleasure of reading this play, is yours, no matter what your background or previous knowledge. When you find enjoyment in Calderón's plays, and you can identify what about the plays produces your enjoyment, you will have important things to say about them.

CHARACTERS

José He is the son his father Jacob loves most. José has extraordinary dreams and has great skill in interpreting the dreams of others.

Castidad and Asenet Castidad is the embodiment (or allegory) of chastity. Asenet's father was an Egyptian priest who worshiped the sun. The same actress would play these two characters. During part of the play, Castidad appears as Asenet. But at another moment, the real Asenet appears on stage (still played by the same actor).

El Sueño The embodiment of dreaming. Sueño and Castidad often appear together in the play and form an unlikely pair.

El Copero (Also called Siquén) The Copero (cupbearer) to the king or pharaoh was responsible for serving the wine. When the play begins, the Copero is in prison with José.

El Panadero A baker that José meets in prison.

Jacob José's elderly father.

José's brothers: (Rubén, Zabulón, Judas, Gad, Benjamín Aser, Neftalí, Manasés, Isacar, Simeón, Leví). José has eleven brothers by four
mothers. Together, these 12 brothers go on to become the patri-
archs of the 12 tribes of the Israel. During Calderón's lifetime, these
twelve brothers had literal or historical significance, but they also
had "typological" significance, meaning that they prefigured Jesus'
twelve disciples (something suggested in the book of Revelation
21:9-14).

El Rey The Pharaoh of Egypt. José is able to interpret his dreams. For
this, the pharaoh rewards José with power.

Bato The "gracioso" or comic relief of the play, Bato is Jacob's servant.
He is not part of the Biblical story. Bato's rustic pronunciation is
played for comic effect.

La Fe An embodiment of the Christian faith. Fe is true religion itself.

What is "sacramental" about an *auto sacramental*?

If you have ever read a novel about lovers—whether by Jane Austen
or more recent authors—you know the promise of a wedding is the
perfect way to wrap up the plot. (It is true of movies, too, especially
romantic comedies.) Many people who do not believe that marriage
is a religious sacrament (or do not believe in marriage at all) love novels that end with weddings in a church. We enjoy feeling that there
is a moment of social integration, and even healing, at the end of a
novel: the happy couple gets together and marriage is the sacrament
that weaves their lives into the broad fabric of society.

A sacrament, in the broadest sense, is simply a rite or ritual that
the Church has designated as particularly important. Roman Catholics generally say that a sacrament is an "efficacious sign of grace," or a
way that the souls of human beings and the grace of God come into
particular contact through a religious ritual like marriage and bap-
tism. An *auto sacramental*, like many novels, ends with the promise
of a sacrament, but instead of the sacrament of marriage there is the
"blessed sacrament," called the Eucharist. Roman Catholics believe
that through the Eucharist believers partake of the body and blood
of Jesus Christ. Just as the body of Christ becomes part of the body of

the believer, the believer becomes part of the mystical body of Christ: the Church. So like the promise of marriage at the end of a novel, the promise of the Eucharist at the end of an *auto sacramental* signals social and spiritual integration: receiving the Eucharist is one of the ways that believers are initiated into the Church.

What if you don't know very much about religion or you aren't interested in theology? Well, just as you can read a novel and root for the wedding (even if you think that marriage is just a contract) you can find the promise of the sacrament at the end of *Sueños hay que verdad son* satisfying. The play is a lot of fun. It tells a story about family jealousies and betrayal, as well as what families can overcome through forgiveness. It is about drought and the stresses that extreme weather places on societies. And, of course, it is a play about faith and how religious rituals bind faith communities.

HISTORICAL BACKGROUND: THE WORLD OF 1670

Calderón wrote *Sueños hay que verdad son* for Madrid's Corpus Christi festival of 1670. If *En la vida...* is about finding an heir to the throne (and reflects the world of 1659) *Sueños hay que verdad son* is about a trusted advisor to the king (reflecting new worries). The Spanish monarchy desperately needed a good advisor and trustworthy guidance because things in Spain were even worse in 1670 then they had been in 1659.

The king of Spain and ruler of its vast empire was the eight-year-old Charles II (Carlos II), who had been king for just over four years. Charles may have suffered from a developmental disability due to generations of inbreeding, but we know for certain that he was intellectually limited and was ultimately unable to have children. Obviously, a child king was not making the important decisions regarding the future of the empire. His mother, a fascinating woman named Mariana de Austria, served as "queen regent" and was the effective ruler in 1670.

Charles' father, Philip IV, had passed away in 1665. The theaters were closed for years by law as a show of mourning. 1670 marked the return of *autos sacramentales* and Spain's vibrant theatrical culture after five dreary years. Although people were looking forward to the play in Madrid, the monarchy was suffering some of its darkest days. In 1668 Spain finally conceded that Portugal had won its independence (following conflicts that began almost three decades before, in 1640). At the very moment that Calderón was writing his play, Spanish diplomats were negotiating the Treaty of Madrid, which would recognize English territorial claims in the Caribbean, including the island of Jamaica. The empire seemed to be crumbling, with bits and pieces breaking off with terrible regularity.[9] The real damage of these losses had been done earlier, but the year 1670 found Spain dealing with the psychological blows of publically recognizing its political problems. Things had gotten so bad that Charles' half-brother, Juan José de Austria marched troops toward Madrid in 1669 and brought the country to the brink of civil war. It was a time of incredible intrigue and high-stakes political gambles, none of which seemed to benefit the people of Spain.

Calderón turned 70 years old in 1670 and by that time he had been an important playwright for over forty years. Perhaps reflecting on Spain's precarious situation, Calderón returned to one of his favorite dramatic subjects in *Sueños hay que verdad son*: how to advise a king. José, the protagonist of *Sueños hay que verdad son*, is an advisor to the ruler of Egypt. Through his interpretation of dreams, José is able to predict the future and avert disaster. This must have been an appealing fantasy in 1670. It was little more than a fantasy, however, and in Charles II's case disaster was not averted. His limitations and incapacities were so obvious and notable that people wondered whether he might be under a spell or curse; Charles was known as "el Hechizado" (the Bewitched). When Charles II died in 1700 he had no children and the Hapsburg dynasty in Spain came to an end.

BIBLIOGRAPHY AND FURTHER READING

Amadei-Pulice, María Alicia. *Calderón y el barroco: Exaltación y engaño de los sentidos*. Purdue University Monographs in Romance Languages, 31. Philadelphia: John Benjamins, 1990.

---

9 Calderón uses phrases like "desmenuzado a trozos," or "crumbling into pieces," that recall these anxieties (496).

Arellano, Ignacio. *Historia del teatro español del siglo XVII.* Madrid: Cátedra, 2002.

Armona, José Antonio de. *Memorias cronológicas sobre el origen de la representación de comedias en España (año de 1785).* Ed. Charles Davis and John E. Varey. Woodbridge: Tamesis, 2007.

Bartra, Roger. *The Artificial Savage: Modern Myths of the Wild Man.* Ann Arbor: University of Michigan Press, 1997.

Bataillon, Marcel. "Essai d'explication de l'auto sacramental." *Bulletin Hispanique* 42 (1940): 193-212. Rpt. as "Ensayo de explicación del auto sacramental." Trans. José Pérez Riesco. *Calderón y la crítica, historia y antología.* Ed. Manuel Duran, and Roberto González Echevarría. Biblioteca románica hispánica, II, Estudios y ensayos; 238. 2 vols. Madrid: Editorial Gredos, 1976. 455-480.

Blue, William R. *The Development of Imagery in Calderón's Comedias.* York, SC: Spanish Literature Publications Co., 1983.

Caballero, Ernesto and Víctor Velasco. "Precursor y artífice de la modernidad: *En la vida todo es verdad y todo mentira* de Pedro Calderón de la Barca." *ADE teatro: Revista de la Asociación de Directores de Escena de España* 140 (2012): 137-140.

Calderón de la Barca, Pedro. *Autos sacramentales, alegoricos y historiales...* Ed. Pedro Pando y Mier. Madrid: Manuel Ruiz de Murga, 1717.

———. *Comedias. Hado y divisa de Leonido y Marfisa.* Ed. Santiago Fernández Mosquera and Luis Iglesias Feijoo. Biblioteca Castro. Comedias vol. 5. Madrid: Fundación José Antonio de Castro, 2010.

———. *El médico de su honra.* Ed. Carol Bingam Kirby. Newark, DE: European Masterpieces, 2007.

———. *En la vida todo es verdad y todo mentira.* Ed. Don William Cruickshank. London: Tamesis, 1971.

———. *La vida es sueño.* Ed. Vincent Martin. European Masterpieces, 2006.

———. *Obras Completas: Tomo III, Autos sacramentales.* Ed. Ángel Valbuena Prat. 2nd ed. 3 vols. Madrid: Aguilar, 1967.

————. *Sometimes Dreams Come True*. Trans. Michael McGaha. *The Story of Joseph in Spanish Golden Age Drama*. Lewisburg, PA: Bucknell UP, 1998. 145-185.

————. *Sueños hay que verdad son*. Ed. Michael McGaha. Zaragoza: Universidad de Navarra, 1997.

————. *Teatro cómico breve*. Ed. María-Luisa Lobato. Kassel: Reichenberger, 1989.

Cascardi, Anthony J. *The Limits of Illusion: A Critical Study of Calderón*. Cambridge: Cambridge UP, 1984.

Cotarelo y Mori, Emilio. *Bibliografía de las controversias sobre la licitud del teatro en España*. Archivum. Spain: 1904. Facsimile edition. Granada: U of Granada, 1997.

Cruickshank, Don William. "Introduction." *En la vida todo es verdad y todo mentira*. By Pedro Calderón de la Barca. Ed. Don William Cruickshank. London: Tamesis, 1971. xi-cxxxix.

Davis, Charles and John E. Varey. "Calderón in the Country: Corpus Christi Performances in Towns around Madrid, 1636–60." *Bulletin of Hispanic Studies* 77 (2000): 289-316.

Díez Borque, José María. "El auto sacramental y el imaginario visual religioso: Antiguo Testamento." *Estado actual de los estudios calderonianos*. Ed. Luciano García Lorenzo. Teatro del Siglo de Oro, Estudios de Literatura, 50. Kassel: Edition Reichenberger, 2000. 35-60.

Gallego Roca, Miguel. "*La rueda de la fortuna* de Mira de Amescua y la polémica sobre el Heraclio español." *RILCE* 7.2 (1991): 311-24.

Gilbert, Françoise. "El Sueño como personaje alegórico en dos autos de Calderón: La siembra del Señor (antes de 1655) y Sueños hay que verdad son (1670)." *Bulletin of the Comediantes* 60.1 (2008): 91-126.

————. "Funciones del sueño en un auto de Calderón: *Sueños hay que verdad son* (1670)." *Bulletin of the Comediantes* 57.2 (2005): 441-89.

Glaser, Edward. "Calderón de la Barca's Sueños hay que verdad son." *Zeitschrift für Romanische Philologie* 82 (1966): 41-77.

Gonano, Eleonora C. "Teorías del poder en Calderón de la Barca: *En esta vida todo es verdad y todo es mentira*." *Estudios críticos de lite-*

ratura española. Ed. Edith Marta Villarino Cela and Elsa Graciela Fiadino. 2 vols. Mar de Plata: Facultad de Humanidades, Universidad Nacional de Mar del Plata, 2003. 97-106.

Gracián, Baltasar. *Agudeza y arte de ingenio,* in *Obras completas, vol. 2.* Madrid: Turner, 1993. 301-800.

Greer, Margaret. *The Play of Power: Mythological Court Dramas of Calderón.* Princeton: Princeton UP, 1991.

Guerra y Ribera, Manuel de. "Aprobación." In: Rodríguez de Monforte, Pedro. *Sueños mysteriosos de la escritura en discursos sagrados, politicos y morales.* Madrid: Imprenta de Antonio Roman, 1687.

Hildner, David. "*En la vida todo es verdad y todo es mentira*: ¿hacia la tragedia o hacia la farsa?" *Hacia la tragedia áurea: Lecturas para un nuevo milenio.* Ed. Frederick A. de Armas, Luciano García Lorenzo, Enrique García Santo-Tomás. Madrid: Iberoamericana; Frankfurt am Main, Vervuert, 2008. 407-416.

Hivnor, Mary. "*En la vida todo es verdad y todo mentira*: Calderón's Prince Defined by Faith." *Bulletin of the Comediantes.* 37.2 (1985): 249-261.

Juana Inés de la Cruz. *Obras completas.* México: Porrúa, 1992.

Kurtz, Barbara E. *The Play of Allegory in the* Autos Sacramentales *of Pedro Calderón de la Barca.* Washington, D. C.: Catholic U of America P, 1991.

Lorea, Antonio de. *El siervo de Dios.* Madrid: Juan García Infanzón…, 1676.

McGaha, Michael. "Introducción." *Sueños hay que verdad son.* By Pedro Calderón de la Barca. Ed. Michael McGaha. Zaragoza: Universidad de Navarra, Edition Reichenberger, 1997. 9-76.

———. *The Story of Joseph in Spanish Golden Age Drama.* Lewisburg, PA: Bucknell UP, 1998.

———. "La comedia de Mira de Amescua *El más feliz cautiverio* modelo de *Sueños hay que verdad son* de Calderón." *Divinas y humanas letras, doctrina y poesía en los autos sacramentales de Calderón.* Ed. Ignacio Arellano, et al. Pamplona: Universidad de Navarra; Kassel: Edition Reichenberger, 1997. 279-301

———. *Coat of Many Cultures: The Story of Joseph in Spanish Literature 1200-1492*. Philadelphia: The Jewish Publication Society, 1997.

Mira de Amescua, Antonio. *Teatro completo*. Ed. Agustín de la Granja. Granada: Universidad de Granada, Diputación de Granada, 2001-2012.

Mujica, Bárbara. "The Skeptical Premises of Calderón's *En esta vida todo es verdad y todo mentira*." *Texto y espectáculo: Selected Proceedings of the Symposium on Spanish Golden Age Theater*. Lanham: UP of America, 1989. 117-126.

Parker, Alexander A. *The Allegorical Drama of Calderón: An Introduction to the Autos Sacramentales*. Oxford: Dolphin, 1943.

———. "Segismundo's Tower: a Calderonian Myth." *Bulletin of Hispanic Studies* 59.3 (1982): 247-256.

Peña Fernández, Francisco. "Violencia y reconciliación: La transformación de la historia de José y sus hermanos en el teatro hispánico del siglo XVII." *eHumanista* 9 (2007): 196-217.

Pratt, Dale. "*Felix Culpa*: Allegory and Play in Calderón's Autos." *Bulletin of the Comediantes* 55 (1999): 37-53.

Regalado, Antonio. "Sobre puesta en escena, verosimilitud, y *admiratio*." *Estudios sobre Calderón*. Ed. Javier Aparicio Maydeu. Madrid: Istmo, 2000. 97-113.

Rice de Molina, Robin Ann. "José como prefiguración de Cristo en dos autos sacramentales: *Sueños hay que verdad son* de Calderón de la Barca y *El cetro de José* de Sor Juana Inés de la Cruz." *Actas del XV Congreso de la Asociación Internacional de Hispanistas*. Ed. Beatriz Mariscal, and María Teresa Miaja de la Peña. México, D.F: Fondo de Cultura Económica, 2007. 459-474.

Rodríguez de Monforte, Pedro. *Sueños mysteriosos de la escritura en discursos sagrados, politicos y morales*. Madrid: Imprenta de Antonio Roman, 1687.

Ruano de la Haza, José María, and John J. Allen. *Los teatros comerciales del siglo XVII y la escenificación de la comedia*. Madrid: Castalia, 1994.

Rull Fernández, Enrique. "Composición de la historia bíblica de José en la obra de Calderón *Sueños hay que verdad son*." *La Biblia en *el teatro español.* Ed. Francisco Domínguez Matito, and Juan Antonio Martínez Berbel. Pontevedra: Academia del Hispanismo, 2012. 469-478.

Shergold, N. D. and John E. Varey. *Teatros y comedias en Madrid, 1651-1665.* London: Tamesis, 1973.

Sullivan, Michael. "Glossing Scripture: Calderón's Sonnet Artistry in *Sueños hay que verdad son.*" *Journal of Christianity and Foreign Languages* 4 (2003): 28-39.

Varey, John E. *Cosmovisión y escenografía en el teatro español en el siglo de oro.* Madrid: Castalia, 1987.

————."The Staging of Calderón's *La cena del rey Baltasar.*" *Aureum Saeculum Hispanum: Beiträge zu Texten des Siglo de Oro: Festschrift für Hans Flasche zum 70.* Ed. Karl-Hermann Körner and Dietrich Briesemeister. Wiesbaden: Franz Steiner Verlag, 1983. 299-311.

Voros, Sharon D. and Ricardo Sáez. *Aquel breve sueño: Dreams on the Early Modern Spanish Stage.* New Orleans: UP of the South, 2004.

Wardropper, Bruce W. *Introducción al teatro religioso del Siglo de Oro: la evolución del auto sacramental (1500-1648).* Madrid: Revista del Occidente, 1953.

Ynduráin, Domingo. "Estudio Preliminar." *El gran teatro del mundo.* By Pedro Calderón de la Barca. Ed. Domingo Ynduráin. Madrid: Alhambra, 1981. 3-126.

Pedro Calderón de la Barca

En la vida todo es verdad y todo mentira

Personas:

Focas (emperador)

Cintia (princesa de Trinacria)

Ismenia (criada de Cintia)

Libia (hija de Lisipo)

Luquete (gracioso)

Sabañón (gracioso)

Eraclio

Leónido

Astolfo

Lisipo (un mago sabio)

Federico (sobrino de Mauricio)

Músicos y Damas

Jornada primera

Dentro a una parte cajas y trompetas, y a otra parte instrumentos músicos,
y salen por una parte soldados y Focas, y por otra parte damas y detrás Cintia.[1]

Soldados	(*Dentro°*) ¡Viva Focas! offstage
Focas	"Cintia viva,"
	decid,[2] soldados, al verla.

1 **Dentro a una…***Offstage, on one side (parte) of the stage, drums and horns are heard; on the other, musical instruments are heard. Focas and the soldiers enter the stage on one side, while Cintia and the women enter the stage from the opposite side.* Imagine that Focas enters first, giving instructions for how to greet Cintia to the soldiers who are still offstage (*dentro*). Cintia enters after this and speaks to the women who are also still offstage. This visually elaborate scene is mirrored in the complicated language used by the characters.

2 **Decid** is a *vosotros* command (infinitive *decir*), so Focas is telling the soldiers what they should say when they see Cintia. You will recognize *vosotros* commands because they end in "d." "Comer"

Damas	(*Dentro*) ¡Viva Cintia y Focas viva!	
Cintia	Repitan las voces vuestras.	
Unos	(*Dentro*) ¡Vivan Cintia y Focas!	
5 Otros	(*Dentro*) ¡Vivan!	
Focas	Y hagan salva a su belleza[3]	
	los militares estruendos°	noise
	de cajas y de trompetas.	

Ahora salen cantando las Damas.

Cintia	Y hagan a su vista salva,	
10	himnos, canciones y letras.	
Músicos	(*Cantan*) *El nunca vencido° Marte,*[4]	conquered
y Damas	*el siempre vencedor César,*	
	a los montes de Trinacria°	Sicily
	en hora dichosa° venga.	fortunate
15 Cintia	ˋVenga en hora dichosa,°	welcome
	tanto que halle a su obediencia,[5]	
	con siempre rendido afecto,	
	su patria ˋa sus plantas° vea.	at your feet
	ˋEn fe de° cuyas lealtades°	As proof of, loyalties
20	tengo de[6] ser la primera	
	yo, que besando su mano,	
	mi corona a su pie ofrezca.	
	Porque postrándome yo[7]	

---

becomes "comed," "ir" becomes "id," "alzar" becomes "alzad." When pronouns are added to the end of a *vosotros* command, the "d" is sometimes dropped, "alzad + os" becomes "alzaos."

3   **hagan salva...***pay tribute to (or salute) her beauty*

4   **Marte** or Mars is the god of war. Here it is used as an epithet to honor the warlike Focas.

5   This play was written in 1659, but not published until 1664 when it appeared along with other plays by Calderón, in a collection entitled the *Tercera parte de comedias de don Pedro Calderón de la Barca.* In this edition, when the footnotes refer to the *Tercera parte* it will simply be notated as *Tp.* (See introduction for more about differences between the *Tercera parte* and early manuscripts of the play.) Footnotes beginning with *Tp* indicate significant differences between the manuscript and the *Tp.* Here, for example, the *Tp* reads, "Tanto, que allá su obediencia" and the manuscript says "tanto que halle a su obediencia." "Hallar" means "to find" so the manuscript makes more sense.

6   **tener de** *to have to* (like "tener que")

7   **Porque postrándome...***Such that by throwing myself at your feet...*Cintia may actually kneel before Focas, but this was generally a manner of speaking.

25	(*Ap.°*) (¡oh temor cuánto me fuerzas, — an aside (aparte)

       (*Ap.°*) (¡oh temor cuánto me fuerzas,   an aside (aparte)
25   viendo el poder de un tirano°!)   tyrant
       a la Majestad suprema
       de tan glorioso héroe, el mundo
       en mi rendimiento° vea,   submission
       que toda Trinacria en mí
30   \`yace rendida° y sujeta,   lies defeated
       diciendo en la voz de todos,
       ufana,° alegre, contenta: proud
Músicos (*Cantan*) *El nunca vencido Marte,*
y Cintia *el siempre vencedor César,*
35   *a los montes de Trinacria*
       en hora dichosa venga.

                Tocan cajas.

Focas Fuerza es[8] que en hora dichosa
       venga, hermosa Cintia bella,
       quien viene a \`lograr aplausos,°   win praise
40   donde pensó hallar° ofensas.   to find
       Bien temí, aunque coronado
       de tantos laureles[9] venga
       a ver la eminente cumbre,
       que fue mi cuna primera,[10]
45   hallar en sus campos antes
       oposiciones que fiestas.
       Porque nadie es en su patria
       tan feliz como en la ajena,[11]
       mayormente,° cuando vuelve   even more so

---

8 **Fuerza es** generally means "it is necessary," but here it is closer to "it is the case" or "it is true." This reflects a philosophical way of thinking about necessity that has less to do with need than with what happens necessarily (or happens in every case).

9 **coronado de...***crowned with so many laurels* It was customary to crown victors and leaders with laurels.

10 **cuna primera** *cradle or birthplace* Focas grew up on the flanks of the high peak (or "eminente cumbre") of the volcano called Mount Etna.

11 **feliz** here means something more like *fortunate* than *happy*. The sense of the passage is that Focas did not expect such a warm welcome. Focas' lines subtly allude to an idea that was quite common and even appears in the Bible: "a prophet hath no honor in his own country" (John 4:44).

50	tras° tantos años de ausencia:	after
	pero viendo, que ha sabido,	
	políticamente cuerda,°	clever
	la razón de estado[12] hacer	
	sacrificio de la fuerza	
55	en premio° del rendimiento,	reward
	con que me admites y aceptas,	
	palabra, Cintia, te doy	
	de que en la paz te mantenga	
	de tu Reino, sin que en ti	
60	satisfaga, ni en tu tierra,	
	la hidrópica sed[13] de sangre	
	de mi heredada soberbia.	
	Y porque[14] conozcas si es	
	`tan nunca usada° clemencia	such extraordinary
65	privilegio que ninguno	
	hasta hoy gozó, escucha atenta,	
	que quieren mis vanidades,	
	ya que mi origen me acuerda	
	estos páramos, gloriarse[15]	
70	de que a mí solo me deba,	
	y no al lustre de mi sangre,[16]	
	las adquiridas grandezas,	

---

12 **razón de estado** *reason of state*. Reason of state is a political philosophy that emphasizes pragmatism. So, Focas really says that he knows two things: first, he knows that they do not like him in Trinacria (they have good reason to hate him), and second, he can see they have decided to do the pragmatic thing and welcome him warmly even though they hate him. Cruickshank explains that Focas "assumes that Cintia is giving him a friendly welcome only because she lacks the military strength to do otherwise"(xcviii).

13 **hidrópica sed** *(figuratively) unquenchable thirst*. Focas suggests that he is bloodthirsty by nature (his "soberbia" or arrogance is inherited, or "heredada"). But note that he is promising *not* to seek bloodshed.

14 **Porque** *In order that*. The meaning of "porque" when followed by the subjunctive is the same as "para que."

15 **mis vanidades…** This passage contains not only hyperbaton (an unexpected or unconventional word order) but also a complicated form of metaphorical transference. The subject of this clause is "mis vanidades," by which Focas means "my vain thoughts or passions." These prompt him to "gloriarse" or revel in his own actions.

16 Focas is from humble origins. Everything he has achieved has been thanks to his own efforts ("a mí solo") and not to the nobility of his family ("y no al lustre de mi sangre").

con que aborto destos montes,[17]
doy a estos montes la vuelta.
75 Aquellas dos altas cimas,°   peaks
que en desigual competencia
de fuego el volcán corona,
corona de nieve el Etna,[18]
fueron mi primera cuna,
80 ya lo dije, sin que en ellas
tuviese más padres, que
las víboras° que en sí engendran.°   vipers, engender
Leche de lobas° infante   female wolves
`me alimentó° allí en mi tierna°   nourished me, young
85 edad, y en mi edad adulta
el veneno° de sus hierbas°...   poison, herbs
En cuya `bruta crianza°   savage upbringing
dudó la naturaleza,
si era fiera° o si era hombre,   wild animal
90 y resolvió,° al ver, que era   decided
hombre y fiera, que creciese
para Rey de hombres y fieras.
Y así, en primer vasallaje,°   servitude
me juraron° la obediencia   swore
95 cuantas, desnudas las garras,[19]
cuantas, armadas las testas,°   heads
tributaron, destroncadas°   killed
a mi sañuda° obediencia,   cruel
vestido y vianda en piel
100 y cadáver,[20] de manera,
que a mi furia `sin segunda,°   without equal
dos frutos° daba mi diestra,°   results, right hand

---

17 Focas is the "aborto" or monstrous birth of "destos montes." He grew up in these mountains.

18 **Etna** is a famous volcano on the island of Sicily that has a snow-capped peak.

19 **garras** *claws* The animals are the first to be subject to Focas' power.

20 Through his domination of the animals, Focas gains two things. The first is clothing ("vestido") which he makes from their "piel" or skins. The second is food ("vianda"), which he takes from their meat (here, gruesomely referred to as "cadáver"). These two things—food and clothing—are the "dos frutos" he'll mention just below.

en el horror que me adorna[21]
y el manjar° que me alimenta.   food
105   En esta, pues, crianza bruta
me halló bandida° la fiera   banded together
milicia de unos soldados,
que en la `intrincada maleza°   thick underbrush
del monte se mantenía
110   de hurtos,° robos y tragedias.   thefts
De la justicia acosados°   pursued
iban, de una en otra tierra,[22]
cuando encontrando conmigo,
absortos° a la extrañeza   dumbfounded
115   de ver racional lo bruto,
para que los defendiera,
me hicieron su Capitán,
cuya cuadrilla[23] pequeña,
a mi fama, en pocos días,
120   creció a copia° tan inmensa,   abundance
que puse en contribución,[24]
no solo de las aldeas°   villages
vecinas,° temido el vulgo,°   nearby, commoners
mas° pasando mis empresas°   but, undertakings
125   a populosas Ciudades,
las reduje a mi obediencia.[25]
Dejemos[26] en este estado
tiranizadas violencias,
sin que tu padre,[27] que entonces
130   reinaba en la Isla, pudiera
de mi orgullo resistir
la traidora inobediencia,

---

21   The "horror" with which he is adorned are the animal skins.

22   **de una en...**_from one land to the next_ This refers to the roving of the renegade soldiers who eventually join Focas' gang or "fiera milicia."

23   *Tp* "familia"

24   **puse en contribución** *I demanded or extorted payment from*

25   **las reduje...***I subjected (the populous cities) to my rule*

26   **Dejemos...***Let's leave (this story).* Focas will now tell what was happening elsewhere.

27   **tu padre** *Cintia's father*

y vamos a que Mauricio,
de Constantinopla César,°   emperor
135 a Italia pasó, en venganza
de que negaba soberbia
los feudos del sacro Imperio,[28]
talando tan sin defensa
sus campañas, que no hubo
140 plaza que en torres y almenas[29]
que no viese tremolada°   waving (on a flag)
la Águila de sus banderas.[30]
Tu padre, atento al peligro,
que ya llamaba a sus puertas,
145 con `generales perdones,
(¡oh razón de estado[31] necia°!   foolish
¿qué no harás, di, si hacer sabes
del delito° conveniencia°?)   misdeed, tool
llamó auxiliares° mis tropas   reinforcements
150 en su favor, y yo, al verlas
empleadas en más noble,
generoso asumpto,° vuelta   matter
lo que empezó por infamia°   disgrace
en blasón,° salí con ellas,   public honor
155 incorporado en las huestes[32]
de sus `milicianas levas°   calls to arms
al oposito a Mauricio,
con tan favorable estrella,
que de poder a poder,
160 medidas entrambas ° fuerzas,   both
murió° en campaña a mis manos,   [murió Mauricio]
con que sus `pompas deshechas,°   splendor destroyed

---

28 Mauricio attacked Italy with "venganza soberbia" because the Italians refused to pay tribute to the empire.

29 *Tp* "entonces muro, ni almena,"

30 The eagle is the traditional symbol of empire.

31 Here, political pragmatism (or expediency) is a mistake. You'll remember that Focas' gang is made up of renegade soldiers. Cintia's father, the king of Trinacria, promised to forgive the soldiers with "generales perdones" if they helped him fight Mauricio.

32 **huestes** *hosts* (in the sense of armies)

  desvanecidos° sus triunfos,   faded
  aclamándome la inmensa
165 voz de tantos su caudillo,[33]
  ya por mar, y ya por tierra,
  pude ˋseguir el alcance,°   pursuing (his goal)
  hasta dar vista a la excelsa°   magnificent
  Corte de Constantinopla,
170 que soberbiamente opuesta
  a tanto raudal de estragos,[34]
  trató ponerse en defensa.
  Real sitio° planté[35] a sus muros, siege
  sin que retirar pudieran
175 mis armas de sus recintos
  de cinco estíos,[36] la fiera
  saña° del Sol, ni de cinco   rage
  hibiernos° la helada hierba,   winters
  ira° de nieve y escarchas,   anger
180 hasta que en ruinas envuelta,
  desahuciada del hambre,[37]
  y de las armas opresa,
  a pesar de mil lealtades,
  me coronó por su César.
185 En cuyas altas conquistas,
  desde la facción° primera,   act of war
  hasta la última, que fue
  dejar reducida y quieta
  la Oriental parte de Europa,
190 seis lustros° gasté, por ˋtreinta five-year periods
  círculos que vi del Sol°,   thirty years
  testigos las canas sean,[38]
  que la mano desaliña,°   disorders

---

  33 **aclamándome la inmensa…***la inmensa voz de tantos aclamándome su caudillo…* Everyone in Sicily proclaimed Focas their leader after they saw him defeat Mauricio.

  34 **raudal de estragos** *the terrible abundance of war's destruction*

  35 *Tp* "plantó"

  36 **cinco estíos** *five summers* (the siege of Constantinople lasted five years)

  37 **en ruinas envuelta…***hopeless and crushed by hunger*

  38 **testigos las canas…***let these gray hairs be a witness*

	cuando juzgo que las peina.°	combs
195	Y aunque volviendo a Trinacria	
	hoy, bastante viso° tenga	reason to suspect
	en la presunción de que	
	vengo a conseguir° en ella	to achieve
	la vanidad de que quien	
200	bandido me vio, me vea	
	coronado Rey,³⁹ hay otras	
	dos razones que me muevan,	
	para cuyas dos contrarias	
	proposiciones opuestas,	
205	del rencor° y amor. Segunda	resentment
	vez te he menester atenta.⁴⁰	
	Audocia,⁴¹ que de Mauricio	
	tan amante esposa era,	
	que en las lides° le seguía,⁴²	battles
210	la noche, según me cuentan,	
	dicen dos vasallos suyos,	
	que él murió, en `su fuga° ella,	Audocia's escape
	con `los dolores del parto,°	birth pangs
	ni bien viva, ni bien muerta,	
215	en brazos de Astolfo–un noble	
	anciano cuya experiencia,	
	antes de dar la batalla,	
	en no sé qué conveniencias°	negotiations
	vino a hablarme embajador,⁴³	
220	`de suerte que° si le viera,	such that

---

39   The first reason that Focas has returned to Trinacria is that he wants everyone who knew him back when he was a bandit to see him crowned king. But he explains two more reasons in the following verses.

40   **te he menester...**_I need you to pay close attention_

41   Audocia was the wife of Mauricio. See introduction.

42   **en las lides...**Audocia followed Mauricio to his battles. The story that Focas tells in the following passage is broken up into a succession of short, choppy phrases of varying length. Sometimes Calderón will signal a change in action, subject, or mood through a change in meter (from hendecasyllabic to octosyllabic verse, for example). At other times, as in this case, Calderón indicates a change by changing rhythmic structures.

43   **vino a hablarme...**_[Astolfo] vino a hablarme [como] embajador_

le conociera[44]–dio a luz,
si es que hay luz en las tinieblas,[45]
un tierno infante, y con él
la vida,[46] el cual, viendo apenas
225   de su dueño en su poder
el hijo[47] con ʻtan deshecha
fortuna,° porque jamás   *great misfortune*
a dar en mis manos venga,
dicen que con él del monte
230   se retiró a la aspereza,
donde hasta hoy no se ha sabido
que uno ni otro viva o muera.[48]
Quédese esto aquí y pasemos
a otra noticia,[49] aún más que ésta
235   estraña,[50] y a nadie cuerdo[51]
inverosímil parezca
que concurran parecidos
dos sucesos,[52] que no hubiera
admiración, si tal vez
240   la historia más verdadera

---

44 **de suerte que...**Focas met Astolfo once and Focas would recognize Astolfo if they met again.

45 **luz en...***light in the darkness.* This is a play on "dar a luz" (to give birth) and an allusion to the gospel of John, chapter 1: "And the light shineth in darkness, and the darkness comprehended it not." This sort of Biblical reference does not mean that Focas is a Christian (this play makes little direct reference to religion).

46 **con él...**Audocia gave birth, then gave her life (she died shortly after giving birth).

47 This is confusing, but the sense of it is that Audocia gives her son to Astolfo so that the son (the true heir to Mauricio) will not be killed by Focas. To understand the lines, think of it this way: "su dueño" refers to Audocia ("dueño" was always masculine in the seventeenth century), and "en su poder" means "in Astolfo's care."

48 **no se ha sabido...***no one knows whether either of them* (Astolfo and the child) *are alive or dead*

49 Focas is changing subjects again. Just to help you keep track of things, the first story Focas told was about growing up in Trinacria and rising to fame and power, the second story was about the birth of Mauricio's son, and now he's starting the third story. This long backstory can seem like clumsy exposition, but the point is not what happened to Focas in the past. The point is what his storytelling communicates to us about him *now*.

50 **aún más que...***even stranger than the last story*

51 *Tp* "ya nadie"

52 **a nadie cuerdo...***It should not seem unbelievable to any wise person that two events seem so similar.* (He's about to tell a story very similar to Audocia's.)

       no se hiciera sospechosa[53]
       en los prodigios que cuenta.
       Irífile, una aldeana°   villager
       tan divinamente bella
245   que, a ser la hermosura imperio,
       la jurara Amor por reina,[54]
       dueño fue de mi albedrío,[55]
       que no hay tan ruda fiereza,°   savagery
       que no se rinda al amor,
250   ni tan constante belleza,
       que dominada del trato,°   dealings
       a quien la adore aborrezca.[56]
       Ésta, pues, el día que yo
       llamado vine,[57] en su aldea
255   encinta° quedó, asistida   pregnant
       de quien con mi confidencia,
       atento me aseguró que
       apenas llegó la nueva°   the news
       de mi vitoria a su oído,
260   cuando sintiendo la ausencia,[58]
       que el alcance ocasionaba,
       trató seguirme, resuelta[59]
       a no quedarse sin mí,
       al preciso riesgo expuesta
265   de sus deudos con el parto,°   birth
       que ya esperaba tan cerca,
       y que con ella viniendo,
       erró del monte la senda,[60]

---

53 *Tp* "provechosa"

54 **la jurara Amor...***the god of love (Cupid) would make her queen (or judge her worthy of being queen).* Today, we would use a different grammatical construction with the imperfect subjunctive and the conditional to express an idea that is contrary to fact: "si la hermosura fuera imperio, Amor la juraría reina."

55 **dueño fue...***she was in control of my will* (she captivated me or figuratively, "I loved her").

56 **ni tan constante...***[no hay] belleza que aborrezca a quien la adore*

57 **el día que...***the day I was called to battle*

58 **sintiendo la ausencia...***not liking to be away from me*

59 **resuelta** refers to Irífile. She is *resolved* or determined not to be away from Focas.

60 Irífile's guide took the wrong mountain trail.

        donde, cerrando la noche,

270   entre dos ʿincultas peñasº   wild mountains

        la asaltaron[61] los dolores,

        y él,º con la súbita pena   (the guide)

        de su desabrigo,º yendo   lack of shelter

        a ver si ʿpor dichaº hubiera   by chance

275   donde albergarla,º siguió   shelter her

        una luz, en cuya ausencia,

        (según ella dijo cuando

        volvió con gente por ella),

        un hombre llegó al gemido,º   groans

280   a quien, turbadaº o atenta,   confused

        porque el interés o el miedo

        de mi nombre le pusiera

        en mayor obligación,

        le reveló cuyo era

285   el fruto infeliz,[62] que ya

        lloraba sobre la hierba,

        añadiendo, que si acaso

        la dejaba el dolor muerta,

        para que fuese creído

290   de mí, le daba por señas

        una cifra de mi nombre

        en una lámina impresa

        de oro,[63] que yo la había dado

        de mi matrimonio en prendas:

295   y que finalmente, oyendo

        gente, se volvió a la sierra,

        ladrón del parto y la joya,[64]

        sin que por más diligencias

        que hiciesen, lo que duró

300   la vida a Irífile bella,

        y a él fuese posible el hacer,

---

61   *Tp* "soltaron"

62   **le reveló cuyo era**...*she told the man whose unfortunate child (fruto infeliz) it was*

63   **una cifra de**...*my name spelled out on a thin piece of gold*

64   **se volvió a**...*he returned to the mountain, stealing the baby and the jewelry (the* lámina*)*

que hurto ni ladrón parezca.[65]
Y siendo así, que hasta hoy
no me dio el valor licencia,
305 para que dejar pudiese
tantas vitorias suspensas.°   unfinished
Ya que, como he dicho, todo
el Levante° a mi orden queda,   eastern Mediterranean
vuelvo con los dos afectos
310 de amor y odio, ʿira y terneza,°   rage and tenderness
a buscar hoy en Trinacria
dos vidas que me atormentan
ignoradas[66]: Una, en fe
de la medrosa° sospecha   scary
315 de que haya de Mauricio
sucesión° que alterar° pueda   heir, disturb
en ningún tiempo el Imperio,
que le toca por herencia:
y otra, en fe del sentimiento
320 de que ʿla mía perezca.°   my heir might be dead
Y así, para coronar,
o sea varón o sea hembra,
a quien con mis señas halle,[67]
y dar muerte a quien sin ellas
325 halle también,[68] vengo expuesto
a que en la Trinacria esfera
no me ha de quedar poblado,°   dwelling place
monte, risco,° gruta° y peña,   chasm, cavern
que no registre, no busque,
330 no solicite, no inquiera,[69]
tronco° a tronco, y rama° a rama,   tree trunk, branch

---

65   This is a complicated passage. Try it this way: "sin que fuese posible hacer que parezca hurto (that which was stolen) ni ladrón (the thief) por más diligencias que hiciesen [durante] lo que duró la vida a Irífile bella."

66   **dos vidas...**the two lives, about which I know nothing, that torment me

67   **a quien con...**the child who looks like me (i.e. the child who is mine and therefore my heir)

68   *Tp* "halle. También..."

69   **que no registre...**These verbs take on the force of impersonal constructions, there will be neither mountains nor valleys that are not searched, checked, examined, and so on.

            hoja a hoja, y piedra a piedra,

            hasta que hallado° o no hallado,   found

            en el uno el temor° venza,   fear

335   o en el otro la esperanza,

            o bien se logre, o se pierda.

CINTIA   Si yo estuviera capaz

            de iguales causas,[70] yo hubiera

            hecho sin ti, en busca suya,

340   señor, cuantas diligencias

            al humano poder fuesen

            posibles: mas ya que llega

            tan tarde a mí la noticia,

            lo que puedo hacer en ella,

345   es asistirte, y en tanto

            que general bando se echa,

            con premio y castigo a quien,

            o sospechoso lo sepa,

            u obediente lo descubra.[71]

350   Ven donde descansar puedas

            de tantas prolijas marchas.

FOCAS   ¡Qué descanso habrá que tenga,

            quien temeroso° imagina,   fearful

            ni quien codicioso[72] piensa!

355   Mas vamos, Cintia, porque

            la primera diligencia

            empiece el bando.

CINTIA   Vosotras,

            para que desde aquí vean

            el alegre regocijo,°   rejoicing

360   con que mi Corte le espera,

            como a primicias del gozo,[73]

---

70 **Si yo estuviera...***Had I been aware of this situation...* An old meaning of "capaz" is informed or instructed.

71 There will be a "premio" for whoever finds one of the children (obediente lo descubra) and a "castigo" for whoever hides their whereabouts (sospechoso lo sepa).

72 **codicioso...***anxious for the outcome I hoped for.* Usually, "codicioso" means greedy. Here, it indicates that Focas intensely wants to find his lost son.

73 **primicias del gozo...***first fruits of happiness*

		volved al tono° y la letra.°	song, lyrics
FOCAS	Y vosotros a la salva	
	de cajas y de trompetas.	
CINTIA	Diciendo en sonoros° ecos...	musical

          volved al tono° y la letra.°   *song, lyrics*

FOCAS   Y vosotros a la salva
       de cajas y de trompetas.

365 CINTIA Diciendo en sonoros° ecos...   *musical*

FOCAS Diciendo en voces diversas...

DAMAS (*Cantan*) *El siempre vencedor Marte,*
      el nunca vencido César,
      a los montes de Trinacria
370   *en hora dichosa venga.*

SOLDADOS ¡Viva Cintia!

DAMAS   ¡Cintia viva!

SOLDADOS ¡Viva Focas!

TODOS   ¡Viva!

Vanse todos al son de cajas y guitarras, y vuelven a la voz de Libia.

LIBIA   (*Dentro*) ¡Muera!

FOCAS ¡Oíd, esperad, ʿsuspended
     el rumor°! ¿Qué voz es esta   *stop making noise!*
375   que, desmandada° del eco,   *disobedient*
     no es lo que oye lo que alienta?
     Sino antes tan al contrario
     articula la respuesta,
     que al decir que Focas viva
380   ella ha repetido...[74]

LIBIA   (*Dentro*) ¡Muera
     a manos de mi desdicha!°   *misfortune*

CINTIA A lo que de aquí se deja
     ver, fugitiva hermosura,
     desde en una en otra peña,
385   para descender al llano,
     buscando viene la senda,[75]
     tan ciegamente turbada,
     tan turbadamente ciega,

---

74 Focas believes that Libia has cried "¡Muera!" in response to the cheers of "¡Viva Focas!"

75 Cintia says that she sees in the distance ("de aquí se deja ver") a beautiful woman high in the mountains, blindly stumbling and trying to find a trail ("buscando viene la senda") that would let her descend to the plain ("descender al llano").

          que es el monte el que la busca,

390   y es el aire quien la encuentra,

          pues precipitada de él,

          cayendo va.

FOCAS   A socorrerla,

          por desmentir el agüero,[76]

          llegaré el primero. (*Vase Focas*)

LIBIA   (*Dentro*) Muera

395   a manos de mi desdicha,

          y no a manos de una fiera.[77]

FOCAS (*Dentro*) No harás, que en mis brazos yo,

          del cielo de tu belleza

          Atlante,[78] sabré parar

400   el rumor de su violencia...

         Sale Focas con Libia en los brazos.

          ...y pues, ya estás socorrida,°   rescued

          `cóbrate ánima y alienta.°   catch your breath

LIBIA Mal podré, que aunque de ti

          favorecida me vea,

405   no asegurada del riesgo

          que me sigue.

CINTIA   Qué es nos cuenta.[79]

LIBIA Libia, del sabio Lisipo,

          –aquel que en mágicas ciencias,[80]

          fue `aborrecido portento°   detested wonder

410   de Calabria,[81] porque en ella

          predijo° a su excelso Duque,[82]   predicted

          no sé qué infeliz tragedia,

---

76 **por desmentir...***to give the lie to the evil omen* (Cruickshank's paraphrase, xcvii).

77 It is finally clear that Libia speaks about her own death when she cries "muera."

78 **Atlante** *Atlas* In mythology, Atlas was the titan who held up the heavens. Focas says that he is like Atlas because he is holding the "cielo de tu belleza."

79 **Qué es nos...***Cuéntanos qué es.*

80 "Ciencia" formerly meant any certain knowledge (irrespective of the method by which it was derived). "Mágicas ciencias" means knowledge of sorcery.

81 Calabria is the region of Italy closest to the island of Sicily (called Trinacria in this play).

82 This is Federico, the "duque de Calabria" (see introduction).

en orden a que negaba
dar a Focas la obediencia—[83]
415 hija soy, que de sus ruinas
cómplice, le asisto[84] en esta
soledad, donde tomó
puerto su infeliz tragedia
el día que echado al mar,
420 sin norte, aguja, ni vela,
timón, ni jarcias[85] encallando°   coming ashore
en las tostadas arenas
desa° playa, abandonó   [de esa]
los poblados[86] por las selvas.°   jungles or forests
425 Aquí, pues, sin más caudal,°   resources
más patria, casa, ni hacienda°   wealth
que sus libros y sus tablas,
sus orbes, globos y esferas,
astrolabios y cuadrantes,[87]
430 y aquella choza° pequeña,   hut
que parece que del monte
ha descendido la cuesta,°   hillside
según en su verde falda[88]
como cansada se asienta,[89]
435 vivimos los dos, partiendo°   divvying up
él el cielo y yo la tierra,
pues yo la° cuento sus riscos,   [la tierra]
y él sus luceros° le cuenta,   rays
siendo pautado° carácter   marked

---

83   This passage explains that Lisipo foretold (*predijo*) that the duke (Federico) would be defeated if he fought Focas.

84   *Tp* "he visto"

85   **sin norte, aguja…***with neither compass, nor sails, nor rudder, nor rigging.* Lisipo sails from Calabria to Sicily without any of the necessary equipment. Although Calabria (on the mainland) is less than two miles from the island of Sicily, the Strait of Messina that separates them is notoriously treacherous due to its strong currents and whirlpools.

86   **abandonó los…***he left behind the populated places*

87   These are the tools of astronomical or astrological observation.

88   **verde falda** *the green base of the mountain (or the green that skirts the mountain)*

89   In this whimsical description of the lowly hut where Libia lives with her father, it is as if the hut plopped itself down tired at the foot of the mountain.

440	de sus líneas y mis flechas,°	arrows
	en mí el vulgo de las flores,	
	y en él el de las estrellas.⁹⁰	
	Con esta inclinación – si es	
	que es inclinación la fuerza,⁹¹	
445	pues no hay otra compañía,	
	que mi soledad divierta –	
	salí hoy al monte, seguida	
	de la montaraz caterva	
	de sabuesos y ventores,⁹²	
450	que atraillaba° la simpleza	had leashed
	de dos rústicos villanos,°	villagers
	que son la familia nuestra.	
	Y habiendo sido el primero	
	lance° una manchada cierva,⁹³	incident
455	a quien prestaron mis plumas	
	añadida ligereza,⁹⁴	
	tras ella, siguiendo el rastro	
	de la sangre por la hierba,	
	por el aire del latido,	
460	me hallé, perdida la senda,	
	sola en lo más intrincado	
	de unas marañadas breñas,⁹⁵	
	cuyo umbroso° laberinto	shadowy

---

90   **el vulgo de...** The "vulgo" generally means common folk, but here "el vulgo de las flores" is a metaphorical way of referring to the living things that populate the earth. While Libia concerns herself with what is on the ground (the flowers) her father concerns himself with the stars. It was common during the seventeenth century to compare stars and flowers, or to speak about flowers as "earthly stars" and stars as "heavenly flowers."

91   Libia's use of the terms "inclinación" and "fuerza" reflects common beliefs about astrology. The stars can "incline" us or give us an inclination to do something, but they cannot *force* us. Libia says that she might as well not have free will at all because her life is so isolated and lonely that she does not really have any choices to make.

92   **la montaraz caterva...** *a pack of mountain hounds* ("sabuesos" and "ventores" are hunting dogs)

93   **manchada cierva** *spotted doe*

94   **a quien prestaron...** the deer ran faster because it has been wounded by arrows, and it is as if the feathers (*plumas*) fletching the arrows gave the deer wings.

95   **lo más intrincado...** figuratively, the dense underbrush of a rough, mountainous land

cerraba el paso a la vuelta.[96]

465 Aquí llegaron los ecos
de dos cláusulas[97] tan nuevas,
como son en estos montes
oír de una parte trompetas
y cajas, y de otra parte

470 instrumentos, con que llena
de admiración° y de asombros°   surprise, amazement
estuve un rato suspensa,[98]
hasta que entre horror y halago°   delight
de la paz y de la guerra,

475 tercera voz decidió
la duda, escuchando della°   [de ella]
dos nombres, cuyo sentido
agora° no se me acuerda.[99]   [ahora]
Basta saber que, aplicando

480 el oído, de la espesa°   thick
maraña° las ramas quise   tangle
apartar, cuando funesta
boca—a quien dura mordaza
de un risco tenía entreabierta,

485 como esperezo[100]—por quien
melancólico bosteza
el monte arrojó de si,[101]
embrión de su pereza,
una fiera en forma de hombre,

490 un hombre en forma de fiera.
Vivo caduco° esqueleto[102]   dead

---

96   **cerraba el paso...***it was impossible to return by the same path because of the thick brush*

97   **cláusulas** *words* Libia is surprised to hear two human voices so deep in the wilderness.

98   **estuve un rato...***I stopped a moment to listen*

99   **dos nombres...***I do not remember now what those two names were*

100   **funesta boca...**This is the "boca" or mouth of a mountain pass, from which there rises a rocky spire (a "mordaza" or bit such as a horse wears in its mouth). With "funesta boca" Calderón starts to recall famous passages from his earlier play, *La vida es sueño*.

101   **por quien...***a man emerged like the gasp from the mouth of the mountain*

102   **Vivo caduco esqueleto...**This antithesis—a skeleton that is at the same time alive and dead—recalls Segismundo's description of himself in *La vida es sueño*: "un esqueleto vivo," and "un animado muerte."

el espectáculo era
de animada anatomía,[103]
sobre cuya piel grosera
495   barba y cabello nevaban
desmelenados a crenchas,[104]
llena de arrugas la faz,°   *face*
que el tiempo en la humana tierra,
–mal labrador, dejar sabe
500   a medio arar la tarea
de los sulcos[105] de la vida,
pues los abre y no los siembra—
del desplomado edificio[106]
nudoso puntal,[107] la seca
505   mano, al revés de otros troncos,
trataba al que le sustenta,
pues de corteza° y raíz°   *bark, root*
equivocadas las muestras,
donde iban las manos, iban
510   la raíz y la corteza.[108]
Vióme, y la voz perturbada,°   *disquieted*
\`tardo el paso,° macilenta°   *walking slowly, gaunt*
la faz, viniéndose a mí,
fue tal mi temor que...

FOCAS   ¡Espera!

515   ¡No prosigas! Que no sabes
cuánto en mi ofuscada idea
\`revuelves de° confusiones,   *stir up*
mujer, con lo que me cuentas.

---

103   The person appears as an "animada anatomía" in the sense that he is so thin that all of his bones can be seen. The description goes on to describe his wild hair and wrinkled appearance.

104   **cabello nevaban...***his disheveled hair fell (like white snow), roughly parted (as hair is parted)*

105   **surcos** *furrows*, these are the wrinkles in the man's face, that are like the furrows left by an inexpert farmer ("mal labrador") who plows but plants nothing.

106   **desplomado edificio...***fallen down building, a derelict*

107   **nudoso puntal** A "puntal" is the support that holds up a building that is falling down, "nudoso" means "knotty." So the hand is like a knotty support holding up a derelict building.

108   **al revés de...**This is a complicated image, but Libia says that this man was like an upside down tree because his hands were like roots. It is actually a very old convention to describe a person as an upside down tree or *arbor inversa*.

    ¿Especie de fiera y hombre

520   todavía se conserva

    donde hombre y fiera nací?[109]

    ¡Qué fuera, Cintia, qué fuera

    que donde vengo a buscar

    mi perdida descendencia°   *offspring*

525   con mi ascendencia° encontrara,   *ancestry*

    y que ese prodigio fuera

    origen de tan estraña,

    tan nunca vista, tan nueva

    naturaleza, como hoy

530   mi semejante me acuerda!

    Y así, soldados, conmigo

    venid, porque hasta que sepa

    qué `parecido portento°   *such a wonder*

    guarda mis primeras señas,[110]

535   no he de pasar adelante.

CINTIA   Ya que averiguarlo quieras

    si las cajas y las voces

    le sacaron[111] de su cueva,

    haz que prosigan, porque

540   su música le divierta,

    engañado, sin saber,

    que el monte en su busca cercas.°   *you surround*

FOCAS   Dices bien, y así, entre tanto,

    que yo sus cervices venza,[112]

545   prosigan entrambas salvas.

LIBIA   Yo seré, ya que eso intentas,

    la que procure guiarte,

    dando hacia el sitio la vuelta.[113]

---

109 **¿Todavía se conserva…**Focas says "nací" because he was also, according to his own account, born on that mountain. Focas described himself in similar terms ("si era hombre o si era fiera," verse 89).

110 **primeras señas** *signs of or keys to my origins*

111 **si las cajas…***if the drums and singing drew him (the skeletal old man) forth*

112 **cervices venza…***triumph over their necks* Just as you yoke an ox at the neck to control it, Focas will make everyone bow their necks to his domination. He's lording his power over Cintia and the people of Trinacria.

113 **dando hacia…***dando la vuelta hacia el sitio [donde vi al anciano]*

FOCAS Guía, pues. Tú, hermosa Cintia,
550   dispón, ya que aquí te quedas,[114]
       que el aparatoso° ruido   *spectacular*
       de cajas y voces vuelva.[115]

Vase con los Soldados.[116]

CINTIA Disponerlo si haré, pero
        quedarme no, porque `atenta
555   a complacer° a un tirano,   *attentive to pleasing*
        cuando él sube por aquella
        parte, `lisonjeando el riesgo,°   *courting danger*
        tengo de subir por esta.
ISMENIA Y todas procuraremos,°   *endeavor*
560   pues todas arcos° y flechas   *bows*
         manejamos, en su busca
         ser señora, las primeras.[117]
CINTIA Pues seguidme, sin que cesen
        voces, cajas y trompetas,
565   que yendo delante yo,
        quizá será la acción nuestra.
MÚSICOS (*Cantan*) *El siempre vencedor Marte,*
         el nunca vencido César,
         a los montes de Trinacria
570   *en hora dichosa venga.*
UNO ¡Viva Focas!
OTRO   ¡Cintia viva!

Vanse, repitiendo la música y la caja, y salen vestido de
pieles Astolfo viejo, Eraclio y Leónido galanes.[118]

---

114 **te quedas...** This is indicative, but Focas means it as a command: you stay (and see to it that the drums and singers return to where Libia saw the old man).

115 In short, Focas' plan is to return to the place where Libia saw the old man. They will do what she did, and proceed with drums and music, hoping to lure the person to their sounds.

116 Remember that this means that Focas exits the stage ("vase" or "se va") with his soldiers. Note how differently Cintia speaks when Focas is not around.

117 The verb "procurar" in verse 559 goes with "ser" in 562: *procuraremos ser las primeras* (we will endeavor to get there before the men).

118 The action now takes place in the mountains.

ASTOLFO Eraclio, oye...

ERACLIO   Padre, ¡suelta°!   let go!

ASTOLFO Detente° Leónido...   stop

LEÓNIDO   ¡Aparta!

ASTOLFO ¿Es posible, que tan ciega
575   resolución, excediendo
             los cotos de mi licencia,[119]
             hoy, temeraria,° mi vida   bold
             así aventure° y la vuestra,   risk
             llegando donde...?

Cantan dentro.

LEÓNIDO   ¿Qué quieres,
580   si esa música que suena
             tan nuevamente[120] a mi oído,
             apacible° y lisonjera,°   gentle, pleasant
             tanto mi espíritu mueve,
             tanto mi atención eleva,
585   y tanto mi afecto° inclina,   emotions
             que tras su acento° me lleva   tones, sound
             absorto y suspenso?[121]

Dentro suenan cajas.

ERACLIO   ¿Qué
             quieres,[122] si ese horror,[123] que llena
             de nuevo escándalo el aire,
590   tanto de mí me enajena,[124]
             tanto de mí me arrebata,°   works me up

---

119   **los cotos de...***the limits of my permission* (i.e. what I allow you to do)

120   **nuevamente** The music sounds "new" or "novel" in the sense that he's never heard anything
like it.

121   **tras su acento...***[la música] me lleva absorto tras su acento*

122   Both Leónido (verse 579) and Eraclio (verse 587) begin with "Qué quieres?" In what follows,
the two young men echo one another's cadence and speech.

123   **horror...**the military sounds of the soldiers' drums.

124   **tanto de mí...***so drives me out of my mind*

y tanto de mí en mi fuerza,	
que tras su estruendo, inflamado	
de no sé qué ardor,° intenta	fiery passion
595 ser ʼboreal[125] imán° de todos	magnetic north
mis sentidos y potencias?	
LEÓNIDO Pero ¿ʼqué mucho?° Si habiendo	is it any surprise?
tantas veces oído en esta	
soledad la dulce salva,	
600 con que la aurora° despierta,[126]	dawn
cuando en ʼla edad más florida°	the greenest stage
de la hermosa primavera,	
con más suavidad° las auras°	gentleness, breezes
y los cristales concuerdan,°	harmonize
605 cláusulas a cuyo blando	
compás,° con arpadas° lenguas	rhythm, musical
las aves° la bienvenida	birds
dan a rosas y azucenas,[127]	
risa° a risa y llanto° a llanto,	laugh, cry
610 flor a flor y perla a perla,	
nunca en su métrico canto	
oí música que suspenda	
tanto como esta,[128] hasta que hoy,	
con la ventaja° que lleva	advantage
615 lo sentido a lo trinado,[129]	
se entiende sin que se entienda.	

Dentro música.

ERACLIO Mas, ¿qué mucho? Si yo, habiendo	
tantas veces, en la densa°	dark

---

125   *Tp* "volcán,"

126   **dulce salva con…**The music that one hears at dawn: breezes, birdsongs, and so on.

127   **con arpadas lenguas…***las aves dan la bienvenida a rosas y azucenas con arpadas lenguas* (the birds of the morning welcome the opening roses and lilies with their song)

128   **nunca en su…***I've never heard music like this, music that makes me stop so completely what I'm doing*

129   **trinado** *warbling of birds* (the music he is hearing is greater than the warbling of birds he is accustomed to)

estación del año, oído
620 el rumor con que se quejan
atormentadas las copas°   treetops
de las ráfagas° violentas   gusts
de los vientos, las montañas,
de las avenidas fieras
625 de los arroyos,[130] las nubes,
de las cóleras° inquietas   fits
de los relámpagos°, nunca,   lightning
por más que unas estremezcan,°   shudder
otras crujan° y otras giman,°   creak, moan
630 oí estrépito,° que mueva   crash
tanto, como de ese que hoy
trueno° de nube serena...   thunder

Cajas dentro.

...parece que al corazón
enciende, anima y alienta.
635 ASTOLFO ¡Ay de mí! que esos dos ecos,
que uno irrita,° otro recrea,°   enflames, delights
temo que han de ser la ruina
de los tres.[131]
LOS DOS   ¿De qué manera?
ASTOLFO Porque saliendo a buscaros,
640 al ver que de mí os alejan,
me vio en esa ʽinculta estancia°   uninhabited place
una mujer,[132] y es bien tema,
que con el asombro° diga,   amazement
que me vio y que...
ERACLIO   Aguarda,° espera,   hold on
645 ¿por qué, si una mujer viste,
no me llamaste ʽa que° viera   so that

---

130 **avenidas fieras...**_the sounds of wild, rushing brooks_
131 **los tres** _all three (Astolfo, Eraclio, and Leónido)_
132 A reference to Libia.

yo cómo es la mujer?[133] Puesto
que de cuantas cosas cuentas
que hay en el mundo, ninguna,
650   siempre que la nombras, llega
a igualar con el halago,°   praise
la caricia° y la terneza   deep regard
con que su nombre se escucha,
pues, a modo de eco[134] deja
655   segundo ruido en el alma,[135]
que sin dar `razón entera°   complete explanation
de lo que quiere decir,
aun con la mitad deleita.

LEÓNIDO   Yo te agradezco, que a mí
660   no me llamases al verla,
porque al contrario parece
que en mí sus efectos muestra.
Pues siempre que "mujer" dices,
al oír su nombre tiembla°   trembles
665   el corazón, como que
de algún contrario° se acuerda,°   adversary, remembers
dejándome su sonido
no sé qué susto,° qué pena,   fright
que acá en el alma parece
670   que aun no sabida, atormenta.

ASTOLFO   ¡Ay Eraclio, qué bien juzgas!
¡Ay, Leónido, qué bien piensas!

ERACLIO   ¿Cómo puede ser, si son
contrarias las ansias nuestras,

---

133   Stories about boys brought up without ever having seen a woman—and as a consequence being unable to understand what a woman is when they see one—are very old. The fourteenth-century author, Giovanni Boccaccio, tells a famous version of such a story in the *Decameron* (Day IV). In Calderón's Spain, people would have learned a story about a boy who grew up in total darkness without ever casting eyes on a woman from a famous collection of tales called *Barlaam y Josephat*. Gracián, one of the great prose writers of Calderón's period, recounts the story of this boy in *Agudeza y arte de ingenio* (chapter 57). Scholars continue to debate whether or not these fantasies of an exclusively male space are misogynist. On the influence of *Barlaam y Josephat* on Calderón, see Bartra's *The Artificial Savage* (96).

134   *Tp* "dello"

135   **a modo de…**While he would have liked to have seen the woman to whom Astolfo refers, just hearing about her "second hand" (like a echo) stirs his soul.

675   que él diga bien, y yo y todo
      juzgue bien?
      Astolfo   Como es cualquiera
      mujer, pintura a dos visos,[136]
      que vista a dos haces[137] muestra
      de una parte una hermosura,
680   y de otra parte una fiera,
      sin que se sepa en cuál puso
      el arte más excelencia.
      El más familiar amigo[138]
      de nuestra naturaleza
685   es y el enemigo más
      familiar de la fe° nuestra: faith
      la media vida del alma
      es tal vez, tal vez la media
      muerte del alma. No hay
690   regalo,° Eraclio, sin ella,   happiness
      y sin ella no hay, Leónido,
      dolor ni ansia, de manera
      que, mirada a entrambas luces,[139]
      hace bien el que la tema,°   fears
695   y hace bien el que la estime.
      Cuerdo° es el que `se fía° della,   wise, trusts
      y cuerdo el que desconfía°,   mistrusts
      porque en `igual competencia,°   equal measure
      ella da la vida y mata,
700   ella es la paz y la guerra,

---

136 **a dos visos** *from two perspectives* Calderón often compared natural things to paintings. Here, however, he makes a special comparison: women, Astolfo says, are like anamorphic paintings. When you look at them one way, you see something positive, when you look at them from a different angle, you see something frightening. In botany, anamorphosis is when one species has characteristics that make it look like a different species. Astolfo's passage helps introduce a theme in the play: things that seem to be one thing, but turn out to be another when viewed differently. For a study of this language, see Amadei-Pulice (209).

137 **haces** plural of "haz" (i.e. "cara")

138 Astolfo is talking about "woman" as an abstraction and not women as people, which is why he uses the masculine "amigo" and "enemigo."

139 **a entrambas luces** *from both perspectives* See also, *Sueños hay que verdad son* for similar references to paintings and perspective (330-341).

          la cura y la enfermedad,

          la alegría y la tristeza,

          la triaca° y el veneno,[140]   antidote

          la quietud° y la tormenta,   calm

705   y para decirlo todo,

          bien y mal de contingencias,[141]

          que, árbitro del bien y el mal,

          da el honor y da la afrenta,[142]

          que es cuanto hay que dar, de suerte

710   que, a imitación de la lengua,

          loable° o nociva,° no hay   praiseworthy, harmful

          cosa en el mundo que sea

          tan mala como la mala,

          tan buena como la buena.

715   LEÓNIDO   Ya que de hoy la novedad

          facilita la materia

          a que nos hables más claro

          que otras veces,[143] no se pierda

          la ocasión° de verte afable.   opportunity

720   Si hay bien y mal, ¿por qué niegas

          a los dos del bien las dichas,

          ni del mal las experiencias?

   ERACLIO   Has dicho bien. ¿Hasta cuándo,

          padre, negarnos intentas

725   la libertad? ¿No es ya hora

          de que sepamos quién seas,

          y quién somos y por qué

          a vivir así nos fuerzas?

   ASTOLFO   ¡Ay, hijos! Sin que hoy

730   esa novedad me mueva,

---

140   *La cura y la enfermedad* and *El veneno y la triaca* are titles of plays written by Calderón.

141   **bien y mal...***good and bad, depending on the circumstances*

142   Women were often described as the repositories or sources of honor. Women, unlike men, could bring dishonor on their families if they had sex before or outside of marriage. Other plays by Calderón (e.g. *El médico de su honra*) portray men who kill their wives, mistakenly believing that the wives have brought dishonor on the men's houses through sexual infidelity.

143   **ya que de...***Since the novelty (of seeing Libia) has encouraged you to speak to us more plainly than in the past*

la de mi cercana° muerte   impending
os adquiere la respuesta.
Y pues ya, jóvenes ambos,
mi vida mi edad abrevia,°   cuts short
735   oíd quien sois, y el peligro
que al salir de aquí os espera,
y la razón porque tuve
vuestras fortunas suspensas.
El Emperador, Mauricio,
Cristiano Atlante...

740   HOMBRES   (*Dentro*) ¡A la selva!
      MUJERES   (*Dentro*) ¡A la cumbre°!   peak
      HOMBRES   (*Dentro*) ¡Al monte!
      MUJERES   (*Dentro*) ¡Al llano!
      ASTOLFO   ¡Ay de mi! ¿qué voces truecan[144]
los pasados ecos?
      LEÓNIDO   Toda
la montaña está cubierta
de gente.

745   ERACLIO   Y venciendo vienen
su cumbre[145] tropas° diversas   troops
por ambas partes.
      HOMBRES   (*Dentro*) ¡Al risco![146]
      MUJERES   (*Dentro*) Al valle.
      ASTOLFO   Sin duda aquella
mujer contra mí amotina°   stirs up
ese vulgo.°   mob of people

750   LOS DOS   ¿Qué hay que temas?
      ASTOLFO   Que aunque tan desemejado
monte, edad, traje me tengan,[147]
como haya quien me conozca,

---

144   The sounds that Astolfo heard previously have returned but are confused or mixed up.

145   **venciendo vienen...***they are coming over the mountaintop*

146   The world "risco" gives a sense of the steepness of a mountainside or a chasm. In that sense, it can mean both a mountain and a deep valley.

147   **aunque tan desemejado...***although they will find me in an unlikely place and much changed in my dress and much older*

peligra una vida vuestra.[148]

755 ERACLIO Aunque hasta aquí es para mí
enigma cuanto nos cuentas,
no en defensa de mi vida,
mas de la tuya en defensa
al paso° les saldré, en tanto   mountain pass
760 que con Leónido a la cueva
vuelves, y de hojas y ramas
la escondida boca cierras.[149]

LEÓNIDO ¿Por qué has de pensar de mí
que huya° yo si tú te arriesgas,   flee
765 cuando primero° que tú
les saldré al paso por esta
parte.

ERACLIO   Pues yo por estotra.[150]

ASTOLFO ¡Leónido oye! ¡Eraclio espera!

LEÓNIDO Si el riesgo es que te conozcan,
huye tú.

ASTOLFO   Yo...

ERACLIO   ¡Espera!

770 LEÓNIDO   ¡Suelta!

ASTOLFO Ved, mirad.

LOS DOS   Salva tu vida,
que importa más que la nuestra.

Vanse por dos partes los dos, y salen Luquete y Sabañón, villanos.

ASTOLFO ¡Ay de mí! Que aunque seguirlos
mi caduca planta quiera,
no puedo.

775 LUQUETE   Hacia aquí una voz
se oye.

SABAÑÓN   Hacia aquí un eco suena.

ASTOLFO ¡Leónido! ¡Eraclio!

---

148 **como haya quien...***if they've brought someone who knows who I am, one of your lives is in danger*

149 In Eraclio's plan, Leónido will disguise the mouth of the cave where they dwell.

150 **estotra...***esta otra (parte)* The two young men head in opposite directions.

LUQUETE	Aunque no	
	sea Leónido...	
SABAÑÓN	Aunque no	
	sea Eraclio...	
LUQUETE	...sepa de quien	
	le llama el camino.	

780   SABAÑÓN   ...Sepa
la senda° de quien le llama.[151]   path
LOS DOS ¡Decidme, por vida vuestra!
LUQUETE Mas, ¿qué es esto?
SABAÑÓN   Lo que es estotro.
ASTOLFO Teneos.°   halt
LUQUETE   ¿Qué manda?
SABAÑÓN   ¿Qué ordena?
785   ASTOLFO ¿Quién sois, que hasta aquí vinisteis?
LUQUETE Un gran asno.[152]
SABAÑÓN   Una gran bestia.
ASTOLFO ¿Quien sois? digo otra vez.
LUQUETE   Yo,
otras veinte...
SABAÑÓN   Yo otras treinta...
LUQUETE ...que un mentecato.°   fool
SABAÑÓN   ...que un tonto.
790   ASTOLFO ¿A qué por aquestas tierras
vinisteis?
LUQUETE   A ver visiones.
SABAÑÓN A cazar° almas en pena.[153]   hunt
ASTOLFO ¿Cómo os llamáis?
LUQUETE   Yo Luquete.
SABAÑÓN Sabañón yo.
ASTOLFO   De ambos sepa,
795   ¿qué trompas y cajas son,
que se han escuchado, ésas?

---

151   Luquete and Sabañón are lost. They've heard Astolfo cry out and they want to find him in order to figure out where they are.

152   Luquete and Sabañón are comic relief. Luquete says Sabañón is an ass because he got them lost in the forest. Sabañón makes the same accusation.

153   **almas en pena** *souls in Purgatory*

	LUQUETE	Yo no entiendo bien de cajas,	
		que no sean de conserva.[154]	
	SABAÑÓN	Ni yo bien de trompas, que	
800		trompas de París[155] no sean.	
	ASTOLFO	¿Qué gente es esa, que el monte	
		corre?	
	LUQUETE	¿Quién hay que lo entienda?	
	SABAÑÓN	Pastores fuimos los dos.	
	LUQUETE	Dejando cabras y ovejas,	
805		dimos en servir a un magro.[156]	
	SABAÑÓN	No quitando su presencia.[157]	
	LUQUETE	Este tal tiene una hija...[158]	
	SABAÑÓN	...marimacha° destas selvas...	tomboy
	LUQUETE	...saltamonta° destos campos.	grasshopper
810	SABAÑÓN	Viniendo `a caza° con ella,	hunting
		perdimos ambos su voz...	
	LUQUETE	...sin saber que causa tengan...	
	SABAÑÓN	...esotras,° que van diciendo...	those others
	UN HOMBRE	(*Dentro*)¡Sube al monte!	
	UNA MUJER	(*Dentro*) ¡El risco cerca°!	surround
	UN HOMBRE	(*Dentro*) Que allí hay gente.	
815	UNA MUJER	(*Dentro*) Que allí hay ruido.	
	ASTOLFO	Ya se escuchan de más cerca.	
		(*Aparte*) (¡Ay de Leónido y Eraclio,	
		si estos hombres los encuentran!	
		Y pues seguirlos no puedo,	
820		que intente ocultarme es fuerza,	
		pues no hay contra ellos[159] indicio,°	evidence

---

154 "Cajas" can mean drums, but it can also mean jars used for jams and sweets (conserva).

155 The "trompa de París" or "trompa gallega" is a kind of single-stringed mouth harp. The instrument may have originated in Africa.

156 This is another joke. "Magro" is a cut of meat, so perhaps the men left their flocks for meat (maybe a better job). However, as they go on to hint, the "magro" they serve is Lisipo, who is a "mago" (a wizard) not a "magro."

157 This means something like "no offense to you." "Magro" also means skinny and we know from Libia's description that Astolfo is very skinny.

158 Lisipo's daughter is Libia. From her account, we know that she loves to hunt. Luquete and Sabañón frequently finish one another's sentences, which may help you understand the dialog.

159 **ellos** *Leónido and Eraclio*

mientras que yo no parezca.
Pero estos° dirán de mí...   Luquete and Sabañón
Mas ¡buen remedio!) (*Áselos*)[160]
LOS DOS   ¿Qué intenta?
825   ASTOLFO   Que a esta cueva entréis conmigo.
SABAÑÓN   Escusada diligencia[161]
es, cuando de nieve somos,
el llevarnos a la cueva.[162]
LUQUETE   Más sanos del tiempo estamos.[163]
ASTOLFO   Entrad, villanos.
830   LOS DOS   Advierta,
si es porque no nos dañemos,
que ya es tarde.

Astolfo los lleva a la cueva.

CINTIA   (*Dentro*) La primera
`tengo de° ser, pues allí   [tengo que]
anda gente, que trascienda
835   lo intrincado de sus senos.[164]
ERACLIO   (*Dentro*) No harás, que hay quien lo defienda.

Sale Cintia.

CINTIA   ¿Quién podrá contra mis iras?[165]

Sale Eraclio.

ERACLIO   ¿Ni quién se opondrá a mis fuerzas?

---

160   **Áselos** *Astolfo grabs Luquete and Sabañón*
161   **Escusada diligencia** *An unnecessary effort*
162   They are "nieve" in the sense of being white with fear. Snow was frequently stored in caves or pits called "neveras" to be used to cool drinks in summertime.
163   **Más sanos...** *We will be safer at room temperature* (a playful reference to Sabañón's earlier statement about being like snow)
164   **que trascienda...** *who climb through the dense depths of the forest*
165   **iras** *impetuousness or passion (driving the character).* Generally "ira" means unrestrained anger. This ire or wrath is one of the seven deadly sins. However, in the plural, it often refers to a passionate or excessive desire, whether for something negative (vengeance) or something positive (justice).

                  (*Ap.*) (Mas ¡qué miro!)

Cintia   (*Ap.*) (Mas ¡qué veo!)

Eraclio (*Ap.*) (¡Qué bello animal!)

840 Cintia   (*Ap.*) (¡Qué fiera
     tan espantosa!)

Eraclio   (*Ap.*) (¡Divino
     asombro!)

Cintia   (*Ap.*) (¡Horrible presencia!)

Eraclio (*Ap.*) (Cuanto animoso° esperaba,   *eagerly*
     tanto ya cobarde tiembla
     el corazón.)

845 Cintia   (*Ap.*) (Cuanto vine
     osada,° altiva y resuelta,   *arrogant*
     tanto ya tímida dudo.)

Eraclio (*Ap.*) (¡Qué hermosura!)

Cintia   (*Ap.*) (¡Que fiereza°!)   *savageness*

Eraclio Cizaña[166] de dos sentidos,

850   pues con hurtados despojos,[167]
     antes de verte los ojos,
     te miraron los oídos:
     ¿Quién eres, que suspendidos
     los dejas?

Cintia   ¿Quién he de ser?

855   Quien sin llegarse a valer
     de honor, que después sabrás,
     es una mujer no más.[168]

Eraclio Y ¡que más que una mujer!
     Y si todas son así,

860   ¿cómo hubo hombre que vivió?

Cintia Luego ¿no has visto otra?

Eraclio   No,
     aunque presumo,° que sí.   *assume*

Cintia ¿Cómo?

---

166 **cizaña** is a weed that chokes out good crops. Here, Cintia's beauty is a force that prevents Eraclio from perceiving properly.

167 **hurtados despojos** *stolen treasure* (figuratively, the sound of her voice)

168 This passage—"¿Quién he de ser?...es una mujer no más"—inverts verses from Tirso de Molina's *El burlador de Sevilla*: "¿Quién ha de ser? Un hombre y una mujer."

	ERACLIO	Como al cielo vi,	
		y siendo el hombre en el suelo	
865		breve mundo en su azul velo,°	veil
		bien que vi a la mujer fundo,[169]	
		pues si el hombre es breve mundo,	
		la mujer es breve cielo.[170]	
	CINTIA	Y tú, que ignorante incurres°	take up (a subject)
870		en lo que atento mejoras,	
		pues si como bruto ignoras,°	do not know
		no como bruto discurres°:	speak
		¿quién eres, que ʿal paso ocurres°	come to the pass
		tan fiero?	
	ERACLIO	No sé.	
	CINTIA	¿Quién fue	
875		un anciano, que escuché	
		ser deste monte horror fuerte?	
	ERACLIO	No sé.	
	CINTIA	¿Cómo desta suerte	
		en el vives tú?	
	ERACLIO	No sé.	
	CINTIA	¿Nada sabes?	
	ERACLIO	No indignada	
880		culpa tus iras me den,	
		que no sabe poco quien	
		sabe que no sabe nada.[171]	
		Y aunque estuviera informada[172]	
		de mí mi ignorancia...	
	CINTIA	Di.	
885	ERACLIO	...volviera, al ver que te vi,	
		a ignorar.	

---

169   **fundo** *I deduce or I surmise*

170   This is a reference to the idea that human beings were a microcosm ("breve mundo") of the universe or macrocosm. The lines recall Segismundo's in *La vida es sueño*: "era el hombre, por ser un mundo breve... la mujer, pues ha sido un breve cielo."

171   This idea—that the greatest knowledge is to know that one knows little or nothing—was attributed to Socrates by Plato.

172   It is his "ignorancia" that would be "informada." Eraclio speaks about his own ignorance as if that ignorance were external to him. He says, in other words, "even if my ignorance were informed by me... (my ignorance would end up not knowing)."

CINTIA	¿De qué manera?	
ERACLIO	Como de mí no supiera,	
	aunque supiera de mí.	
CINTIA	Pues yo tengo de saber	
890	quién eres, o de tu vida	
	mi valor me hará homicida.°	killer
ERACLIO	¡Qué poco tendrá que hacer!	

Cintia flecha el arco, cáese la flecha,[173] y al tomar otra se caen las demás.

CINTIA	El temor me hizo perder	
	las flechas.	
ERACLIO	¿Menos las echas?[174]	
CINTIA	¿Pues no?	
895 ERACLIO	No, que si aprovechas	
	los ojos en dar desmayos,[175]	
	quedándote con sus rayos,[176]	
	¿qué falta te hacen las flechas?	
CINTIA	En tu aspecto° lo feroz,	appearance
900	cuando en tu estilo lo fiel,	
	o esa voz `no es de° esa piel,	doesn't match
	o esa piel no es de esa voz:	
	Con que el discurso veloz°	fast
	de una en otra fantasía,	
905	de nieve una estatua fría	
	en mí va labrando ciego.	
ERACLIO	En mí de nieve y de fuego.	

Estando suspensos Eraclio y Cintia, salen al otro lado Leónido y Libia.

LEÓNIDO	Bello escándalo[177] del día,

---

173 **cáese la flecha** *she drops the arrow*

174 **Menos las echas?** *Do you really need them?*

175 **No, que si...***you do not need arrows because your eyes are enough to make me faint*

176 Today, we understand that we can see because light enters the eye. For much of human history, however, people believed that the eye emitted rays (rayos) in order to see (somewhat similar to the way a bat emits sounds in order to echolocate).

177 **escándalo** *something astounding*

que has venido anticipado°							before
a esa gente que te sigue,
porque el mirarte me obligue
a que me halle mi cuidado[178]
suspenso, absorto y turbado.
¿Quién eres?

LIBIA					Quien a buscar
vino a otro y en su lugar
te halla,[179] porque en susto tanto,
doblándose en ti el espanto,
en mi se doble el pesar.°							regret

LEÓNIDO ¿A otro buscas y no a mí?
Segundo susto eres ya.

LIBIA ¿Pues qué cuidado te da,
que no busque a quien no vi?

LEÓNIDO No sé, pero aunque temí
que a darme muerte venía
tu arrogancia,[180] como veía
cuan dulce muerte me daba,
sentía que me mataba,
sin sentir que lo sentía.
Mas cuando buscando vas
a otro,° tan otro° el mal es,						another, different
que echo menos que me des
la muerte que no me das.
¿A quién, di, buscando estás?

LIBIA A un anciano, que hoy aquí
en tu fiero traje vi.

LEÓNIDO ¿Luego tú vienes a ser,
bello hechizo,° la mujer,							spell
que él dice que le vio?

LIBIA					Sí.

LEÓNIDO Luego bien conmigo lucho,

---

178 **cuidado** often means "worry" during the period, but here, it means something closer to "thoughts."

179 **Quien a buscar...***I am she who came in search of another but found you instead.* Remember that Libia is searching for Astolfo, whom she saw earlier.

180 **a darme muerte...***tu arrogancia venía a darme muerte*

940		si ser vida y muerte creo.
	UNA MUJER	(*Dentro*) ¡Bella Cintia!
	ERACLIO	Mas ¿qué veo?
	FOCAS	(*Dentro*) Libia hermosa.
	LEÓNIDO	Mas ¿qué escucho?
	ERACLIO	Mucho es mi recelo.° — suspicion
	LEÓNIDO	Mucho mi temor.
	UNA MUJER	(*Dentro*) ¡Espera!
	UN HOMBRE	(*Dentro*) ¡Aguarda!
945	CINTIA	Gente es que viene en mi guarda.[181]
	LIBIA	Gente es que seguirme intenta.
	ERACLIO	Pues si tu luz me amedrenta°... — terrifies me
	LEÓNIDO	Pues si tu luz me acobarda°... — intimidates
	ERACLIO	...presto verás que no ha sido
950		vil° temor el que me ha helado... — base
	LEÓNIDO	...presto verás que el que ha estado suspenso lidia atrevido...[182]
	ERACLIO	...que de cuantos te han seguido ninguno aquí ha de llegar. (*Vase Eraclio*)
955	LEÓNIDO	...que ninguno ha de pasar el término° que pasaste. (*Vase Leónido*) — border
	CINTIA	Corazón, el temor baste.
	LIBIA	Recelo, baste el pesar.
	CINTIA	Y pues, saliendo al camino,
960		con otras dará, de él quiero huir, que a su asombro muero.

Truecan puesto las dos.[183]

---

181 To understand this part of the play, you should visualize that on one part of the stage Cintia is still talking with Eraclio. On another part of the stage (unaware of the presence of Cintia and Eraclio) Libia is speaking with Leónido. These are essentially two simultaneous but distinct interactions.

182 **el que ha...***he who has been stopped in his tracks* (suspenso) *with amazement fights daringly* (lidia atrevido)

183 The two women switch places (perhaps as they wander, absorbed in thought). They are still unaware of one another. Remember that Cintia was the first woman Eraclio ever saw, and Libia the first woman Leónido saw. But now the women have switched places, so when Eraclio emerges from where he exited the stage (see below) he will see Libia, not Cintia. Leónido will have a parallel experience, finding Cintia where he left Libia.

Libia	Y pues a otras manos vino,	
	huir su vista determino.	
Una mujer	(*Dentro*) ¡Cintia!	
Un hombre	(*Dentro*) ¡Libia!	

Vuelven Leónido y Eraclio y encuentran a Cintia y Libia trocadas.

Eraclio	Desmandada	
965	la gente, sin que la entrada	
	halle a este sitio, volvió.	
Leónido	Solo aquí la voz llegó,[184]	
	y pues por agora nada	
	hay que temer, vuelva a ver	
970	al encanto desta selva.	
Eraclio	Y así de un riesgo a otro, vuelva	
	al que da más que temer.	
Leónido	(*A Cintia*) Imán fue tu rosicler.[185]	
Eraclio	(*A Libia*) Norte° ha sido mi deseo.	North Star
975	Leónido Que aquí lo que dudo creo.	
Eraclio	Que aquí lo que toco admiro.	
Cintia	(*Ap.*) (¡Cielos, nuevo monstruo veo!)	
Libia	(*Ap.*) (¡Cielos, nuevo monstruo veo!)	
Leónido	¿Cómo en tan breves instantes	
980	truecas las señas° primeras?	features
	Bien me dijeron, que eras	
	animal de dos semblantes.°	appearances
Eraclio	Justo es, que al verte me espantes,	
	que aunque las rudezas mías	
985	ya sabían, que podías	
	mudar la cara a dos haces,[186]	

---

184 **Solo aquí…** *Only the voices or sounds of the people (and not the people themselves) made it here*

185 **rosicler** *the rosy color of dawn* Figuratively, "rosicler" means her complexion, which Leónido says drew him back like a magnet (imán). Neither Leónido nor Eraclio realize they are speaking to different women.

186 **haces** is in this instance, the plural of "haz" (appearance). In the next line it will be a conjugated form of the verb "hacer." This play on *haces* (from *haz*) and *haces* (from *hacer*) is a pun, the technical term for which is *paronomasia* in both English and Spanish.

          no sé si bien o mal haces
          en trocar la que tenías.
LEÓNIDO Más justo es agradecer
990   la mudanza,° que hallo en ti,   *change*
          pues aunque bella te vi,
          más bella te llego a ver.
ERACLIO Y pues vuelvo a pretender,°   *aspire to*
          cobradas° flechas y aljabas,°   *recovered, quiver*
995   la muerte que antes me dabas.
          Porque la agradezca más,
          no me mates como estás,
          mátame como te estabas.
LIBIA Yo soy quien debía estrañar°   *[extrañar]*
1000   el verte ʿtan[187] otro° aquí.   *so changed*
CINTIA Yo soy quien podía de ti
          las nuevas señas dudar.
LIBIA Mas, no es tiempo de apurar°... (*Yéndose*)   *insist*
CINTIA Mas, no es tiempo de argüir... (*Yéndose*)
1005   LIBIA ...de tu bruto discurrir
          la causa.
CINTIA   ...de tu rudeza
          la ocasión.
LEÓNIDO   No tu belleza
          se ausente.
ERACLIO   No te has de ir.
LIBIA Ten la mano,° pues dejarte   *hands off*
1010   basta sin darte la muerte.
CINTIA No me toques, que en tan fuerte
          riesgo basta el no matarte.
LEÓNIDO No has de irte.
ERACLIO   No has de ausentarte.

Eraclio y Leónido intentan detenerlas.

UNO (*Dentro*) ¡Libia!
OTRO   (*Dentro*) ¡Cintia!
1015   LIBIA   ¡Hacia este puesto

---

187 *Tp* "con"

venid!

CINTIA			¡Llegad, llegad presto!

LAS DOS	¡Que aquí las fieras están!

Salen Soldados y Focas y los demás por otro lado.

FOCAS		Voces Libia y Cintia dan.
			¡Acudid todos!

TODOS					¿Qué es esto?

LAS DOS	Que habiendo el monte corrido...

1020	ERACLIO	(*Ap.*) (`Dame albricias,° corazón...		[exclamation of joy]

LEÓNIDO	(*Ap.*) (Alma, dame albricias...

ERACLIO							...que
			dos los semblantes no son...

LEÓNIDO	...que no son dos las mudanzas...

LOS DOS	...sino las mujeres dos.)

1025	CINTIA	En esta parte encontré
			a este espanto.

LIBIA				Yo a este horror,
			sin que el anciano parezca.

FOCAS		Fieras, en quien viendo estoy
			de mi primero linaje°						lineage

1030			la bruta especie,° ¿quién sois?				species

ERACLIO	No sabemos de nosotros
			más de que solo nos dio
			este monte la primera
			cuna,° alimento el verdor°					cradle, green

1035			de sus plantas, y este traje
			de sus brutos lo feroz.

FOCAS		Hasta ahí supe yo de mí,
			pero vosotros mejor
			lo sabréis, pues un caduco

1040			anciano hay `más que° los dos,				in addition to
			¿dónde está?

LEÓNIDO				De él no sabemos.

ERACLIO	Ni tú sabrás.

FOCAS		(*A Eraclio*) ¿Cómo no?

   (*A los soldados*) Registrad grutas y quiebras[188]
   deste risco, que mostró
1045 que por mas impenetrable
   será en él° su habitación.   [en el risco]
UN SOLDADO Aquí, de ramos cubierta,
   una boca° está.   mouth of the cave
LIBIA   Y si yo
   vuelvo a recorrer° las señas,   run my eyes over
1050 ella es de donde salió.

    Pónense Eraclio y Leónido a la boca de la cueva.

FOCAS Entrad, pues, mirad su centro.°   innermost part
LEÓNIDO `Nadie ose° llegar, si no   let no one dare
   quiere antes morir.
FOCAS   ¿Pues quién
   lo impedirá?°   oppose, impede
LEÓNIDO   Mi valor.
1055 ERACLIO Y el mío, porque primero,
   que a esta `lóbrega mansión°   dark dwelling
   ninguno entre, en su defensa
   hemos de morir los dos.
FOCAS Dos veces brutos, ¿no veis
1060 cuanto vuestra pretensión°   attempt
   es imposible?
LOS DOS   Llegad,°   come at us
   y lo veréis.
FOCAS   A un error
   tan desatinado,° mueran.   foolhardy
CINTIA No quede `acerado[189] arpón,° sharpened arrow
1065 que no se vibre en sus pechos.
TODOS ¡Mueran pues!

  Al ir a dispararlos, sale Astolfo, y pónese delante de Eraclio y Leónido.

ASTOLFO   Aqueso no.

---

188 **Registrad grutas...**_Search the caves and cracks in the mountain_
189 *Tp* "flechado"

Si ellos han de morir, menos
importa que muera yo,
matadme a mí y ellos vivan.

Quédanse suspensos todos, mirándole a Astolfo.

1070 Focas ¿Qué es lo que mirando estoy?
       Libia Al que yo vi.
      Cintia   ¡Qué portento!
Un hombre ¡Qué asombro!
 Una mujer   ¡`Qué admiración°!   how astounding!

Salen Sabañón y Luquete.

  Sabañón Apunten bien los que hubieren
           de tirar, por solo un Dios,
1075   porque me darán a mí,[190]
           según desgraciado soy.
   Luquete Que a mí me apunten les pido,
            pues con eso mi temor
            sabrá, que han de dar a otro:[191]
1080   mas, ¿qué es lo que viendo estoy?
  Sabañón   ¿Qué hace aquí con tanta gente
            nuestra ama?[192]
   Luquete   ¿Qué sé yo?
            Ítem,[193] dos salvajes más,
            a avisar a mi amo voy,
1085   de que tu hija entre salvajes
            se queda en conversación.
  Sabañón   Dices bien, pues, para que
            la saque desta aflicción,
            o es mágico, o no es mágico.

Vanse Luquete y Sabañón.

---

190   **Apunten bien...***Aim well or you'll shoot me (instead of Astolfo)*
191   **han de dar...***they'll probably end up shooting someone else (if they aim at me)*
192   **ama** *the woman in charge (i.e. Libia)*
193   **Ítem** is legalistic language, kind of like a verbal bullet point. It's used here for comic effect.

1090	**CINTIA** (*Ap.*) (¿Quién igual letargo° vio,	daze
	como el que ha quedado Focas?)	
	LIBIA (*Ap.*) (¿Qué será esta suspensión?)	
	FOCAS Yerto[194] cadáver en quien,	
	—ʿa despecho° del veloz	in spite of
1095	tiempo, a pesar de las canas°	gray hairs
	y injurias° de escarcha° y sol—	assaults, frost
	todavía en mi memoria	
	guarda la imaginación	
	aquellas primeras señas,	
1100	con que te vi embajador[195]	
	como aquí. Pero no quiero,	
	que te asuste° mi rigor°	scare, harshness
	cuando debo, agradecido	
	al no esperado favor	
1105	del hallarte, las albricias.	
	Alza° del suelo y tu voz	arise
	me diga si es de Mauricio	
	el hijo que reservó	
	de mis iras tu lealtad,	
	uno déstos.[196]	
1110	**ASTOLFO** Sí, señor,	
	uno de los dos es	
	hijo de mi Emperador,	
	a quien–porque nunca diera	
	en manos de tu furor–	
1115	crié° en estos montes, sin que	I raised
	sepa° quién es ni quién soy.	[sepa el hijo]
	Porque el tenerle así tuve	
	a ʿinconveniente menor°	lesser evil

194   **yerto** *stiff and cold* "Yerto" is most commonly applied to dead bodies. Astolfo only appears to be a cadaver.

195   Astolfo was Mauricio's ambassador.

196   **si es de...***dígame tu voz si uno de estos [jóvenes] es el hijo de Mauricio que tu lealtad reservó de mis iras.* One of the things that makes passages like this one difficult is that Focas does not command Astolfo by saying "dime" (tell me). Instead, he says "tu voz me diga" (let your voice tell me), commanding the voice rather than the person. Similarly, Focas does not say that *Astolfo* saved Mauricio's son, Focas says Astolfo's *loyalty* saved Mauricio's heir (tu lealtad reservó el hijo). A character's qualities and capacities are often spoken of, addressed, and commanded as if they were independent of the character.

1120		que el mirarle en tu poder,	
		ni de una gente que dio	
		obediencias a un tirano.	
	FOCAS	Pues mira cuán superior	
		el hado° a la diligencia°	fate, human efforts
		manda: ¿cuál es de los dos?	
1125	ASTOLFO	Que es uno dellos diré,	
		pero cuál es dellos, no.[197]	
	FOCAS	¿Qué importa que ya lo calles,	
		si es inútil pretensión°	attempt
		para que no muera? Pues	
1130		matando a entrambos,° estoy	both
		cierto de que muera el uno,	
		el que aborrezco,° y que no	hate
		turbará° nunca el Imperio.	stir up
	ERACLIO	`A menos costa° el temor	with less difficulty
		podrá asegurar.°	reassure
1135	FOCAS	¿Cómo?	
	LEÓNIDO	Vengando en mí[198] ese rencor.	
		Que yo, a precio de ser hijo	
		de un supremo Emperador,	
		daré contento la vida.[199]	
1140	ERACLIO	Si en él dicta la ambición,	
		en mí la verdad.	
	FOCAS	¿Por qué?	
	ERACLIO	Porque yo sé que lo soy.	
	FOCAS	¿Tú lo sabes?	
	ERACLIO	Sí.	
	ASTOLFO	¿Pues quién	
		te lo ha dicho?	
	ERACLIO	Mi valor.	
1145	FOCAS	¿Entrambos, para morir,	
		competís por el blasón°	honor
		de hijos de Mauricio?	

---

197 This sets in motion a great deal of the plot. Astolfo knows the truth, but he will not tell Focas.

198 **Vengando en mí...**_Taking your bitterness and hatred out on me (choosing to kill me)_

199 **a precio de...**Leónido says he would gladly die if it meant that he would be recognized as the legitimate son of the true emperor, Mauricio.

LOS DOS	Sí.
FOCAS	(*A Astolfo*) Di tú, ¿cuál es de los dos?
LOS DOS	¡Yo!
ASTOLFO	Que es uno[200] mi voz ha dicho.

1150   Cuál es no dirá mi amor.

FOCAS   Eso es querer, por salvar

               uno, que perezcan° dos: die

               y pues entrambos conformes°   in agreement

               estáis en morir, no soy

1155   tirano, pues que la muerte

               que ellos me piden les doy.

               Soldados, mueran entrambos.

ASTOLFO   Tú lo pensarás mejor.

FOCAS   ¿Por qué?

ASTOLFO   Porque no querrás,

1160   ya que el uno te ofendió

               en vivir, te ofenda el otro

               en morir.

FOCAS   ¿Pues por qué no?

ASTOLFO   Porque es el otro tu hijo,

               de cuya verdad te doy,

1165   para testimonio, esta

               lámina, que a mí me dio (*Dale una lámina*)[201]

               con él, y con la noticia

               de ser tuyo, la aflicción

               de aquella villana, en quien

1170   fue tan parlero° el dolor,   expressive

               que por no reservar nada,

               el hijo aun no reservó.

               Agora, con el resguardo°   documentation

               que el uno en el otro halló,

1175   sabiendo que es tu hijo el uno,

               podrás matar a los dos.

FOCAS   ¿Qué escucho y qué miro?

CINTIA   ¡Estraño

               suceso!

---

200   **es uno…***it is one of the two young men* (either Eraclio o Leónido)

201   See verses 292-293 for the story of the "lámina."

FOCAS ¿Quién, cielos, vio
que cuando de mi enemigo,
1180 y mía buscando voy
la sucesión,²⁰² que afligía° agitated
mi `vaga imaginación,° restless thoughts
tan equívocas encuentre
una y otra sucesión,
1185 que impida el golpe del odio
el escudo° del amor? shield
Mas tú dirás, uno y otro,
quién es.

ASTOLFO Eso no haré yo:
tu hijo ha de guardar al hijo
1190 de `mi Rey y mi señor.° [Mauricio]

FOCAS `No te valdrá° tu silencio, [it] won't work
que la natural pasión
con experiencias dirá
cuál es mi hijo y cuál no,²⁰³
1195 y entonces podré dar muerte
al que no halle en mi favor.

ASTOLFO No te creas de experiencias
de hijo a quien otro crió,²⁰⁴
que apartadas crianzas° tienen upbringings
1200 muy sin cariño el calor
de los padres y quizá,
llevado de algún error,
darás la muerte a tu hijo.

FOCAS Con eso en obligación
1205 de dártela° a ti me pones, [darte la muerte]
si no declaras quién son.

ASTOLFO Así quedará el secreto
en seguridad mayor,

---

202 **cuando de mi...**_cuando voy buscando la sucesión mía y de mi enemigo_ "Sucesión" means successor or heir.

203 Focas believes he'll be able to tell which is his son, and which is Mauricio's, based on their nature, their personalities, and other telling signs. "Experiencia" often means "test" or "experiment." It is a conscious, directed form of experience, not just what happens by chance.

204 **No te creas...**_Do not think you can put heredity to a test, when you did not raise your son._

que los secretos, un muerto
1210 es quien los guarda mejor.
FOCAS Pues no te daré la muerte,
caduco, loco, traidor,

Écha a Astolfo en el suelo y levántanle Eraclio y Leónido.

sino guardaré tu vida
en tan mísera prisión
1215 que lo prolijo en morir[205]
te saque del corazón
a pedazos el secreto.
ERACLIO No le ultraje tu furor.[206]
LEÓNIDO No tu saña le maltrate.
1220 FOCAS Pues ¿qué? ¿Amparáisle[207] los dos?
LOS DOS Si él nuestra vida ha guardado,
¿no es primera obligación
de todas guardar su vida?
FOCAS Luego ¿a ninguno mudó°   moved
1225 la vanidad de que pueda
ser mi hijo?
ERACLIO   A mí no,
porque más quiero, otra vez
digo, morir al honor
de ser legítimo hijo
1230 de un supremo Emperador,
que vivir de una villana
hijo natural.°   born out of wedlock
LEÓNIDO   Y yo,
que aunque ser tu hijo tuviera
a soberano° blasón,   sovereign, supreme
1235 no me ha de exceder a mí
Eraclio en la presunción

---

205 **prolijo** means talkative or wordy, but here "lo prolijo en morir" refers to Astolfo's last words or his willingness to reveal the truth on his deathbed (after torture and imprisonment).

206 **No le ultraje...**Do not commit an offense against him (or more literally, *do not allow your fury to commit an outrage against him*)

207 **Amparáisle** *le amparáis* (*amparar* means to help or succor)

	de serlo más.	
FOCAS	¿Y es lo más	

FOCAS   ¿Y es lo más
Mauricio?

LOS DOS   Sí.

FOCAS   ¿Y Focas?

LOS DOS   No.

FOCAS ¡Ah venturoso° Mauricio!   fortunate

1240   ¡Ah infeliz Focas! ¿Quién vio,

que para reinar° no quiera   rule, govern

ser hijo de mi valor

uno, y que quieran del tuyo

serlo, para morir, dos?

1245   (*A Astolfo*) Y pues de tanto secreto,

que ya pasa a ser baldón,°   insult, affront

solo eres dueño, volviendo

a mi primera intención,

te harán hablar hambre y sed,

1250   desnudez, pena y dolor.

(*A los soldados*) Llevadle preso.°   prisoner

LOS DOS   Primero,

restados en su favor[208]

nos verás.

FOCAS   Eso es querer,

que abandonado el amor

1255   con que al uno busqué, en ambos

se vengue mi indignación.

A todos tres los prended.°   seize

Embisten[209] los Soldados a prenderlos, y ellos los retiran peleando.

ERACLIO Primero pedazos yo

me dejaré hacer.

LEÓNIDO   Primero

1260   moriréis todos.

FOCAS   ¡Su error

los castigue°! ¿Qué esperáis?   punish

---

208 **restados en...***we will fight to see he is not taken prisoner*

209 **Embisten** *they attack or set upon (their enemy)*

       si no se dan a prisión,
       mueran.

ASTOLFO   ¡No mi vida, hijos,
       así os empeñe!

CINTIA y
 LIBIA   ¡Señor!

1265 FOCAS Nada me digáis, que al ver,
       que hay quien desdeñe° mi honor,   spurns
       tengo un volcán en el pecho,
       y un Etna en el corazón. (*Vase*)

 CINTIA ¡O quién pudiera impedir
1270   tantas desventuras° hoy! (*Vase*)   misfortunes

 LIBIA ¡Quién embarazar[210] pudiera
       de tanta fiera cuestión°   quarrel
       los peligros!

    Vanse todos. Salen Sabañón, Luquete y Lisipo.

SABAÑÓN   Llegad, presto,
       que donde Cintia quedó
1275   es donde se escucha el ruido
       de las armas.

 LUQUETE   Y si no
       me engaño, ella en medio anda.

 LISIPO Yo llego en mala ocasión,
       pues que todo cuanto encuentro
1280   es ira, saña y furor.

 LUQUETE Los salvajes° se defienden,   [Eraclio y Leónido]
       pero como menos son,
       no tienen muy ‘buen partido.°   defensible position

 SABAÑÓN Y ‘no es poca admiración,°   not unsurprising
1285   ‘que una vez de° los salvajes   [supuesto que]
       sea el número menor.

 LISIPO ¡O qué de vidas peligran!
       Si viendo este estrago° estoy,   havoc
       ¿para cuándo de mis ciencias
1290   los raros prodigios son?

---

210 **embarazar** *to present an obstacle to*

Pongan, pues, paces las sombras,
y anticipado el horror
de la noche, al parecer,[211]
obedezcan a mi voz,
1295   con relámpagos y truenos,
nube, cielo, luna y sol.

Dentro terremoto, y salen todos confusos, tropezando unos con otros.[212]

FOCAS   ¿Qué nuevo escándalo, cielos,
de un instante a otro turbó
la luz, que ninguno ve
1300   con quién lidia, ni quién no?
CINTIA   ¿Qué se nos ha hecho el día,
que de vista se perdió
de un punto a otro?
ERACLIO   ¿Qué portento
nos `apaga el resplandor°   snuffs out the light
1305   de los rayos?
LIBIA   ¿Qué prodigio
nos niega `el mayor farol?°   the sun
LEÓNIDO   ¡Qué no imaginado eclipse!
ASTOLFO   ¡Qué no esperado pavor°!   terror
UNA MUJER   (*Dentro*) ¡Qué asombro!
OTRA   (*Dentro*) ¡Qué ansia!
OTRA   (*Dentro*) ¡Qué espanto!
1310   LUQUETE   ¡Que andaluvio![213]
SABAÑÓN   ¡Que antuvión°!   blow
FOCAS   ¡Libia!
LIBIA   ¡Focas!

---

211   **anticipado el horror…***may the horror of night appear to arrive during the day* Lisipo, the wizard, is conjuring a storm. Critics have suggested that this may simply be a sudden and terrifying eclipse and not the work of Lisipo's magic (Gonano 99). However, the first act of *Hado y divisa de Leónido y Marfisa* (a play that has much in common with *En la vida…*) also ends with a storm explicitly conjured by magic.

212   **Dentro terremoto…***Offstage, we hear an earthquake, and everyone takes the stage, chaotically tripping over one another.*

213   What Luquete means is "diluvio" or "flood." "Andaluvio" is a nonsense word.

Focas	¡Cintia!	
Cintia	¡Ismenia!	
Unos	¡Al monte!	
Otros	¡A la población!	
Otros	¡A la choza!	
Otros	¡Al risco!	
Otros	¡Al llano!	

       Libia Pues en tanta confusión,

1315   embarazando las iras,

           buscan todos su mansión,[214]

           `en lo que paran,° dirá   *how they end up*

           `otra vez que° salga el Sol.   *when*

Jornada segunda

Salen Cintia y Libia, delante de la cabaña de Lisipo.

       Cintia Pues en todo este coto°   *territory*

1320   solo tu albergue,° hermosa Libia, ha sido   *lodging*

           en quien Focas y yo vemos vencido

           el ceño° del pasado terremoto.[215]   *threat*

           Ya que de cerca tus fortunas[216] noto,

           compadecida,° quiero   *moved to pity*

           procurar enmendarlas.°   *improve*

1325   Libia   Bien infiero

           el que huéspedes° tales   *guests*

           `no acaso° pisan míseros umbrales.[217]   *not by chance*

       Cintia Parecidas fortunas

           dan a entender ser las estrellas unas,[218]

---

214 **mansión** *hiding place, safe spot*

215 We know why the storm and earthquake did not affect the place where Libia and Lisipo live: because Lisipo caused the storm.

216 **tus fortunas...***your fortunes.* Fortune can be good or bad.

217 **míseros umbrales** *lowly or humble doorways*

218 **estrellas unas** *the same stars* Having the same stars or same astrological influences explains why, Cintia suggests, she and Libia have the same fortunes.

1330	y desta simpatía	
	se engendran los cariños.	
LIBIA	¿Pues la mía°	[mi fortuna]
	en que, señora, pudo confrontada	
	simbolizar la tuya?	
CINTIA	En la pasada	
	acción, donde llegando las primeras	
1335	fuimos las que de aquellas creídas fieras[219]	
	el centro descubrimos,	
	y las primeras que en su estilo vimos	
	que tenía tratable° la rudeza,°	docile, roughness
	escondida no menos estrañeza°	surprise
1340	que la que el caso infiere,	
	y por si alguna vez hablar quisiere	
	(sobre tenerme—que es lo más—tu vida,	
	como te dije ya, compadecida)[220]	
	en lo turbada que mirar me tuvo,	
1345	antes tan fiero,[221] al que después estuvo	
	conmigo tan rendido,°	submissive
	con sus noticias tan desvanecido,°	haughty
	con Focas tan severo	
	que osó° morir primero	dared
1350	que creer lo menos noble a su destino,	
	y en fin tan leal, tan fino,	
	con la piedad° del `venerable anciano°,	mercy, [Astolfo]
	es bien que a ti `te tenga° más a mano,	[yo te tenga]
	porque una admiración, Libia, tan grave	
1355	aun no la sabe oír quien no la sabe:[222]	
	y así, por uno y otro, he de llevarte	
	conmigo.	
LIBIA	Otra, y mil veces a besarte	
	vuelvo la mano. Pero cuando `se halla°	discovers
	mi padre...	

---

219 **creídas fieras** *what we believed to be beasts*

220 **sobre tenerme...***tenerme compadecida tu vida* Libia's life causes Cintia to feel compassion.

221 She's speaking here of Eraclio.

222 **una admiración...***something so extraordinary, Libia, cannot be understood by anyone who does not know what we know (or see what we've seen)*

CINTIA	No prosigas,° cesa, calla,	continue

CINTIA No prosigas,° cesa, calla,   *continue*
1360 que la gente dejando,
Focas con él viene en secreto hablando.[223]

LIBIA Pues si es secreto, `demos
para él lugar,° de aquí nos retiremos.   *let's give them space*

CINTIA Cuánto será mejor, ya que aquí estamos,
pues es secreto...

LIBIA   ¿Qué?

1365 CINTIA   ...que lo sepamos.
Que no hay más gusto, Libia, te prometo,
que saber, sin fiármele, un secreto.[224]

LIBIA Pues si de eso te agradas,
desde aquí los oigamos, amparadas
1370 deste verde cancel,[225] que ha dividido
nuestro pequeño albergue.

Escóndense detrás de unos árboles, y salen Focas y Lisipo.

FOCAS   Agradecido,°   *thankful*
Lisipo, a la ocasión de tu destierro
—que ya sé que fue en orden a que el yerro
`del de Calabria° amenazó tu ciencia,   *[Federico]*
1375 por negar de mis feudos la obediencia—
te estoy,[226] pero aunque desto
a darte el galardón° estoy dispuesto,   *prize*
otro es el fin° con que hoy honrarte trato.   *goal*

LISIPO A tanto honor no me hallarás ingrato.

FOCAS Yo vine...

1380 LISIPO   Ya lo sé, con ansia fuerte
de dar una corona y una muerte.[227]

---

223 **que la gente...***leaving the other people behind, Focas is speaking secretly with Libia's father, Lisipo.*

224 **Que no hay...***There is no greater pleasure than knowing a secret that I was not supposed to know (that was not entrusted to me).*

225 **verde cancel** *the screen formed by the green branches*

226 **Agradecido, Lisipo...***te estoy agradecido* Focas is grateful to Lisipo for the prophecy that resulted in Lisipo's exile from Calabria (that Federico could not defeat Focas).

227 This is what Focas explained in verses 320-325. Lisipo was not present then.

	FOCAS	Cuando tarde° esperaba...	late in life
	LISIPO	...que hallase tu deseo a quien buscaba...	
	FOCAS	...con ello di casi al primero paso.	
1385	LISIPO	Estudio es de los cielos el acaso.°	luck
	FOCAS	Mas con tan clara confusión tan nueva...	
	LISIPO	...como es el no saber a quien se deba	
		el odio, ni el amor.	

FOCAS   A aquese efecto...[228]

LISIPO   ...prender mandaste al \`dueño del secreto.°   [Astolfo]

1390   FOCAS   Pusiéronse los dos en su defensa.

LISIPO   Fue noble acción.

FOCAS   Así el valor lo piensa,

        juzgando, al ver aun contra mí los bríos,°   nerve

        que eran entonces ambos hijos míos.

        Sobrevino° a la lid° el terremoto...   overcame, fighting

1395   LISIPO   Ya un eje° y otro vi del cielo roto.   axis

FOCAS   ...con que en tu albergue Cintia y yo amparados...

LISIPO   ...tienen sitiado el monte tus soldados.[229]

FOCAS   Con orden...

LISIPO   ...que al que encuentren muerto o preso

        traigan. ¿Qué lo repites, si el suceso

1400   nadie hasta aquí lo ignora?[230]

FOCAS   Pues lo que no se sabe empieza agora.

        Yo sé que la experiencia,

        Lisipo, de tu ciencia

        lo más oculto alcanza,

1405   y así libro en tu ciencia mi esperanza,[231]

        \`tú has de° decirme de ellos,   you must

        ¿quiénes son?

LISIPO   Sí diré, y antes de vellos°   [verlos]

        sabido lo tendrás.

CINTIA   ¡O quién pudiera,

---

228 **A aquese efecto...**_to that end_

229 The soldiers have laid siege to the mountain because Leónido and Eraclio escaped.

230 **¿Qué lo repites...**_Why do you repeat what everyone knows?_

231 **libro en tu...**_I'm basing my hopes on your wisdom and knowledge_ ("libro" here is from the verb "librar" meaning to free or liberate).

        Libia, estorbarlo![232]

LIBIA   Yo.

CINTIA   ¿De qué manera?

1410   LIBIA   Puesto que a mis engaños
tardará con el peso de los años,
habla a mi padre tú, mientras retiro
a Focas yo.[233] (*Vase Libia*)

FOCAS   Si en tu noticia miro
logrado mi deseo,[234] que has de verte
piensa...

LISIPO   ¡No más! El que...

1415   LIBIA   (*Dentro*) ¡Que me dan muerte!
¡Focas! ¡Padre! ¡Señor!

LISIPO   ¡Ay de mi! Aquella
voz es de Libia.

FOCAS   ¿Cómo a socorrerla
no voy? (*Vase*)

LISIPO   ¿Y cómo torpe° mi pie tarda   clumsy
en no ser yo el primero?

Lisipo quiere irse, pero Cintia sale y lo detiene.

CINTIA   Espera, aguarda.

LISIPO   Si ves...

1420   CINTIA   Cobra la acción helada y fría,
que esa voz no es de Libia, sino mía.[235]

LISIPO   ¿Tuya?

CINTIA   Sí, si con ella a estorbar° llego   obstruct
que pueda tu noticia hacer que, ciego
de ira, Focas dé muerte

---

232 Cintia and Libia are still hiding while they spy on Focas and Lisipo.

233 **puesto que a...**Only part of what Libia means is clear at this point. She says that Lisipo will move slowly because of his age ("tardará con el peso de los años"). Libia is about to exit the stage and scream for help, this is her trick or "engaño."

234 **si en tu...***if I find my wishes fulfilled in what you tell me (if I get the information I want from you).*

235 **esa voz no...**Cintia says that Lisipo has heard her voice, not Libia's, which is not literally true. Cintia and Libia are acting together (and in the figurative sense, speaking with one voice).

1425	al hijo de Mauricio, que es muy fuerte	
	dolor que, cuando el desengaño acuda,	
	valga una vida menos que una duda.	
	Y pues al cielo ofendes si a él le obligas,	
	muévate la piedad, no se lo digas,[236]	
1430	o verás, siendo otro tu homicida,°	murderer
	si es buen precio una duda de una vida.[237]	

LISIPO Pues como si...

Cintia se esconde. Salen Focas y Libia.

FOCAS   (*A Lisipo*) Detente,°   stop
        no tu cansada edad el paso aliente,[238]
        desvía ya el temor, delirio ha sido
        de un sueño.

1435   LIBIA   Tan ladrón de mis sentidos
        robada me tenía
        con las especies que en la fantasía
        —llenas de confusiones,
        variedades, ideas e ilusiones,
1440   prólogos de tan nunca vista historia—
        informes° conservaba la memoria,[239]   without form
        que debieron veloces,°   fast
        (yo no lo sé) de interrumpir en voces.

        LISIPO En albricias del gusto
1445   de verte libre, te perdono el susto
        que, de mi vida dueño,
        aun guarda en mí las sombras de tu sueño.[240]

---

236 **no se lo digas...***do not tell Focas (whether Eraclio or Leónido is his son)*

237 This passage (1422-1431) is a window into Cintia's character and the quality of her thought. She appeals to Lisipo as a father (stressing her relationship with Libia), then she appeals to Lisipo as a human being who will value an innocent life; to conclude, however, she threatens Lisipo's life.

238 **cansada edad...**Here, "cansada edad" means old age, and "el paso" is "your steps." So the meaning is, roughly, "do not worry and feel like you need to hurry (or rush your steps) to save your daughter, old man (it was nothing)."

239 **Tan ladrón de...**The memory of the storm conjured by Lisipo has robbed Libia of her senses (or so she claims).

240 **el susto que...***el susto que guarda en mí las sombras de tu sueño.* Lisipo claims to have been shaken up by Libia's cries for help. However, he knows that it was a trick.

Retírate de aquí.

Libia se acerca a la escondida Cintia.

LIBIA	(*a Cintia*) ¿Qué ha sucedido?°	happened
CINTIA	Que ya está del silencio prevenido.	
1450	Vuelve a escuchar, veremos[241] que han logrado	
	tu industria, bella Libia, y mi cuidado.	
FOCAS	Pues el daño, Lisipo, que esperamos	
	fue una ilusión. Prosigue.	
LISIPO	¿En qué quedamos?	
FOCAS	En que aun antes de vellos	
	los he de conocer.[242]	
1455 LISIPO	Sí, porque dellos	
	tu hijo es...[243]	
CINTIA	(*Ap.*) (¡Ay infelice!°)	[infeliz]
LISIPO	...él que...	
CINTIA	(*Ap.*) (Sobre mi aviso° se lo dice.)	warning
LISIPO	...él que...	
FOCAS	¿Qué te enmudece?[244]	
LISIPO	No sé, solo sé que me estremece°	makes me shudder
	al nombrarle un temblor.°	trembling
1460 FOCAS	¿Qué te acobarda?°	intimidates you
LISIPO	Cierta deidad que esotra vida guarda.[245]	
	Tú no la ves, yo sí, la vi enojada, y bella,	
	con el dedo en los labios los míos sella.°	seals
	No me aflijas, pues ves que te obedezco.	
1465	No me amenaces, pues por ti enmudezco.[246]	
	Y pues primero el cielo,	
	entupecido° el `cristalino velo,°	clogged, the sky

---

241 *Tp* "creemos"

242 **antes de vellos...**Focas paraphrases Lisipo's words from verses 1407-1408.

243 This stopping or breaking off in mid sentences is called aposiopesis.

244 **¿Qué te...***What is keeping you from speaking?*

245 **Cierta deidad...***Some deity guards the other life* (In other words, some divinity is preventing Lisipo from telling Focas which is his son.)

246 **No me aflijas...***Do not hound me, you see that I obey you! Do not threaten me, for you I am silent!* These two verses are spoken to the "deidad." Cruickshank suggests that at this moment, Cintia may be standing behind Focas where he cannot see her but Lisipo can.

en su favor nubes amotina,°   stirs up
y ahora auxiliar alta, deidad divina,
1470   me niega la asistencia
del espíritu impuro
que, a la callada voz de mi conjuro°   spell
invocado, dictaba en obediencia
del explícito pacto de mi ciencia.
1475   No me mandes que diga,
pues a callar otro poder me obliga,
lo que ni sé, ni puedo.
¡Qué ansia! ¡Qué espanto! (*Vase*)

FOCAS   ¡Y qué pavor, qué miedo
es el que ha introducido
1480   tu asombro° en mí! Mas ¿cómo yo a partido   astonishment
doy mi furor, si todo el cielo opuesto
a mí no ha de poder?²⁴⁷

Salen Cintia y Libia.

LAS DOS   (*a Focas*) Señor, ¿qué es esto?
CINTIA   ¿Tú, la voz destemplada?
LIBIA   ¿Tú, perdido el color?
LAS DOS   ¿Qué ha sido?
FOCAS   Nada.
1485   Quise, que me dijera
Lisipo, por su mágica, cuál era²⁴⁸
el hijo de Mauricio,
y perturbado° de un letargo el juicio,   disrupted
no sé qué alto poder convierte en hielo
su voz.²⁴⁹

---

247   **Mas ¿cómo yo...**_How can I surrender (dar a partido) when the heavens that oppose me will not back down?_

248   *Tp* "por su mágica esfera"

249   Scholars who notice similarities between *En la vida...* and Mira de Amescua's *La rueda de la fortuna* focus on two things: the plots of the plays, because both have to do with Mauricio's offspring, and verses such as "no sé qué alto poder convierte en hielo / su voz." This recalls verses from *La rueda de la fortuna* such as "No sé qué deidad me inclina / a respetar su presencia." The importance of these similarities, however, is a matter of debate.

Cintia	Yo sí.	
Focas	¿Tú?	
Cintia	Yo.	
Focas	¿Quién es?	

1490 　Cintia 　　　　　　　　　El cielo,

que una inocencia ampara.
¿Qué culpa a un desdichado es nacer,[250] para
que a tus cóleras° nazca destinado?　　　　　　*anger*
¿No le basta nacer a un desdichado?[251]

1495　Las políticas leyes[252]
que establecieron Césares y Reyes
dicen que si una herida
en un cadáver se halla, y de homicida
contra dos el indicio°　　　　　　*evidence*

1500　resulta igual, no deban ser en juicio
condenados los dos, porque prudente
tuvo la ley piadosa
por mejor que, en sentencia tan dichosa,°　　　　　　*fortunate*
se libre el delincuente

1505　que no que lo padezca el inocente.[253]
Pues siendo así, tu gracia ambos reciba,
y a sombras del amor el odio viva,
que en juicio tan penoso,°　　　　　　*serious*
mejor será que sepa hacer el hado°　　　　　　*destiny*

1510　un dichoso, señor, de un desdichado,
que hacer un desdichado de un dichoso.
Y en cuanto a que te deje sospechoso
la duda que te queda,
que de Mauricio el hijo alterar pueda

1515　el Imperio, es engaño,

　250　This line recalls, and inverts, Segismundo's complaint in *La vida es sueño*: "pues el delito mayor / del hombre es haber nacido."

　251　**¿No le basta…?** *¿No le basta a un desdichado nacer?* (Isn't being born [punishment] enough for an unfortunate person?)

　252　**políticas leyes** *the laws made by human beings (as opposed to natural or divine laws)*

　253　**si una herida…**Cintia says that, according to the law, if a cadaver is found that shows signs of only one fatal wound then two men should not be punished for the murder. It would be better for the guilty party to go unpunished than for the innocent to be wrongly sentenced. Medical forensics was a subject of considerable interest during the sixteenth and seventeenth centuries.

pues no constando nunca el desengaño,
podrás dejar de tu laurel° la herencia   crown (figuratively)
a quien más te inclinare la experiencia,[254]
que aunque apaguen el fuego las mudanzas
1520   de apartadas crianzas,[255]
¿qué falta el fuego hará, cuando a ver llego
que la sangre no mas arde sin fuego?

FOCAS   Si capaz estuviera
yo de razón, la tuya `me venciera.°   would convince me
Mas, ¿cómo...?

Dentro ruido y salen Sabañón, y Luquete.

TODOS   (*Dentro*) ¡Entrad!
LOS DOS   Albricias,
1525   FOCAS   ¿Qué es aqueso?
LUQUETE   Yo lo diré.
SABAÑÓN   No sino yo.
LUQUETE   Que preso...
SABAÑÓN   ...nuestro placer, señor...
LUQUETE   ...nuestra alegría...
LOS DOS   ...te trae al que encuevados[256] nos tenía.
FOCAS   ¿Adónde le encontrasteis?
SABAÑÓN   No le encontramos.
1530   FOCAS   ¿Dónde, pues, le hallasteis?
LUQUETE   No le hallamos tampoco.
FOCAS   Pues ¿cómo, dime necio, dime[257] loco,
le prendisteis?°   capture
SABAÑÓN   Como otros que allá fueron,
le hallaron, le encontraron, le prendieron.[258]

---

254   **podrás dejar...***podrás dejar la herencia de tu laurel a quien la experiencia más te inclinare.* Cintia suggests Focas can observe Eraclio and Leónido and allow his natural feelings or inclination to identify his heir.

255   A reference to Astolfo's verses 1197-1199.

256   **encuevados** *hidden or held in a cave*

257   *Tp* "como"

258   Luquete and Sabañón are splitting hairs for comic effect. They say, in essence, "we didn't find him (no le encontramos), they did (le encontraron)."

1535   FOCAS   ¿Y de eso las albricias pretendisteis?

LUQUETE   ¿Es novedad, señor, que hombres de chistes,
cuando el gusto complacen,
ganen las gracias de lo que otros hacen?

Salen Soldados y Astolfo.

SOLDADO   Apenas a ꞌla oscura
1540   niebla° siguió del sol la lumbre pura,   Lisipo's storm
cuando al monte volvimos,
y en él a Astolfo, desmayado, vimos,
sin ꞌacudir a reparar° sus daños,   stopping to notice
el fatigado peso de los años,
1545   y como divididos
dejó el nublado a todos, esparcidos
por el monte, ꞌlos dos° no aparecieron,   [Leónido y Eraclio]
que quizá por hallarle le perdieron.

ASTOLFO   Sola esta vez ufano,°   proud
1550   puesto a tus pies, besara yo tu mano.²⁵⁹

FOCAS   ¿Por qué ufano esta vez?

ASTOLFO   Porque me advierte
mi ventura,° que vengo a ver mi muerte.   fortune

FOCAS   Pues mira cuán contrario° es tu recelo,°   mistaken, distrust
a vivir vienes, alza,° pues, del suelo.   rise
1555   Yo, Astolfo, aunque no prudente
sea, hoy he de ꞌparecerlo°   to seem prudent
en mudar° consejo°: ya   change, methods
no solamente me ofendo
de tu lealtad, pero antes
1560   en la parte la agradezco
de la crianza de un hijo,²⁶⁰
bien que implica el argumento
de que ꞌle tenga° por ti,   I have my son
cuando por ti no le tengo.

---

259   **besara yo...***would I kiss your hand* The imperfect subjunctive (besara) is used instead of the conditional. Astolfo is the living image of antithesis: thrown down at the feet of Focas but feeling pride.

260   **ya no solamente...***no longer do I simply take offense at your loyalty to Mauricio, now I'm also grateful for that loyalty because it led you to raise my son.*

1565		Y pues el semblante° miras	expression
		mudado con el consejo,	
		dime cuál es de los dos,	
		y con el otro° te ofrezco	[el otro joven]
		`templar la cuerda° al enojo.	moderate
1570	Astolfo	Si yo, señor, poco atento	
		a Dios, a mi fe y a ti,	
		tratara engañarte, es cierto,	
		que con trocar° a los dos,	switch
		viera al hijo de mi dueño,°	[Mauricio]
1575		aunque con nombre de tuyo,	
		restituido° en su imperio,	crowned
		y que si al otro matabas	
		matabas al tuyo.[261] Pero	
		—sobre que no quiera Dios,	
1580		que dé, ni que quite reinos—[262]	
		es tan igual, es tan una	
		la fe con que a `los dos° quiero,	[Leónido y Eraclio]
		como en fin quiero a los dos	
		que he criado, que primero	
1585		que mi silencio aventure	
		el uno, moriré. Y puesto	
		que no tengo de mentirte,	
		ni decirte verdad tengo,	
		toma la resolución	
1590		que quisieres, advirtiendo,	
		señor, que no será mucho	
		que, cuando leal y cuerdo	
		te da mi silencio un hijo,	
		des otro tú a mi silencio.[263]	
1595	Focas	¡Cuántas razones escucho	
		y cuántas acciones veo!	

---

261 This is the opposite of "razón de estado" (see verse 53). Astolfo rejects even the just outcome if it is reached by underhanded means.

262 **sobre que…** *because God does not want me to be the one who decides who rules and who does not* (I will not feed you misinformation that would cause you to kill the wrong man).

263 **no será mucho…** *it won't be surprising if my loyal silence leads you to infer the wrong son* Astolfo says that Focas can conclude nothing from his (Astolfo's) silence.

Todas me arguyen y todas
me convencen, y aunque tengo
tan en el alma arraigado
el rencor, esta vez quiero,
—de Lisipo atento al pasmo,°   *awe*
de Cintia al discurso atento,
de Astolfo atento al amor—
deponer° mis sentimientos.   *control*
Vive tú, pues, y ellos vivan,
hasta que diga el afecto
de la sangre la verdad.[264]
Y pues ya conmigo intento
que asistan° los dos y sean   *accompany me*
iguales sus tratamientos,
dime con este seguro,[265]
¿donde los hallaré?

ASTOLFO   Eso
mal puedo saberlo yo,
pues los buscara, a saberlo,
antes de dar en tus manos.

FOCAS   Pues fuerza será, volviendo
al monte, buscarlos todos.

CINTIA   Quizá, señor, es perderlos,
pues no sabiendo a qué fin
vuelven gente, armas y estruendos
a la fuga, a la defensa
los aventuran.

LIBIA   Es cierto.

FOCAS   Pues, ¿qué he de hacer?

ASTOLFO   Yo señor,
ya que reducido creo
tu enojo al mejor partido,[266]
daré para hallarlos medio.[267]

---

264   **hasta que...***until the natural affinity of the blood declares itself* (or, until it's clear which of the two has my blood due to the natural affection of a father for his son)

265   **seguro** *assurance* Focas assures Astolfo that he will treat Eraclio and Leónido equally.

266   **reducido creo...***now that I believe you've calmed down*

267   **daré para...***te daré medio para hallarlos* "Medio" here means "a way" or "a means."

Tú no has de ir, ni tus soldados,
porque al verte a ti y a ellos,
como has escuchado, es fuerza[268]
que tan ventajoso[269] riesgo
los oculte. Los `vecinos
de la tierra° han de ir y estos   common folk
con muchas señas de paz,
y para mostrar el serlo[270]
manda que dulces clarines
y músicos instrumentos
sonoros suenen, bien como
otra vez que los oyeron,
que no dudo que, escuchando
festivos sus dos acentos
lo que hizo el acaso antes,
agora lo haga el intento,[271]
que fue, absortos los sentidos,
dejarse atraer suspensos,
cuál del escándalo y cuál
de la suavidad del viento.
Con que advertirlos podrá
cualquiera que llegue a verlos
de tu resguardo.[272]

FOCAS   Bien dices.

LIBIA   Pues si te agrada el consejo,
supuesto que no has de ir
tú con tu gente, me ofrezco
a ir con la música yo. (*Vase Libia*)

CINTIA   Ya que ella eligió primero,[273]

---

268   *Tp* (verses 1629-1631) "es forzoso, que no esperen / a tan ventajoso riesgo. / Mejor es que los vecinos"

269   **ventajoso** *clear, obvious* Calderón draws on the root of "ventajoso," which is "avanzar." Leónido and Eraclio will know they are outmatched by the advancing soldiers and will hide.

270   **mostrar el serlo** *to show that they are peaceful*

271   **lo que hizo…***what was done before by accident can now be done on purpose* (i.e. luring the young men to the sound of music and drums)

272   **Con que…***Con que cualquiera que llegue a verlos podrá advertirlos de tu resguardo.* Anyone who sees Leónido and Eraclio can alert them to your promise of protection.

273   Note the differences in the way that Libia and Cintia address Focas.

1655	con tu licencia, porque	
	no me acusen mis deseos	
	omisión en la fineza	
	con que obligarte pretendo,[274]	
	aunque tema la censura	
1660	escrúpulos del respeto,	
	por ser la acción varonil°	manly
	y ser tan digno el empleo	
	como hallar un hijo tuyo	
	la salva, por otro puesto	
1665	iré con gente y clarines. (*Vase Cintia*)	

FOCAS   A entrambas os lo agradezco.

(*A Astolfo*) Y tú, `porque no presumas,°`   so you do not think

que a vista de igual suceso

estás preso° ni estás libre,   prisoner

1670	partidos los dos estremos,°	extremos
	no te pondré de soldados	
	guarda, que fuera estar preso,[275]	
	ni te dejaré sin ella,°	[guarda]
	que fuera estar libre, esos	
1675	dos villanos,[276] que no son	
	guardas ni dejan de serlo,	
	no te han de perder de vista.[277]	

LUQUETE   Nosotros sí perderemos,

como haya quien nos le gane.[278]

1680   FOCAS   Ea, villanos, id presto,

llevadle de aquí.

SABAÑÓN   ¡Luquete!

LUQUETE   ¡Sabañón! ¿Sabes qué es esto

---

274   **porque no me...**_so that my own desires to serve you do not accuse me of failing in my service to you, the service with which I intend to win your approval_ "Fineza" and "fino" are important words that are difficult to translate, they tend to suggest dutifulness and loyalty. You might think of "fineza" as perfection in rendering to a another what is owed, whether what is owed is service, loyalty, or devotion. Sometimes it can be translated "the care that someone takes" (roughly "esmero"). It is related to finesse—in the sense that it implies skill—but finesse is not an exact cognate of "fineza."

275   **que fuera...**_that would make you a prisoner_

276   **dos villanos** _Luquete and Sabañón_

277   **no te han...**_will not lose sight of you_ (this carries the force of a command)

278   **como haya...**_if there is anyone who wants to win him from us_

	de guardas de vista?	
Sabañón	Sí.	
	Guarda tú el ojo izquierdo	
	y yo el derecho.	
1685 Luquete	(*A Astolfo*) Vusted,[279]	
	pues es llave de un secreto,	
	nos conozca por sus guardas.	
Astolfo	¡Ay, lealtad, en que me has puesto!	
	¡En qué me has puesto, fortuna!	

Vanse Luquete, Sabañón y Astolfo.

1690 Focas	¿No me dirás, pensamiento,[280]	
	cuál experiencia° con los dos	test
	hiciera,° que fuera medio	I could do
	de dar luz al desengaño?[281]	

Sale Lisipo.

Lisipo	(*Ap.*) (A buscar a Focas vuelvo,	
1695	y pesaroso° de haber	disappointed
	perdido, por el respecto	
	de Cintia, ocasión° de que	opportunity
	logre su° agradecimiento,	[de Focas]
	con que vengará, quizá,	
1700	del de Calabria el desprecio.[282]	
	Y pues no estoy obligado	
	más que a guardar el secreto,	
	y le guardo, ¿por qué no	
	trataré de mis aumentos?[283])	
1705 Focas	Ninguna° hay que... Mas, Lisipo,	[Ninguna experiencia]
	¿aquí estabas? ¿Qué hay de nuevo?	
Lisipo	Que apenas, señor, cobrado°	recovered

---

279 **Vusted** *vuestra merced* or "your honor"
280 Focas here addresses his own thoughts in an apostrophe.
281 **que fuera...***that would be a way to find out the truth?*
282 Remember that Lisipo originally served the duke of Calabria.
283 **¿por qué...***why not try to get ahead?*

de aquel frenesí° violento   frenzy
me hallo, cuando cuidadoso
1710   de haber visto a Astolfo preso,[284]
a saber lo que resulta
de tan gran novedad vengo.
FOCAS   ¿Qué ha de resultar, sino
que—a pesar del sufrimiento—
1715   haya de capitular
con la pereza el incendio?
Siendo ansí, que en mí no habrá
minuto, instante, momento
que no sea siglo, hasta que
1720   aquilatados los pechos[285]
en la forja° de las horas,   the forge
que son cristales del tiempo,
muestren el oro y la liga,[286]
amor y aborrecimiento.
1725   LISIPO   Aunque todavía me tiene
temeroso aquel supremo
poder que a mi ciencia niega
quiénes son, con todo eso
he de ver si también manda°   [manda el poder]
1730   que no `se anticipe el tiempo.°   see the future
¿`Tendrás ánimo°...?   would you be up for
FOCAS   ¿Qué dices?
¿Estás `sin juicio?° ¿Sin seso?   out of your mind
¿Si tendrá ánimo preguntas
a Focas?
LISIPO   Oye, te ruego,
1735   que tiene el frase[287] en que dudo
énfasis con que prevengo.
¿Tendrás ánimo de ver

---

284   *Tp* "de haber visto a Astolfo, *presto*"

285   **aquilatados los pechos** Focas says he wants to assay or determine the worth of the hearts of Eraclio and Leónido as if they were gold. "Quilates" in Spanish are carats (of gold), so "aquilatar" is to find out how pure the gold is. This is a complicated way of saying he wants to find out which is his son.

286   **liga** *a metal (such as copper or silver) that is alloyed with gold* "La liga" is the less valuable metal.

287   "Frase" was occasionally a masculine noun in seventeenth-century Spain.

en fantásticos efectos,
a la breve edad de un día
1740 reducido hoy el entero
círculo de un año,[288] en que
`representados sucesos,°   simulated events
antes de verle, te digan
todos los acaecimientos,°   events
que en el año vieras?°   [verías]
1745 FOCAS   Ya,
cuanto al ánimo, te tengo
respondido, y así paso
a otra objeción que no entiendo.
Si han de ser fingidas sombras,[289]
1750 sin vida, sin alma, y cuerpo
las° que vea, ¿como yo,   [las sombras]
de ellas haré juicio, puesto[290]
que obrando sin albedrío
los que a ley de tu precepto°   commandment, rule
1755 representen a los dos,
ni saber, ni inferir puedo
los que ellos con él obran?
LISIPO La objeción es buena, pero
fácil la respuesta.
FOCAS   ¿Cómo?
1760 LISIPO Como han de ser ellos mesmos.[291]
FOCAS ¿Ellos mesmos?
LISIPO   Sí.
FOCAS   Otra vez,
y mil, ¿cómo (a dudar vuelvo)

---

288 **¿Tendrás ánimo…***Are you willing (or brave enough) to see through magic (fantásticos efectos) what would normally take a year in only one day?* These verses recall Act I of another play, *La prueba de las promesas* by Juan Ruiz de Alarcón (in turn based on an earlier text by Juan Manuel). In Ruiz de Alarcón's play, the character Don Illán is able to "cifrar muchos días, / y epilogar muchas leguas / en la esfera de esta casa." In other words, Illán magically condenses time and space to reveal the true nature of another character. This sort of effect—in which time happens differently in the literary work than it does in our daily experience—is a building block of many great texts.

289 **fingidas sombras…***mere appearances (false or imaginary appearances)*

290 *Tp* "dellas a su juicio opuesto,"

291 **ellos mesmos** *the men themselves (not appearances of the young men)*

               sombra y realidad podrán
               avenirse?[292]

LISIPO   Como dentro
1765   del encanto han de ser reales
               personas.

FOCAS   ¿Quién?

LISIPO   Tú, yo y ellos.°   [Eraclio y Leónido]

FOCAS Ellos, tú y yo... ¿cómo?

LISIPO   Finge,
               buscando divertimientos
               a tus penas, una caza,[293]
1770   y en alcance de un ligero
               bruto, te hallarás adonde,
               perdido de tus monteros,
               verás una sumptuosa
               fábrica,° que sobre el viento   building
1775   fundada... Mas, gente viene.

Dentro ruido.

FOCAS Pues de aquí nos retiremos,
               no te oigan.

LISIPO   (*Ap.*) (Fortuna, si hoy
               obligo a Focas, espero
               enmendarte.[294])

Vase Lisipo.

FOCAS   Si hoy, fortuna,
1780   el curso del año abrevio,
               y en él° me dice un examen   [el curso]
               lo que me calla un silencio,
               yo me vengaré de...

---

292 **sombra y realidad...**_how can appearance and reality be the same thing?_

293 **Finge, buscando...**_Pretend that you want to go hunting in order to distract yourself from your worries._

294 **Fortuna, si hoy...**_Fortune, if I win Focas' favor today, I hope to correct your course._ Lisipo hopes to improve his fortunes by serving Focas.

Eraclio
y Leónido   (*Dentro*) ¡Astolfo!
Focas   Ya me parece que empiezo
1785   a oír proverbios° del encanto.°   words, enchantment
               ¡Qué ilusión! ¡Qué devaneo°!   disorientation
               Voz es, que le nombra acaso.°   by chance

Vase Focas, y salen Eraclio y Leónido por dos puertas.

Leónido   ¡Astolfo!
Eraclio   ¡Astolfo!
Leónido   Aun el eco
               no me responde.
Eraclio   Aun le faltan
1790   suspiros para mí al viento.
Leónido   ¡Eraclio!
Eraclio   ¡Leónido!
Leónido   ¿Ha estado
               contigo Astolfo?
Eraclio   Lo mesmo
               preguntara yo, a tener
               tan bien mandado el aliento.[295]
1795   Desde aquella obscuridad
               que nos dividió, no he vuelto
               a verle.
Leónido   Ni yo tampoco.
Eraclio   ¿Si le han prendido° o le han muerto!   taken him prisoner
Leónido   No sé, pero ¿qué lamentas
1800   ningún infeliz suceso,
               si de ese y de todos tienes
               la culpa?[296]
Eraclio   ¿Yo?
Leónido   Pues ¿no es cierto,
               si tu vanidad fue quien
               más adelantó el empeño?
1805   ¿Tan mal le estaba al que nace

---

295 **Lo mesmo...***I would have asked you the same thing if I could catch my breath as quickly as you.*
296 *Tp* "De todo tienes la culpa."

echado al umbral° de un yermo,°   *threshold, wasteland*
hijo expósito° del hado,°   *abandoned, fate*
hallarse `al viso° de serlo°   *within sight, [hijo]*
de quien coronado César
1810   supo hacerse[297] por sus hechos,
para que estimando más
a Mauricio que a él, el fuego
encendiese de sus iras
el aire de sus desprecios,
1815   tanto, que si no enviara
en nuestro socorro el cielo
la recluta° de las nubes,   *gathering*
hubiéramos todos muerto?[298]

ERACLIO   ¿Por qué, si fue culpa en mi
1820   esa vanidad, tan presto
le seguiste tú?

LEÓNIDO   Porque
debe, aunque conozca el yerro,
noble espíritu seguir
los ejemplares° del riesgo.   *model to imitate*
1825   Que dicen que es más vitoria
lo restado° que lo cuerdo.°   *audacious, sensible*
¿Fuera° bien que presumiera   *[Sería]*
nadie,° cuando tú, soberbio,°   *[alguien], arrogant*
osabas° morir, que yo   *dared*
no osaba?

1830 ERACLIO   Pues según eso,
¿qué culpas que obre lo más?

LEÓNIDO   El que bastaba lo menos.

ERACLIO   Si a ti bastaba, a mí no,
y la plática dejemos,
1835   que el duelo de una porfía

---

297 **supo hacerse...***supo hacerse César* Focas knew how to become emperor (through his own actions).

298 Leónido refers back to what happened in verses 1133-1134, when Eraclio spoke up to Focas: "A menos costa el temor / podrá asegurar."

suele pasarse a otro duelo.[299]

LEÓNIDO ¿Y a quién estaría peor?

ERACLIO No sé si miro...

LEÓNIDO ...si advierto°... perceive

ERACLIO ...que mi ansia...

LEÓNIDO ...que mi pena...

1840 MÚSICOS (*Dentro cantan*) *¡Ay como gime, mas hay como suena!*

LEÓNIDO ¿Pero qué música es ésta?[300]

ERACLIO ¿Cuando esperamos que estruendos
de armas vuelvan a buscarnos,
vuelven voces y instrumentos?

1845 LEÓNIDO ¿Quién de halago° el aire llena? delight

MÚSICOS *El remo a que nos condena.*[301]

ERACLIO ¿Remo y paz? ¿Quién puede ser?
¿Quién mezcla agrado y rigor?[302]

MÚSICOS *El niño amor.*

1850 LEÓNIDO De mí el canto me enajena.° overwhelms me

Salen los Músicos, cantando.

MÚSICOS *Ay como gime, mas ay como suena*
el remo a que nos condena
el niño amor.

LEÓNIDO Sigamos deste rumor
1855 el armonioso acento,[303]
que él, pues que viene de paz,
quizá del cuidado° nuestro concern
nos informará.

---

299 Eraclio plays with the two meanings of "duelo": a duel and sorrow. He warns Leónido that duels with words (arguments, disputes) sometimes lead to real sorrow or pain.

300 Audiences familiar with Calderón's work would have known *exactly* what song the musicians have started to sing. They sing an "estribillo" or chorus of a well-known traditional ballad that had already been used in a famous poem by Luis de Góngora beginning "Contando estaban sus rayos..." Calderón used verses of this song in a number of other plays, including *La vida es sueño.* You might think of this as a kind of inside joke: the fact that Leónido does not recognize the song is further evidence that he has been living in a cave, far from civilization.

301 The allusion is to galley slaves who were forced to row. ("El remo" is "the oar.")

302 **agrado y rigor...***pleasure and discomfort*

303 **Sigamos...***Let's follow the harmonious tones of these sounds*

	ERACLIO	Bien dices,
		y peligro no tenemos,
1860		mientras que calla la duda.
	LEÓNIDO	Pues vamos la voz siguiendo.
	MÚSICOS	*Ay como gime, mas ay como suena*
		el remo a que nos condena
		el niño amor.
	ERACLIO	Vamos.

Suena el clarín dentro.

1865		Mas ¿qué es esto que
		mueve con fuerza mayor?
	MÚSICOS	*Clarín que rompe el albor.*
	ERACLIO	Mejor la cláusula suena
		deste nuevo ruiseñor.[304]
1870	MÚSICOS	*No suena mejor.*

Suena el clarín dentro.

	ERACLIO	Sí suena mejor.
	MÚSICOS	*No suena mejor.*
	LEÓNIDO	O escucha,
		si es que alternados a un tiempo
		vuelven a la competencia
1875		el uno y otro, diciendo:

Suena el clarín.

	MÚSICOS	*Ay como gime, mas ay como suena*
		el remo a que nos condena
		el niño amor.
		Clarín que rompe el albor,
1880		*no suena mejor.*

---

304 **ruiseñor** *nightingale* (a bird famed for its singing). The song contains two kinds of images and is accompanied by two kinds of sounds. The harmonious singing about love appeals to Leónido, while the warlike horn (clarín) appeals to Eraclio.

Suena el clarín.

Eraclio	Sí suena mejor.
Leónido	No suena mejor,
	y si a ti te lo parece,
	síguele tú, que yo el eco
1885	desta dulce suavidad
	he de seguir. (*Vase Leónido*)
Eraclio	Yo el acento
	desta ignorada° armonía.

unheard of

Sale Cintia y Eraclio se detiene.

Cintia	`En tanto que° yo este ameno
	espacio registro,° no
1890	cese° el clarín un momento.

while
survey
cease

Suena el clarín.

Eraclio	(*Ap.*) (Hermosa debe ser
	ave° de tan lisonjero°
	canto... y ¡cómo si es hermosa!)
Cintia	(*Ap.*) (Ya el uno de los dos veo,
1895	y no le pierdo el temor,°
	aunque el asombro° le pierdo.)
Eraclio	Segunda aurora° del día,
	si esas voces, que no entiendo,
	acaso son salva, que hacen
1900	nuevos pájaros a nuevo
	Sol, ¿cómo, di, de una causa
	nacen contrarios efectos?[305]
	Tanto, como que animoso°
	y cobarde a un mismo tiempo,
1905	me aliente° con lo que escucho
	y tiemble con lo que veo.
	Y ¿cómo, habiéndote dado

bird, pleasing

fear
astonishment
dawn

brave

emboldens me

---

305 The twofold cause is the sound of the horn and the sight of Cintia, which Eraclio experiences simultaneously. He explains the two contrary effects in the following lines.

esta fiera[306] tanto miedo,
vuelves,° no digo al peligro,   turn (your face) to
1910   sino al horror del aspecto?°   this appearance
CINTIA   Infeliz joven, en quien
preso° el corazón contemplo,   prisoner
pues ʽacechando resquicios°   glimpsing cracks
anda en la cárcel del pecho,[307]
1915   aunque tu vista° temí,   the sight of you
me aseguró tu respecto
tanto que vuelvo a buscarte.
ERACLIO   Primero° hermoso portento   [Primer]
que vi, y postrero° también   ultimate
1920   que veré, porque no creo
que pueda contigo ir
la perfección en aumento...
(*Ap.*) (o dígalo la hermosura,
que juzgué mudarse° necio,   remain silent
1925   pues al ver un rostro más,
eché muchas gracias menos).[308]
¿Tú a buscarme a mí?
CINTIA   A buscarte,
mas no el desvanecimiento
te persuada a que es favor,
1930   sino cuidado,[309] supuesto
que, si encontrara a tu amigo,
a él le dijera lo mesmo.
ERACLIO   Que no entendido lenguaje
es ese, que le agradezco

---

306   **esta fiera** *Eraclio* He refers to himself as a horrible beast.

307   This is a complicated image. Cintia says that Eraclio's heart is a prisoner in his chest (or his ribcage). This prisoner catches sight of chinks (resquicios), moments of rational illumination or of truth. "Achechar resquicios" also suggests stalking or hunting, waiting for the opportune moment. One way to think about this is that a bigger world of greater possibility is becoming visible to Eraclio; another way to think about this is that he sees only partial glimpses of a world beyond his figurative prison, like shadows on a wall. Hunting is often metaphorically related to acquiring knowledge (see verse 2052).

308   **eché muchas...***eché [de] menos muchas gracias.* Eraclio gets tongue tied.

309   **mas no...***but don't get a swelled head and think it was love, because it was only concern.* Here, "desvanecimiento" draws on an obsolete meaning of desvanecer: to make someone vain.

1935		en una parte y en otra	
		me parece que le siento.	
		¿A mí me buscas, y a él	
		le buscaras? ¿Lo que espero	
		que me digas, le dijeras?	
1940		¡Ay de mí! Que agora veo	
		que ya que mudar semblantes	
		me engañó el primer concepto,	
		no me ha engañado el segundo	
		en cifrar° en un sujeto	combine
1945		la quietud y la tormenta,	
		la tristeza y el contento,	
		la cura y la enfermedad,	
		la triaca y el veneno,	
		y finalmente...	

CINTIA   ¡No más!

1950		Y pues dora atrevimientos[310]	
		quien ignora con quien habla,	
		oye, y sabrás a qué vengo.	
		Habiendo prendido a Astolfo...	
	ERACLIO	¡Ay de mí! ¿Astolfo está preso?	
1955	CINTIA	...persuadido a sus razones,	
		si ya no a las mías primero,	
		Focas envía por ti.	
	ERACLIO	¡Ay de mi! Que según eso	
		debió de decirle que era	
		su hijo yo.	
1960	CINTIA	¿Y qué sientes?	
	ERACLIO	Siento que cuando desvanecido	
		quisiera mi pensamiento	
		ser a tus ojos lo más,	
		es en tus labios lo menos.	
1965	CINTIA	¿Y no pudiera ser que	
		por ti enviara, sabiendo	
		serlo° de Mauricio?	[ser hijo]

---

310 **dora atrevimientos** *gild insolence* Here *dorar* (literally, to gild or cover in gold) is to cover up. Cintia says that Eraclio is being too forward (because, she says, he does not realize to whom he's speaking).

ERACLIO	No.	
CINTIA	¿De qué lo infieres?	
ERACLIO	Lo infiero	

de que por matarme fuera,
1970   y no vinieras tú a eso,
que no quisiera matarme
con tan hermoso instrumento,
que le pudiera decir:
'No blasones° que me has muerto,   *flatter yourself*
1975   que no eres tú el que me matas,
que yo soy el que me muero.

CINTIA   Porque sepas que no es
uno ni otro,[311] a decir vuelvo
que Focas, a mis razones
1980   y las de Astolfo ha dispuesto,
que tú y esotro° Leónido,   *[ese otro]*
si es que del nombre me acuerdo,
vais a su palacio donde
con iguales tratamientos
1985   viváis los dos, sin saber
más de ti que de él, haciendo
razón de estado la duda:
y así, el enojo depuesto,°   *set aside*
con señas de paz por ambos
1990   envía, y pues yo te encuentro,
sea yo la que conmigo
te lleve, porque deseo
que mi fineza[312] se logre.

ERACLIO   Buen arbitrio halló el ingenio,
1995   que me quiso reducir
al yugo de sus imperios,[313]
pues supo hallar el imán°   *magnet*

---

311   **uno ni otro...***I neither came to kill you, nor to make you kill yourself*

312   **fineza** *action undertaken on behalf of another.* Here, once again, Cintia talks about her service to Focas as *fineza*. This *fineza* is often part of an attempt to win favor, in other words, it is something you do in hopes of getting something in return.

313   **Buen arbitrio...***Your ingeniousness (or cleverness) found a perfect means to place me under the yoke of its power (yugo de sus imperios).* In short, you found a great way to make me want to go with you.

de mis sentidos que, ciegos
girasoles,[314] es forzoso
2000 que vayan al Sol siguiendo.
Guía pues, no porque voy,
como dices, a un supremo
alcázar, sino porque
vaya tras ti,[315] que a no ser eso,
2005 primero que a Focas diera°   [daría yo]
—por un natural despego°   coldness
con que aborrezco° su nombre—   hate
ni aun el menor rendimiento°   submission
quizá...
CINTIA   Pues a nadie digas
2010 tu oculto aborrecimiento,
que ignoras lo que aventuras.[316]
Porque vas... Pero no puedo
proseguir, que llega gente.
Mas lo que ahora no te advierto[317]
2015 te diré en otra ocasión,
porque te importa el saberlo.

Salen Libia, Ismenia, música (Damas), y Leónido.

LIBIA   (*a Leónido*) Ya que yo tuve la dicha°   good fortune
de hablarte,[318] con el intento
que te he dicho, de que vas
2020 donde en el palacio excelso
de Focas vivas gozoso,
sígueme.
LEÓNIDO   Ya te obedezco,

---

314   **girasoles** *sunflowers* They were symbols of obedience, because the sunflower always follows the sun.

315   Eraclio explains that he's not going with Cintia to please Focas, but because it is what she wants.

316   **ignoras lo que...** *you do not know what you are risking* (or what you would be risking if you told Focas what you think of him)

317   **lo que ahora...** *what I can't tell you right now* (because people are coming)

318   Libia is summarizing a conversation that took place offstage.

        agradecido a la causa

        que dices, si considero,

2025   dure o no dure la duda,

        que a vivir voy[319] por lo menos

        `este espacio° en reales pompas,   this period of time

        ufano,° alegre y contento.[320]   proud

CINTIA Libia.

LIBIA   Señora.

CINTIA   Pues antes

2030   que lo digas, el efecto°   result

        lo dice, y que a la armonía

        acudió Leónido, a tiempo°   the same time

        que a los clarines Eraclio,

        porque vean que volvemos

2035   gozosas de haber logrado

        de Focas el justo intento,

        volvamos con la alegría

        que venimos, repitiendo

        ambas músicas.

DAMA 1   La parte

2040   que nos toca obedecemos,

        siempre tuyas aunque hoy

        de Libia hemos sido.

ERACLIO   ¡Cielos,

        sin duda la más hermosa

        tiene en las demás imperio,

2045   pues todas se la avasallan°!   obey

LEÓNIDO No solo ya el gozo llevo

        de ir a mandar, sino el gozo

        de que voy adonde puedo

        ver hermosura, a quien todas

2050   parece que pagan feudo.°   respect

Suena el clarín dentro.

---

319 **a vivir voy...***voy a vivir*

320 These lines tell us that Leónido's reasons for accompanying Libia are very different than Eraclio's reasons for following Cintia. It's not love that motivates Leónido, but the desire to live "en reales pompas" (in royal splendor) "ufano, alegre y contento."

Damas	(*Cantan*) *Ay como gime, mas ay como suena...*	
Hombres	(*Dentro*) To, to, Melampo...[321]	
Otro	(*Dentro*)...Barcino.	
Otro	(*Dentro*) Al jaral.°	thicket
Otro	(*Dentro*) Al risco.°	crag
Otro	(*Dentro*) Al cerro.°	hill
Focas	(*Dentro*) Aunque vueles, veloz bruto,	

Focas   (*Dentro*) Aunque vueles, veloz bruto,
2055   iré tus huellas siguiendo.
Sabañón   (*Dentro*) Pues ya acosan los ventores,
        desatraillad todos presto
        los lebreles,[322] a que sigan
        la ladra de los sabuesos.
2060 Todos   (*Dentro*) ¡Al cerro, al jaral, al risco!
        ¡To, to!
Leónido   Villanos, ¿qué es eso?

Salen Sabañón, y Luquete.

Luquete   Que Focas, por divertirse°   distract himself
        de no sé qué sentimientos,
        sabiendo que de monteras,
2065   Libia nos pasó a monteros,[323]
        —pues desde que la servimos,
        andamos dados a perros—[324]
        sacándonos de la guarda[325]
        en que antes nos había puesto,
2070   mandó, que su montería
        traigamos, y en el ojeo°   hunt
        acertó a caer un tigre,

---

321   "to, to" is what people say when calling a dog. "Melampo" and "Barcino" are the names of dogs. Remember that Lisipo's plan was for Focas to stage a hunting expedition (1769-1775). The hunt (*venatio* in Latin) is one of the principal metaphors for the process of acquiring knowledge during the sixteenth and seventeenth centuries.

322   **desatraillad todos...***let loose the hounds!*

323   **de monteras...***we used to be hunters (monteras), but Libia put us in charge of the dogs*

324   **pues desde...***since we started working for Libia our life has gone to the dogs*

325   **sacándonos...***relieving us of our duty to guard Astolfo*

              manchado galán del cierzo,[326]

              si es que hay galanes manchados,[327]

2075   y Focas le va siguiendo,

              no sin gran peligro.

LEÓNIDO   ¡Que oigo!

              Focas en peligro, ¡cielos!

              (*a Luquete*) Ven, villano, hasta ponerme

              en la senda.

ERACLIO   (*a Sabañón*) Haz tú lo mesmo,

2080   que aunque por Focas no fuera,

              por Leónido es fuerza, puesto

              que yo le enseñé a seguir

              los ejemplares del riesgo.[328]

SABAÑÓN   ¿Aun no hemos acabado

              con los salvajes?

2085 LEÓNIDO   Ven presto.

Vanse Leónido con Luquete y Eraclio con Sabañón.

CINTIA Vamos siguiéndolos todos,

              ya que este lance ha dispuesto,

              que sigamos a quien antes

              nos seguía.

LIBIA   Y sea diciendo,

2090   porque alentemos la gente[329]

              con sus alaridos° mesmos.   shouts

Vanse Cintia y Libia.

UN HOMBRE (*Dentro*) ¡To, to, Melampo, Barcino!

---

326 **manchado galán**...*a spotted gentleman who ran like the wind* (i.e. the tiger). In plays such as Mira de Amescua's *La rueda de la fortuna*, the tiger is an animal that is fiercely protective of its offspring and symbolizes a mother's concern for her children.

327 This is a play on the double meaning of "manchado": both spotted and stained.

328 Previously, Leónido used the phrase "ejemplares del riesgo" when he was talking about following Eraclio's lead in verse 1824. In that scene, Eraclio declared that he would rather die the son of Mauricio (and be the legitimate heir to the empire) than live the son of Focas (1133-1147). Leónido patterned his own behavior after Eraclio's risky model.

329 **Y sea**...*And let's shout as we go, to inspire the hunters*

TODOS (*Dentro*) ¡Al jaral, al risco, al cerro!

Salen Leónido con Luquete por una parte, Eraclio con Sabañón por otra parte.

LEÓNIDO ¿Adónde, villano, vas?
2095 Que en vez de haberme traído
donde se escuchaba el ruido,
conmigo en lo oculto das
del monte, donde, ni gente,
ni ladra, ni huella hay.

2100 ERACLIO ¿Dónde, villano, me trae
tu error? Pues no solamente
a la parte me has guiado,
donde la caza se oyó,
pero a sitio, que aun el día,
2105 parece que le ha ignorado,
según lo opaco, y tejido
impide el Sol su boscaje.

LUQUETE ¿Quién de uno en otro salvaje
anda, que no sea un perdido?

2110 SABAÑÓN Pues, ¿qué mucho ha sido errar,[330]
quien a buscar otro viene
en un barrio que no tiene
barbero[331] a quien preguntar?

LEÓNIDO ¿Quién en el monte juzgara
2115 que nací que me perdiera?[332]

Salen Sabañón y Eraclio.[333]

ERACLIO ¿Quién donde viví creyera
que ningún seno° ignorara?   hidden place

LEÓNIDO Desde esta peña° veré   cliff top

---

330 *Tp* "Diles, que no es mucho errar,"

331 **barbero** *barber-surgeon* Barbers were famous for loitering outside their shops, so they were often asked for directions.

332 **¿Quién en...***Who ever thought that I would get lost in the mountains where I was born?*

333 They enter from the other side of the stage from where Luquete and Leónido are. They do not notice one another until later in the scene.

		si senda descubro o gente.
2120	ERACLIO	Desde este risco eminente
		el monte registraré.
	LEÓNIDO	Y no en vano, que en su espacio
		un alto edificio vi.

Mudase el teatro.[334]

LUQUETE   ¿Quién diablos le puso allí?

2125   ERACLIO   Y no en vano, que un palacio
descubro a mi parecer.

SABAÑÓN   Por más que el monte he corrido
nunca yo del° he sabido.   [del palacio]

LEÓNIDO   Sin duda debe de ser,

2130   pues aquella beldad° dijo,   beauty
que a un alcázar° me traía,   fortress
este por quien lo decía.

ERACLIO   Si sus razones colijo,[335]
que a un palacio me guiaba

2135   fue lo que me dijo aquella
divina hermosura bella,
sin duda que deste hablaba.

LEÓNIDO   Y así en el preguntaré,
si acaso llegó primero.

2140   ERACLIO   Y así en él saber espero,
si este el que me dijo fue.

LEÓNIDO   ¿Dónde, Eraclio, vas?[336]

ERACLIO   A ti
te puedes tú responder,
pues una° debe de ser   one and the same
nuestra confusión.

2145   LEÓNIDO   A mí,
después de no haber hallado
a Focas, ni haber sabido

---

334   The stage directions suggest that the scenery should be changed mid-scene. All of a sudden, there appears a palace.

335   **Si sus...***If I understood what Cintia was telling me correctly...*

336   Leónido had not noticed Eraclio until this point.

		dónde el bruto que ha seguido
		le puede haber emboscado,° *ambushed*
2150		la noticia que me dio

dónde el bruto que ha seguido
le puede haber emboscado,°   ambushed
2150   la noticia que me dio
la beldad a quien seguía[337]
a esa fábrica me guía.

ERACLIO   A ese mismo efecto yo
vengo a ella.

LEÓNIDO   De nuestra fama
2155   las fortunas apuremos,
que ignoramos y sabemos.

LOS DOS   ¡Ah del alcázar![338]

MÚSICOS   (*Dentro*) ¿Quién llama?

LEÓNIDO   Quien desea saber.

MÚSICOS   (*Dentro*) Di.

ERACLIO   ¿Quién fue el Sol[339] que de mí huyó?

MÚSICOS   (*Dentro*) Yo.

ERACLIO   Luego no fue ilusión?

2160   MÚSICOS   (*Dentro*) No.

LEÓNIDO   ¿Y el otro° fue verdad?   [otro Sol]

MÚSICOS   (*Dentro*) Sí.

ERACLIO   Según eso, ¿aquí llegó
la que en el monte perdí
por seguir a Focas?

MÚSICOS   (*Dentro*) Sí.

LEÓNIDO   ¿La otra quedóse en él?[340]

2165   MÚSICOS   (*Dentro*) No.

LOS DOS   Pues a una y otra decid
que hemos seguido sus huellas.

Lisipo sale.

LISIPO   (*A los músicos*) Pues han venido tras ellas,

---

337   Leónido and Eraclio got lost while they were following the women.

338   **Ah de...** *Is anyone there (in the palace)?*

339   Figuratively, "el Sol" is the beautiful woman he followed.

340   **¿La otra...***Did the other woman remain on the mountain?* (The alternative being that she came to the palace.)

a recibirlos salid.[341]

Salen en dos tropas todos los Músicos que puedan, y traerán todos
en fuentes[342] capas, espadas, y todo adorno de vestidos.

2170	MÚSICOS	(*Cantan*) *Pues ya de Mauricio*
		y de Focas ya
		la sangre sea heroica,
		que el lustre les da.
	OTROS	*Ambos igualmente*
2175		*reciba triunfal,*
		Trinacria, con fiestas
		pompa y majestad.
	MÚSICOS	*Y pues no se sabe,*
		si es su ʼestirpe realʼ
2180		*mentira o verdad.*
	OTROS	*Mientras que la duda*
		calla, sean sus dichas
		verdad y mentira.
	ERACLIO	¡Cielos! Lo que veo y escucho,
2185		¿es verdad o es vanidad
		de mi fantasía?
	MÚSICOS	Verdad.
	LEÓNIDO	¿Los asombros con que lucho
		son, cuando en tal confusión
		el sentido los admira,
		mentira o verdad?
2190	MÚSICOS	Mentira.
	ERACLIO	¿Verdad y mentira son?
		¿Cómo puede ser?
	LEÓNIDO	¿Quién vio
		la duda en que yo me vi?
	ERACLIO	¿No es verdad lo que veo?

si es su ʼestirpe realʼ — royal lineage

---

341 *Tp* "saldré." Lisipo is commanding his apparitions to enter the stage to receive Leónido and Eraclio at the castle, which is why they immediately appear in the following lines, while Lisipo remains unnoticed by the protagonists.

342 You can imagine that the "capas," "espadas," and "vestidos" are displayed on trays or large plates (*fuentes*).

MÚSICOS	Sí.	
LEÓNIDO	¿No es verdad lo que oigo?	
2195 MÚSICOS	No.	
OTROS	*Que pues no se sabe*	
	si es tu estirpe real	
	mentira o verdad...	
MÚSICOS	*Mientras que la duda*	
2200	*calla sean tus dichas,*	
	verdad y mentira.	
LUQUETE	¿Hubiera el diablo intentado	
	aquestas cosas?	
SABAÑÓN	Sí hubiera,	
	como nuestro amo° fuera	master (Lisipo)
2205	quien se lo hubiera mandado.	
LUQUETE	¡Dicho y hecho! Vesle° aquí.	[Lo ves]
SABAÑÓN	¿Qué dices? ¡Él es, por Dios!	

Sale Lisipo.

LISIPO	(*Ap.*) (Ya que una vez estos dos°	[Luquete y Sabañón]
	pudiendo llegar aquí,	
2210	tuve por mejor que entraran	
	donde este tiempo estuvieran,	
	que no que volver pudieran	
	donde el palacio contaran	
	que vieron,[343] sobre el pesar	
2215	que allá de Focas alcanza,	
	en la perdida esperanza	
	de que le puedan hallar.[344])	
	Príncipes,° a quien el cielo,	Eraclio y Leónido
	con prodigiosa crianza,°	upbringing

---

343 **donde el...**_donde contaran que vieron el palacio._ Lisipo explains why he let Luquete and Sabañon into the palace along with Eraclio and Leónido.

344 **que allá...**These verses present an interpretative challenge. A wonderfully skillful editor of this play, Don William Cruickshank, says in a note, "I do not know what these lines mean" (226). That does not imply that readers should not *try* to understand what they mean. Oftentimes, readers' best interpretations start with problems and obstacles—the deadlock that literary critics call "aporia"—rather than with what they understand easily.

2220	no sin suma° providencia,
	para grandes cosas guarda,
	Focas, reducido° a que
	es más heroica, más clara
	acción honrar a la ajena,[345]
2225	que ver que a su sangre falta,
	por los dos envió, de cuyo
	intento ya en la montaña
	de paz os dieron aviso°
	una y otra dulce salva.
2230	Y aunque por entonces pudo
	el acaso° de la caza,
	divertir la acción, habiéndoos
	guiado el destino las plantas,[346]
	viniendo donde os trujera
2235	quien de buscaros se encarga,
	seáis bien venidos: y puesto
	que de la `sangrienta saña°
	de aquel bruto que siguió°
	triunfante, volvió a este alcázar
2240	adonde con alborozo°
	de igual afecto° os aguarda.
	Entrad, porque, desnudando
	la bruta piel tosca y basta,[347]
	para llegar a su vista°
2245	os adornen ricas galas,
	joyas y plumas: aquella
	es la `prevenida estancia°
	vuestra, Leónido. Esta es,
	Eraclio, la vuestra. Vaya
2250	la música divirtiendo
	a los dos.

Glosses (right margin):
- 2220 suma° — utmost
- 2222 reducido° — convinced
- 2228 aviso° — sign (of peace)
- 2231 acaso° — chance
- 2234 trujera — [trajera]
- 2237 sangrienta saña° — bloodthirsty rage
- 2238 siguió° — [Focas siguió]
- 2240 alborozo° — rejoicing
- 2241 afecto° — affection
- 2244 vista° — [de Focas]
- 2247 prevenida estancia° — prepared room

ERACLIO　　¡Grandeza estraña!

345　**ajena** *ajena sangre* The blood that is not his, Mauricio's blood (i.e. Mauricio's son).

346　**habiéndoos guidado**...*el destino habiendo guiado las plantas* (*destiny having guided your feet*) "Habiéndoos" is "habiendo + os."

347　**basta** *rough* Here "basta" is an adjective modifying "piel" (the animal skins Eraclio and Leónido are wearing).

¿Esto, cielos, no gozó
tanto tiempo mi ignorancia?

LEÓNIDO   Aunque es mucho lo que veo,
2255   o poco me admira o nada.[348]
Porque para mi ambición,
aun más que miro me falta.[349]

TODOS LOS   *Pues ya de Mauricio,*
MÚSICOS   *y de Focas ya,*
2260   *la sangre es heroica,*
que el lustre les da,
a ambos igualmente
reciba triunfal
Trinacria con fiestas,
2265   *pompa y majestad,*
y pues no se sabe
si es su estirpe real
mentira o verdad,
mientras que la duda
2270   *calla, sean sus dichas*
verdad y mentira.

Vase cada uno por su parte con un coro de música.[350]

SABAÑÓN   Luquete, ¿que dices desto?
LUQUETE   ¿Tú sabes lo que nos pasa?
SABAÑÓN   Yo, no.
LUQUETE   Pues ni yo tampoco.

Vanse Luquete y Sabañón.

2275   LISIPO   Señor, ya es tiempo que salgas.

Sale Focas.

___

348   **o poco...***I find this a little impressive, or not at all impressive*

349   These lines are another important passage for understanding Leónido's character. The question is: does Leónido's obvious ambition suggest that he is the son of Mauricio or of Focas?

350   The members of the chorus exit on both sides of the stage, with Eraclio going with one member and Leónido with another. They are taking them away to dress them in proper attire for court.

Focas Aunque culpé que dijeses
tal vez, que si me bastara
el ánimo[351] para hacer
una experiencia[352] tan rara
2280 sin enseñarla, disculpo
la frase ya, porque es tanta
la admiración que `yo solo
me atreviera° a ejecutalla.   I alone would dare

Lisipo Pues ahora, señor, empieza,
2285 que saliendo de sus cuadras°,   rooms, quarters
acabados de vestirse,
los dos a este cuarto pasan.

Por dos partes salen Eraclio y Leónido, vestidos de gala,[353] con criados,
acabando de vestirse, y salen Luquete y Sabañón de lacayos[354] ridículos.

Focas Atendamos[355] mientras llegan.
Criado 1 Toma el sombrero y la capa.
Leónido ¿Cuál es el sombrero?
2290 Criado 1   Este.
Leónido Si remotas no me engañan
las noticias que de él tuve, [356]
a la sombra desta falda
se aloja la cortesía[357]
2295 y la vanidad descansa.
Con gusto a ponerle llego.
¿Es posible, que esto haga?°   [haga yo]
¡O bien vistos, o mal vistos![358]

---

351 **Aunque culpé...**_Although I was mad that you doubted whether I was up for this..._ Focas refers
to his earlier conversation with Lisipo (1731-1744).

352 *Tp* "apariencia"

353 **vestidos de gala** *dressed elegantly*

354 **lacayos...**_dressed as servants (in livery)_

355 *Tp* "Atento, amor,..."

356 **Si remotas...**_Si las noticias remotas que tuve de él no me engañan..._ "Remotas" means distant
in the sense of unclear or uncertain.

357 **a la sombra...**_wherever this cape casts its shadow courtesy or courtliness can be found._ (Leónido
is really enjoying his new clothes!)

358 Leónido compares his new clothes to his old animal skins.

	¡O ceremoniosa alhaja°!	finery
2300	¡Lo que por ti se merece,	
	y se desmerece!³⁵⁹ ¡Que haya	
	quien peligre en cosa que	
	tan fácilmente se manda!	

CRIADO 2   Ciñe° la espada.   *fasten on*

ERACLIO   Con miedo
2305   llego a ceñirme la espada.

CRIADO 2   ¿Por qué?

ERACLIO   Porque en los avisos°   warnings
que della Astolfo me daba
me decía que era ella°   [la espada]
el tesoro de la fama,
2310   en cuyo crédito acepta
valor todas sus libranzas.°   orders of payment
Jeroglífico° que fácil   symbol
hizo el uso, pues te tratan³⁶⁰
muchos como adorno y no
2315   como empeño,° ven fiada   responsibility
en que sé que hubiera pocos,
que ciñeran tu hoja blanca,³⁶¹
si el día que se la ciñen
supieran de qué se encargan.³⁶²

2320   LISIPO   (*a Focas*) Ya a besar tus manos llegan,
en sus acciones repara,°   observe
y sus razones, porque
desde aquí observando vayas
sus genios° y inclinaciones,   temperaments
2325   ya que con esto adelantas
la pereza de los días.³⁶³

---

359   Leónido is speaking to his new clothes. He says that one is either worthy or unworthy (powerful or not) according to one's clothes.

360   Eraclio is now addressing his sword.

361   **hoja blanca** *sword* "Armas blancas" are sharpened weapons or swords to be used in battle, "armas negras" are not sharpened and are used for practice or competitive fencing.

362   **hubiera pocos...** *few would ever put on a sword if they knew what responsibility it entailed.*

363   **adelantas...** *you outstrip or go faster than sluggish time.* This is another reference to not being constrained by the normal unfolding of time.

FOCAS	(*a Lisipo*) Bien les asientan las galas,[364]	
	briosos° son los dos.	spirited
CRIADO 1	El Rey,	
	que llegues, señor, aguarda.[365]	
2330 CRIADO 2	El Rey, que llegues espera.	
ERACLIO y		
LEÓNIDO	Dame, gran señor, tus plantas.[366]	
FOCAS	Ya os habrán dicho, que yo,	
	Príncipes, la `ira templada,°	anger calmed
	quiero más daros honores,	
2335	que tomar una venganza.	
	Ya en un palacio, de donde	
	a la Corte iréis mañana,	
	os halláis, vivid seguros	
	de que vuestras vidas guarda	
2340	en la piedad de una duda	
	el rigor de una esperanza.	
ERACLIO	Otra vez tus plantas beso,	
	(*Ap.*) (Tiranía, ¿qué no arrastras?°)	hold sway over
	y en ellas, agradecido	
2345	a tanto honor, dicha tanta,	
	esclavo, ya que no puedo	
	hijo, te doy la palabra	
	de reconocer la vida,	
	que en mí y Leónido restauras.	
2350	Porque viviendo los dos	
	dos vidas hoy con un alma,	
	cada uno recibe una	
	y queda deudor de entrambas.	
FOCAS	(*Ap.*) (¡Qué bien suena el rendimiento°!)	submission
2355	¿Por qué, Leónido, te apartas,	
	y tú gracias no me das?	
LEÓNIDO	¿De qué te he de dar las gracias?	
	Si es del honor, por cualquiera	

---

364 **Bien les…** *The fine clothes suit them both.*

365 **El Rey…** *El rey aguarda, señor, que llegues (The king is waiting for you to approach)*

366 **tus plantas** *the soles of your feet* They do not actually kiss his feet—it's just a courtly formula—but they do bow deeply.

	lado a mi sangre le alcanza,
2360	si es de la vida, con ella
	más que me obligas me agravias.
	Pues o por ti o por Mauricio,
	acreedor soy a la sacra
	diadema[367], y mientras me pones
2365	en duda dicha tan alta,
	¿para qué quiero la vida?

FOCAS   (*Ap.*) (No suena mal la arrogancia.)

LUQUETE   Y a mí, a quien también han puesto,
señor, estas martingalas...°   incredible clothes

2370   SABAÑÓN   Y a mí, a quien también han dado
librea[368] aquestas fantasmas...

LOS DOS   ¿...no daréis un pie siquiera?[369]

LEÓNIDO   ¡Quita, loco!

ERACLIO   ¡Necio, aparta!

FOCAS   ¿Quién son estos?

LEÓNIDO   Dos villanos

2375   que acaso nos acompañan.

LUQUETE   ¿Ya no nos conoce?

FOCAS   ¿Pues
quién sois?

SABAÑÓN   ¡Lo que hacen las galas!
Los que del monte y de Astolfo
fuimos monteros y guardas.

FOCAS   ¿Qué hacéis aquí?[370]

2380   LUQUETE   Tener miedo.

LISIPO   Ea, villanos, ya basta.

Sale Libia.

LIBIA   Habiendo Cintia sabido...

---

367   **acreedor soy...**_I am heir to the empire (worthy of the crown)_

368   **librea** _livery_ (i.e. the clothes or uniform a nobleman gives to his servants)

369   **¿No daréis...**_Won't you back us up on this?_ (In other words, "don't we look great?") Luquete and Sabañón must start strutting around at this point or doing something else annoying, because Leónido and Eraclio are going to get fed up with them.

370   Lisipo explains why Luquete and Sabañón are there in verses 2208-2217.

	LUQUETE	¿También está acá nuestra ama?	
	SABAÑÓN	¡Ahora digo que es el diablo!	
2385	LIBIA	...después que de la montaña	
		los cotos corrió en tu busca,	
		que ya en esta quinta° estabas	palace
		y los Príncipes contigo,	
		licencia de entrar aguarda	
2390		a darles la bienvenida.[371]	
	FOCAS	Que llegue, `la di.°	[dile]
	LISIPO	Repara,	
		que no son Cintia, ni Libia	
		las dos, sino...[372]	
	FOCAS	¿Qué te cansas	
		en advertirme, si en todo	
		estoy?[373]	
2395	LEÓNIDO	¿Quién es la que aguardan?	
	ERACLIO	¿Quién es la que esperan?	
	LISIPO	Cintia, Reina de Trinacria.[374]	

Salen todas las Damas y Cintia.

	ERACLIO	¿No es la que en el monte vi?
	LEÓNIDO	¿No es la que vi en la campaña?
2400	ERACLIO	Ella es, muera mi deseo...
	LEÓNIDO	Ella es, viva mi esperanza...
	ERACLIO	...pues ya no puede atreverse
		amor a empresa tan alta.
	LEÓNIDO	...pues a no menor asumpto,

---

371 **licencia de...**(*Cintia*) *aguarda licencia de entrar a darles la bienvenida*

372 It may be a little difficult even for the audience to figure out how much of what we are seeing is reality and how much is the work of Lisipo's magic. Clearly, however, Lisipo is at pains to remind Focas that all is not as it seems.

373 **en todo...***I know everything already*

374 This verse is problematic due to the modifications it incurred over the course of time. In the original manuscript, the verse reads, "Doña Cintia, ruina de triaca" ("triaca" means, roughly, "antidote"). It was changed to say, "Doña Cintia, Reyna de Triaca," before its final version in later editions that reads "Cintia, Reyna de Trinacria." It seems to us that later versions make more sense than the original manuscript for a basic reason: Eraclio must learn in this moment that Cintia is a queen. This is something he did not know previously (see verse 1951).

2405		diera yo mi confianza.[375]
	CINTIA	Después, señor, que mis dichas
		dádose el parabién hayan
		de vuestra vida,[376] a quien tuvo
		en leal desconfianza
2410		de aquella fiera el empeño,
		dadme licencia a que añada
		el segundo parabién
		de que merezca mi casa
		dos huéspedes tan gloriosos,
2415		ya que quiso mi tirana
		suerte que ʿno fuese yoʿ _I did not go_
		cuando ellos en demanda
		de vuestra vida acudieron,[377]
		quien a este albergueʿ los traiga. _shelter_
2420	ERACLIO	Solo pudiera, en disculpa
		de dejar la soberana
		vista vuestra, yo... si... cuando...
		(_Ap._) (¡Aliento y voces me faltan!)
		Perdonad, porque el saber
2425		quién sois me turba y espanta
		tanto que aun hablar no puedo.
	LEÓNIDO	Pues diga yo lo que él calla.[378]
		Solo pudiera en disculpa
		de dejar la soberana
2430		vista vuestra, alegar yo,
		lo preciso de la causa.[379]
		Pues por solo dar, señora,
		vida al Rey, me la quitara
		a mí, y si el no conseguir

---

375   **a no menor...**_I would not attempt anything less._

376   **Después, señor...**_Señor, después que mis dichas se hayan dado el parabién de vuestra vida (after my good fortune has congratulated you on being alive)_ She says she's happy that Focas was not killed by the tiger.

377   **en demanda...**_when they rallied to the effort to save your life_

378   **Pues diga...**_Let me say what he does not_

379   **Solo pudiera...**_I can only give as an excuse for having left your sight the importance of the task I was facing_ (i.e. trying to save Focas from the tiger).

2435   el fin de empresa tan alta
          no me valió para dicha,
          para disculpa me valga.
FOCAS   (*Ap.*) (Lo bien y mal explicado
          de los dos también me agrada,
2440   sin que nada inferir pueda
          para el examen del alma.
          Porque no está decidido
          en el duelo de las damas,
          si es cobarde el que se atreve
2445   u osado el que se acobarda.)
          El cuidado de mi vida
          os estimo, y porque haga
          tiempo al descanso quien fue
          de la fatiga la causa,
2450   será bien que acompañándoos
          hasta vuestro cuarto vaya.
          (*Ap. a Lisipo*) (Esto es dar lugar a ver
          que obran sin mí.)

Tocan el clarín.

LISIPO   (*Ap. a Focas*) (Bien lo trazas,
          pero antes has de ver
2455   lo que el tiempo te adelanta.)

Sale un criado.

CRIADO   Un Embajador, señor,
          del Gran Duque de Calabria
          audiencia pide.
FOCAS   Di que entre.

Sale el Príncipe Federico.

LISIPO   (*Ap.*) (Su misma forma retrata,
2460   sucediendo lo que había

	de suceder.)[380]	
FEDERICO	A tus plantas	
	besar tu mano merezca.°	may I deserve
FOCAS	Del suelo, joven, levanta.	
FEDERICO	El Gran Duque Federico,	

FEDERICO El Gran Duque Federico,
2465 sabiendo, que hoy en Trinacria
estás, a ti y a Cintia dos
parabienes dar me manda.
De tu salud y venida
a ti y del honor que gana
2470 con tal huésped° a ella, en cuyo   guest
nombre merezca tu blanca
mano besar. Y pasando
a no menor importancia,
te representa por mí,[381]
2475 que siendo hijo de Casandra,
hermano del infelize
Mauricio, cuya desgracia
el mundo llora, no solo
te debe rendir las parias,°   tribute
2480 que al imperio pagó, pero
que puesto que no se halla
heredero más cercano
el día que el hijo falta,[382]
que dicen que retiró
2485 un vasallo a las montañas,
le toca el laurel,° bien como   kingship
dignidad hereditaria.
Y así, que le° restituyas,   [a Federico]
dice...

FOCAS No prosigas, calla,

---

380 **Su misma...** *This is the very likeness of Federico, and what is happening now is what should have happened in the past.* Lisipo was Federico's advisor and Lisipo counseled Federico to pay tribute (*parias*) to Focas rather than fight.

381 **te representa...** *these are his words I am delivering* (more literally, "he is speaking to you through me"). Federico begins speaking about himself in the third person because he is playing the part of an ambassador.

382 **el día...** *if you confirm that you cannot find your lost son*

2490	que inobedientes locuras,
	tanto como ésa aun palabras
	en respuesta no merecen,
	y esto que le digas basta.
LEÓNIDO	No basta, señor. ¿No tiene
2495	este palacio ventanas,
	por donde volando vuelva
	más presto?[383]
ERACLIO	Leónido, aguarda
	que viene sobre seguro
	de Embajador[384] y no agravian
2500	los motivos de su dueño
	en su boca.
LISIPO	(*Ap. a Focas*) (No reparas
	en la ira y la cordura°
	de los dos?)
FOCAS	(*Ap. a Lisipo*) (Sí.) ¿Pues qué aguardas?
	¿Ya no llevas la respuesta?
2505 FEDERICO	Que sepas que en la campaña,
	última razón de reyes
	son la pólvora y las balas.[385] (*Vase*)
FOCAS	Está bien. Ven, Cintia.
CINTIA	El cielo
	os guarde, y pues obligada
2510	al hospedaje me veo,[386]
	procuraré que no haya
	espacio° en que no os diviertan
	saraos,° paseos y danzas.
FOCAS	No paséis los dos de aquí,
2515	quedaos,° en la hermosa varia

Glosses (right margin): cordura° = good sense; espacio° = moment; saraos° = parties; quedaos° = [quedados]

---

383 Leónido offers to throw Federico out of the window. Segismundo, the protagonist of Calderón's *La vida es sueño* throws a servant out of the window in Act II of the play.

384 **viene sobre...***he comes to us as an ambassador and is protected.* A basic value in international relations for thousands of years has been that ambassadors should never be harmed. (This is reflected in the expression, "don't shoot the messenger!") Federico is playing the role of ambassador, so Eraclio says it would be unwise to hurt him.

385 **última razón...***kings have the right to use gunpowder and bullets as a last resort (when peaceful means are ineffective)*

386 **obligada al...***me veo obligada al hospedaje* I find myself obliged to you for this stay.

estancia destos jardines,
esperad, mientras que salga.

Vanse Focas y las Damas y Lisipo.

Leónido   Siempre yo he de obedecerte.
Eraclio   Siempre haré lo que me mandas.
2520   Leónido   Bien que a pesar de mis penas...
Eraclio   Bien que a pesar de mis ansias...
Leónido   ...pues que siga al Sol que adoro
mi presunción embarazas.°   place an obstacle to
Eraclio   ...pues niegas, que siga al Sol,
2525   que mi temor idolatra.°   worships

Lisipo y Focas al paño.[387]

Lisipo   Desde aquí podrás agora
ver como en un lance andan,
poniéndoles la piedad
en dos iguales balanzas.
2530   Voces   (*Dentro*) ¡Seguidle y donde le hallaréis,
matadle!

Sale Astolfo.

Astolfo   ¡El cielo me valga!
Leónido
y Eraclio   ¿Qué es esto?
Astolfo   Dichoso yo
pues que llegue a vuestras plantas.
Supe de vuestra venida
2535   y, quebrantando las guardas,
rompí° la prisión, no tanto   broke out of
porque esto mi vida salva,
cuanto por ver que logró
mi silencio su esperanza,
2540   pues aunque agora me den

---

387   **al paño** *at the edge of the stage*

una y mil muertes, me bastan
para consuelo el haberos
visto en majestad tan alta.

LEÓNIDO   ¿En qué majestad nos miras,
2545   siendo en una duda fundada?[388]
               ¿Quitas a cuya es la dicha,
               para neciamente darla
               a cuya no es?[389]

ERACLIO   Mal, Leónido,
               lo que le debes le pagas.

2550 LEÓNIDO ¿Qué le debo? Lo tirano
               de una rústica crianza
               en que, ladrón de mi media
               vida, en riscos me la gasta.
               ¿No fuera mejor, pues supo
2555   quién éramos, que empleara[390]
               nuestras fortunas en otros
               ejercicios, que lograran
               la sangre de nuestros pechos
               donde lo que nos quitaba,
2560   el hado por conveniencia,
               restituyese por armas?

FOCAS   (*Ap. a Lisipo*) (Bien discurre por lo altivo
               Leónido.)

ERACLIO   Si es cosa clara,
               que, `conocido él° lo fuera   known to him
2565   el hijo infeliz que ampara
               de Mauricio entre los dos,[391]
               ¿qué lealtad, di, se compara
               al desterrarse° con él?   exile himself
               Y di, ¿qué piedad se iguala,
2570   también entre los dos, que

---

388 Leónido implies that although both he and Eraclio are presently dressed in elegant clothing, they still do not know which of them is heir to the crown.

389 **¿Quitas a…***Are you taking away the happiness that rightfully belongs to one of us and unwisely giving it to one who doesn't deserve it?*

390 *Tp* "empezara"

391 **el hijo…***que [Astolfo] ampara el hijo infeliz de Mauricio entre los dos [i.e. Eraclio y Leónido]*

sabiendo por la aldeana
madre del uno, que era prenda° offspring
de su enemigo, le guardara
con igual fineza?

FOCAS (*a Lisipo*) Bien
2575 por lo cuerdo Eraclio habla.

LEÓNIDO ¿Y es fineza y es lealtad
y es piedad lo que ahora calla?
No. Pues, cuando anda con uno
piadoso, con otro cruel anda,
2580 fuera mejor y era fuerza,[392]
que de una vez se explicara
y muriera el que muriera,
y reinara el que reinara.

ERACLIO No fuera,° pues una vida [fuera mejor]
vale más que un reino.° kingdom

2585 LEÓNIDO Calla,
que el ver que ʼvuelves por él,° you defend him
tanto mi cólera° arrastra, anger
que ʼestoy por°... on the verge of

ASTOLFO ¿Por qué? ¡Di, ingrato!

LEÓNIDO ¡Por serlo, pues me lo llamas:
2590 traidor, tirano, caduco[393]!

Échalo (a Astolfo) en el suelo.

ERACLIO Del suelo, padre, levanta.

ASTOLFO ¡Ay de mi!

ERACLIO Y ya que mi mano
a ti socorrió, mi saña° anger
castigue un tirano aleve.° treacherous

2595 LEÓNIDO No es muy fácil la demanda.

---

392 **fuera mejor...***it would have been better and it was necessary*

393 Leónido uses "caduco" in an obsolete medical sense, in which "caduco" describes the presence of convulsions, spasms, or epileptic seizures, as well as times when the conscious will no longer controls the movements of the body. Leónido knows he has completely lost control of himself.

Riñen[394] *Eraclio y Leónido.*

SABAÑÓN	Ve aquí por lo que no puede
	poner uno a su hijo espada.[395]
LUQUETE	No, que el día que la ciñe,
	no ve la hora de sacarla.

Vanse Luquete y Sabañón.

ASTOLFO	¡Hijos! ¡Hijos!
LEÓNIDO	¡Tropecé° I stumbled
	y caí!

2600 — LEÓNIDO ¡Tropecé° ...   *I stumbled*

*Salen Focas y Cintia. Focas se pone delante de
Leónido. Cintia detiene a Eraclio.*

FOCAS	¡Detente!
CINTIA	¡Aguarda!
FOCAS	¡No le mates!
CINTIA	¡No te empeñes!
ERACLIO	(*A Focas*) Viva, porque tú lo mandas.[396]
	(*A Cintia*) Viva, porque tú lo quieres.
	Ven, Astolfo.

Vase Eraclio.

ASTOLFO	Con el ansia,
	que Focas a socorrer
	a Leónido se adelanta.
LISIPO	Con el afecto que Cintia,
	aun entre las sombras vanas,
	deteniendo a Eraclio, hizo
	lo que yo hiciera.
LEÓNIDO	¡Qué rabia!
ASTOLFO	¡O secreto, lo que dices! (*Vase*)

---

394   **Riñen** *they fight*

395   **Ve aquí...** *This is why you can never give your son a sword (he'll just fight with it).*

396   *Tp* "No haré, pues que tú lo mandas."

LISIPO	¡O secreto, lo que callas! (*Vase*)	
LEÓNIDO	Haber tropezado no es	
2615	flaqueza° sino desgracia°	weakness, bad luck
	y ahora lo verás.	
FOCAS	Detente.	
LEÓNIDO	Nadie impida mi venganza,	
	que he de \`sanear el desaire.°	remedy the insult
FOCAS	¿Ves que soy quien te lo manda?	
2620	CINTIA ¿Ves que soy quien te lo ruega?°	pleads
LEÓNIDO	Ni tu decoro me ataja,°	deter
	ni tu respeto me mueve.	

Vase Leónido.

FOCAS	¡Oye, espera!	
CINTIA	¡Escucha, aguarda!	
	¿Qué te van diciendo, Focas,	
	las experiencias?[397]	
2625	FOCAS Mucho, y nada.	
	Pues que quedo con mis dudas	
	al ver que iguales me agradan	
	en el uno la soberbia	
	y en el otro la templanza.	
2630	CINTIA Pues date prisa a saberlo,	
	que si el término° al día pasa,	period of time
	en un punto que esto sobre[398]	
	verás que todo esto falta.	

Vanse.

---

397 **¿Qué te van…***What are you learning from these experiments, Focas?*
398 **en un punto…***if the time [spent doing these experiments] exceeds even a little*

Jornada tercera

Salen Cintia, Libia, Ismenia y Músicos.

CINTIA	Ya que al conjuro de aquel	
2635	fuerte, poderoso hechizo°	magic spell
	finjamos° lo que no somos,	let's pretend to be
	seamos lo que fingimos.	
LIBIA	Dices bien, y pues al duelo	
	entre los dos Focas hizo	
2640	las amistades,³⁹⁹ sin que	
	de aquel ni otros motivos	
	haya averiguado más	
	que la soberbia en Leónido,	
	y la templanza en Eraclio,	
2645	tratemos de divertirlos,⁴⁰⁰	
	hasta que dé otra ilusión	
	de sus pasiones indicio.°	sign, evidence
ISMENIA	Buena es para descubrir	
	la interior la que Lisipo	
	trazando está.⁴⁰¹	
2650	CINTIA Cantad, pues.	
ISMENIA	Ya `tono y letra° fingimos.	melody and lyrics
MÚSICOS	(*Cantan*) *Los ojos que dan enojos,*	
	al ver y mirar con ellos,	
	más valiera no tenerlos,	
2655	*pero bueno es tener ojos.*⁴⁰²	
	Los ojos que dan enojos...	
LEÓNIDO	(*Dentro canta*) *Los ojos que dan enojos...*	
ERACLIO	(*Dentro canta*) *Al ver y mirar con ellos...*	
LEÓNIDO	*Más valiera no tenerlos.*	
2660	ERACLIO	*Pero bueno es tener ojos.*	

---

399   Remember that at the end of Act II, Leónido and Eraclio were fighting, apparently some time has passed because Libia suggests that Focas has patched things up between them.

400   This desire to distract Eraclio and Leónido explains why the women start singing below.

401   **Buena es...***Buena es la (ilusión) que Lisipo está trazando para descubrir la interior (de Eraclio y Leónido)*

402   These paradoxical verses introduce the central theme of the following scene.

Por una parte salen Leónido y Luquete,
por otra parte salen Eraclio y Sabañón.[403]

LEÓNIDO   Siempre la música fue
el imán de mis sentidos.

LUQUETE   Buena la música° fuera,   female musician
si no tuviera músicos.°   male musicians

2665   ERACLIO   Aunque pudiera este acento
haberme hasta aquí traído,
más a seguirle me mueven
los ojos que los oídos.

SABAÑÓN   Haces bien, porque no hay solfa°   musical notes
como el solfa de lo lindo.

2670   MÚSICOS   (*Cantan*) *Los ojos...*

CINTIA   Oíd, esperad,
que parece que he sentido°   noticed
entre aquellas ramas° gente.   branches

LIBIA   Entre estas también hay ruido.

ISMENIA   ¿Quién está aquí?

2675   LEÓNIDO   Quien llamado
del sonoro acento vino,[404]
porque disculpas del canto
le sirvan para el delito.[405]

ISMENIA   ¿Y aquí quién está?

ERACLIO   Quien no
2680   disculpar su yerro° quiso,   error
pues no le sirvió el acento
más que de darle el aviso.

LEÓNIDO   Culpa que del oído fue,
bien sanearla solicito.[406]

---

403   The women onstage either do not see or pretend not to notice the men take the stage.

404   **Quien llamado...***Quien vino llamado del sonoro acento (One who was called by the beautiful music).*

405   Leónido says that he is drawn to where the women are by the beautiful music. The music is so lovely that he cannot be blamed for intruding.

406   This reference to "culpa" or guilt partly sets in motion the action of the rest of the scene. Essentially, Leónido says that he was tempted by his ears (that he was figuratively "guilty" for giving in to the pleasure that his sense of hearing offered him). However, he wants to be "absolved" of that

2685	ERACLIO	Culpa fue de los ojos,
		mal a negarla me animo.[407]
	CINTIA	Pues porque a cuestión[408] no pase,
		quien mayor fineza hizo,
		él que adelantó la culpa,
2690		o él que la culpa previno,
		cantad, que es muy visto lance° a common dispute
		éste de entre ojos y oídos,
		andar graduando afectos.
	LEÓNIDO	Yo no he de dejar el mío
2695		desairado, y aunque canten,
		sanearle tengo.
	ERACLIO	Lo mismo
		haré yo al compás° del tono. rhythm
	CINTIA	También ese lance es visto.
	LOS DOS	¿Propio o ajeno?[409]
	CINTIA	No sé,
2700		¿mas para qué es el decirlo?
	LEÓNIDO	Para que ajeno es acierto
		ver cuanto mejor elijo.
	ERACLIO	Para que propio no es culpa,
		pues de mi paño me visto.[410]
2705	CINTIA	Con no atender cumplo yo.
		Prosigue, Ismenia.

---

guilt ("sanearla solicito"). As we'll see in Eraclio's response, Eraclio is moved by his sense of sight and physical beauty.

407   **mal me...***I do not want to deny myself the pleasure*

408   "Cuestión" here means a fight or duel. Leónido has said that he is moved most by what he hears, while Eraclio says that it is what he sees that has the greatest power over him. So each will defend the superiority of one of the senses. For her part, Cintia does not want a resumption of the violence between Leónido and Eraclio, so she will propose another kind of contest: a poetic "battle." The two men will compose verses on the theme that has already been introduced by the musicians: "Los ojos que dan enojos..." This kind of poetry, in which the theme of a short number of verses is expounded upon by various poets is called a "glosa."

409   What they ask here is whether or not the verses and ideas they use to gloss the stanza should be original ("propio") or by someone else ("ajeno"). In other words, are they competing in the proper selection and application of verses written by someone else or are they competing in the composition of original poetry?

410   **de mi paño...***I dress myself in my own cloth (figuratively, my verses will be original)*

ISMENIA   Prosigo.
                           (*Canta*) *Los ojos que dan enojos...*[411]
LEÓNIDO   Del placer y del pesar
             árbitros los ojos son,[412]
2710   pues sirven al corazón
             de mirar, ver y llorar:
             Y aunque ya al ver y al mirar
             distintos son sus antojos,
             no al llorar luego en despojos,
2715   siempre unos al peor empeño,
             traidores son a su dueño.

LEÓNIDO y
los MÚSICOS (*Cantan*) *Los ojos que dan enojos...*
MÚSICOS   *Al ver y mirar con ellos.*
ERACLIO   Ver, mirar y llorar, ser
2720   tres cosas no he de dudar.
             Ver, que es ver y no cuidar.
             Mirar, que es cuidar y ver.[413]
             Luego el llorar, sin tener
             glosa,° es quien llega a excedellos,[414]   elaboration
2725   que ojos que lloran al vellos°   [verlos]
             sus ojos ya aliviaron
             el daño que ellos causaron...

ERACLIO y
los MÚSICOS (*Cantan*) *...al ver y mirar con ellos...*
MÚSICOS   *Más valiera no tenellos.*
2730 LEÓNIDO Que el llanto el dolor termina,
             tampoco no he de negar,

---

411   Ismenia is setting the "glosa" in motion, prompting Leónido to explain the paradox contained in the musicians' verses: seeing is believing, but we are deceived by what we see. Leónido and Eraclio will now take turns, each responding to the verse supplied to them (in the next case, Eraclio will respond to "al ver y mirar con ellos"). This kind of poetic contest was a common entertainment for noblemen and intellectuals during the sixteenth and seventeenth centuries.

412   **Del placer...***los ojos son árbitros del placer y del pesar* "Arbitros" has the sense of "arbiters" in English.

413   You may find this distinction between "ver" and "mirar" helpful as you think through the different experiences of perceiving with the eyes in this play.

414   "Excedellos" is a poetic way of saying "excederlos." This becomes very common in the ensuing verses.

             pero error fuera negar,
             en fe de la medicina,
             en ojos que uno imagina,
2735   antes o después de vellos,
             llorallos ya es padecellos,
             y aunque haya de aliviallos
             tenellos para llorallos...

LEÓNIDO y
los MÚSICOS   (*Cantan*) *Mas más valiera no tenellos.*
2740 MÚSICOS   *Pero bueno es tener ojos.*
     ERACLIO   De mi dolor el tormento
             no llego a sentirle yo
             porque le lloro, sino
             le lloro porque le siento.
2745   Y así, si aliviar intento,
             sucedidos los enojos,
             con lágrimas que en despojos
             los ojos dan al pesar,
             malo es tener que llorar...

ERACLIO y
2750 los MÚSICOS   (*Cantan*) *Pero bueno es tener ojos.*
     MÚSICOS   *Los ojos que dan enojos...*

                   Sale Lisipo.

      LISIPO   No prosigáis, porque Focas,
             en el bello laberinto
             que hace en esos cenadores°   bower
2755   la amenidad deste sitio,
             con la dulzura del canto
             rindió al sueño los sentidos.[415]
      CINTIA   Retiraos todos, porque
             si el canto dormir le hizo,
2760   no es bien que el canto le haga
             despertar, que fuera impío
             halago el que convirtiera
             tan presto en pena el alivio.

---

415   A long way of saying that Focas is sleeping and they should not wake him up.

Vanse las Damas.

Luquete	Vamos, Sabañón, a ver	
2765	si hay en jardines tan ricos	
	algo que comer.	
Sabañón	¡Que haya[416]	
	quien plante rosas y lirios,°	irises
	claveles° y tulipanes,	red carnations
	y no coles° y pepinos!	cabbages

Vanse los dos y sale Focas.[417]

2770	Lisipo	Mira, que le has de decir
		a Eraclio lo que te digo,
		que en voz de Cintia[418] le digas.
	Cintia	Sí, diré, pues que te asisto
		para obedecerte.
	Lisipo	Tú
2775		en voz de Libia a Leónido
		lo mismo dirás.
	Libia	Si haré.
	Lisipo	Así veré si consigo
		la última experiencia, ya
		que Cintia callar me hizo.[419]
2780	Focas	Ya a hablarles llegan las dos,
		con que veré si examino
		su amor u odio, a cuya causa,
		para poder asistirlos
		y notarles las acciones,
2785		el sueño° a su vista finjo.
	Libia	Leónido, escucha.

416 **¡Que haya...**No puedo creer que haya

417 This is confusing because Lisipo just said that Focas was asleep. This was part of a ruse.

418 **en voz...**in Cintia's voice You may already understand why Lisipo is saying this. Many readers, however, are confused and confusion, as strange as it may seem, is partly the point. As an audience of readers and spectators, we all have to determine which part of what we are seeing is true and which part is deception.

419 Lisipo refers to Cintia's plea in verses 1422-1431.

Leónido	No, Libia,	
	quieras que el Norte que sigo[420]	
	de vista pierda.	
Libia	Quizá,	
	si oyes lo que solicito,	
	le° alcanzarás antes.	your objective
2790 Leónido	¿Cómo?	
Eraclio	Dijiste—cuando rendido,	
	aún no sabiendo quién eras,	
	seguía tu Sol divino—[421]	
	que en otra ocasión me habías	
2795	de decir un escondido	
	secreto, que embarazó°	impeded
	la gente[422] que entonces vino.	
Cintia	Es verdad, y aunque de paso,	
	decirle ahora determino.	
	Oye, pues...	
2800 Leónido	¿Qué es lo que dices?	
Libia	Lo que mi padre Lisipo	
	por sus ciencias alcanzó,	
	y a mí solamente dijo.[423]	
Cintia	Viéndose de mí obligado,	
2805	cuando preso a Astolfo vimos,	
	porque intercedí por él,	
	o por si moría, me quiso	
	dueño hacer de su secreto.	
Leónido	¿Cielos, qué escucho?	
Eraclio	¿Qué he oído,	
	cielos?	
2810 Leónido	¿De Mauricio	

---

420 **Norte** *the North Star (or a light that guides Leónido's course)* So, "el Norte que sigo" is "the goal I am pursuing." Leónido's words mean roughly, "I won't listen to you because you probably want me to lose sight of my objective."

421 The subject here is "yo": "cuando (yo estaba) rendido, aun no sabiendo quién eras, (yo) seguía tu Sol divino..."

422 **embarazó la gente** *the arrival of the people prevented you from telling me the secret.*

423 Libia and Cintia are acting under instructions (2770-2776). Keep in mind that two conversations are happening simultaneously: Libia is speaking in private to Leónido and Cintia is speaking privately to Eraclio.

el hijo soy?
Eraclio   ¿De Mauricio
soy yo el hijo?
Libia   Sí, y por serlo
te toca el Imperio invicto
de Constantinopla.
Cintia   Sí,
2815   y no solo de mi altivo
valor el Imperio es,
mas de Trinacria el dominio,
que feudataria colonia
es suya.
Libia   Pero es preciso,
2820   que mientras que Focas viva,
esté el secreto escondido,
porque te importa no menos
que la vida.
Cintia   Más convino
guardar el secreto, mientras
2825   viva Focas, porque impío,
hidrópico de mi sangre,[424]
no se cebe° en tu homicidio.   vent itself
Libia   Y así, secreto, y pensar[425]
cómo se podrán tus bríos
declarar...
2830   Cintia   Y así, silencio,
y prevenir° discursivo   prepare
cómo podrás declararte...
Libia   ...que si hallas algún camino...
Cintia   ...que si algún modo descubres...
2835   Libia   ...no dudo, que al punto mismo...
Cintia   ...al mismo instante `no ignoro°...   I know
Libia   ...que te sigan infinitos°...   many follow you
Cintia   ...que haya muchos que te aclamen°...   proclaim
Libia   ...aunque imposible lo miro...
2840   Cintia   ...aunque imposible lo veo...

---

424   "Hidrópico" implies an insatiable thirst or desire. Here, it means "bloodthirsty."
425   **secreto, y pensar** *keep this secret and think*

LAS DOS: ...mientras esté Focas vivo.

Vanse Cintia y Libia.

LEÓNIDO ¡Oye, Libia!
ERACLIO ¡Cintia, espera!
LEÓNIDO Suspenso° con tal aviso...   dumbstruck
ERACLIO Con tal noticia admirado°...   amazed
LEÓNIDO ...triste muero.
2845 ERACLIO ...alegre vivo.
FOCAS Ya deste engaño informados,
y contra mí persuadidos,
es fuerza que en dos afectos
contrarios y tan distintos
2850 como de enemigo y padre,
haga la sangre su oficio.[426]
A hablarles llego ahora, pero
no, mejor es `advertirlos
recatado,° pues es claro   watch them secretly
2855 que disimulen° conmigo,   put on an act
y `a sus solas° no. Y así,   by themselves
otra vez el sueño finjo.
LEÓNIDO Confieso, que tuve a Focas
no sé qué interior cariño,
2860 pero ahora conozco ser
de mi soberbia nacido,
por juzgarme en él más cerca[427]
de la corona a que aspiro.
Dígalo el que, oyendo agora
2865 que me toca por Mauricio,[428]
el que cariño juzgaba
es rencor, cuando imagino
que es° tirano y que me quita   [Focas es]
el Imperio que era mío...

---

426 **haga la sangre...**blood will do its job* The father's blood will be evident in the son's reactions and natural inclinations.

427 *Tp* "por juzgarme el más cercano"

428 **que me toca...**that the empire is mine because I am Mauricio's son (and not Focas')*

2870	ERACLIO	De albricias la vida diera
		—aunque viva aborrecido
		de Focas, tan a su vista,
		en manos de mi peligro—
		por las nuevas que me ha dado.
2875		Pues no importa que el invicto
		laurel que me toca goce,[429]
		tanto como haber sabido°
		la sangre que arde° en mis venas,
		bien que ahora esté el fuego tibio.
2880	FOCAS	Como hablan `entre sí,°
		nada en los dos averiguo,
		con todo vuelvo al acecho.[430]
		¡Qué fuera que de fingido
		a verdadero pasara!
2885		Pues parece que me rindo
		a la pesadez de un sueño,[431]
		que más que sueño es delirio.
	LEÓNIDO	...y pues en mí no hay más ley,
		ni más razón, ni más juicio,
2890		que desear reinar, ¿que hiciera
		para poder conseguirlo?[432]
	ERACLIO	...y pues no hay más ambición
		en mí, ni deseo más digno
		que el de ser quien soy,[433] dejemos
2895		lo demás de mis designios°
		al Cielo, que Él volverá
		por su causa.[434]

found out   *(2877)*
burns   *(2878)*
to themselves   *(2880)*
plans   *(2895)*

---

429   **Pues no importa...***It doesn't matter that he (Focas) enjoys the position that is rightly mine*

430   **con todo...***I'll go back to spying on them despite the fact that I haven't found out much to this point.*

431   Focas has been pretending to be asleep until this point, but now he actually does fall asleep.

432   **¿que hiciera...***what wouldn't I do to become emperor?*

433   "Ser quien es," being who or what you truly are, is a social responsibility frequently discussed in seventeenth century literature. Often, this means being what you were born to be and fulfilling the expectations of your station or social class.

434   **Él volverá...***God will seek His own justice* Eraclio will no longer aspire to be king, but will leave things in God's hands.

Vase Eraclio.

	LEÓNIDO	Ya se ha ido	
		Eraclio, solo he quedado,	
		mas no, que quedan conmigo	
2900		mis confusiones y penas.	
		De tal horror me revisto,°	gather resolve
		al ver al traidor⁴³⁵ por quien	
		el sacro laurel no ciño,	
		que no sé como la saña	
2905		de tanto rencor resisto.	

Sale Eraclio.

	ERACLIO	Por descansar a mis solas	
		huí de aquí, y habiendo visto	
		gente al paso, y por no hablar	
		con nadie, `tuerzo el camino.°	I have turned back
2910	LEÓNIDO	Pero si me dijo Libia,	
		cuando lo demás me dijo,	
		que muerto él,° es fuerza que	[Focas]
		sigan todos mi partido.	
		¿Qué espero? Mas ¡ay! que aquel	
2915		cariño oculto indeciso	
		me tiene.° ¿No vale más	stops me
		un imperio que un cariño?	
		Sí. Pues, ¿qué temo? ¿Qué dudo?	
	ERACLIO	¿Qué es lo que intenta Leónido?	
	LEÓNIDO	¡Muera!	
	ERACLIO	¡No muera!⁴³⁶	
2920	FOCAS	¿Qué es esto?	
	LEÓNIDO	Haber Eraclio querido	

---

435 Leónido says these words while watching Eraclio leave, but it's not entirely clear whether Leónido is speaking about Focas or about Eraclio. Leónido believes himself to be Mauricio's son, and Leónido would then have to conclude that Eraclio is Focas' son. Leónido probably sees both Eraclio and Focas as obstacles to the throne.

436 In this moment, Leónido attempts to kill Focas, but is stopped by Eraclio. Focas is asleep and he does not see what happens.

              darte muerte y ser yo quien

              tan loco furor impido.

ERACLIO Leónido era el que intentaba

2925   matarte y yo quien te libro.

    FOCAS ¡Ay infeliz! Que ni bien

              despierto, ni bien dormido,

              "¡Muera!" y "¡No muera!" en dos voces

              oí, tan a un instante mismo,

2930   que mezclados los metales°   *sounds*

              ninguno sonó distinto,

              de suerte que de su acento

              nada infiero, y si remito

              a la acción el desengaño,

2935   igual en los dos la miro,

              pues miro en los dos igual

              desnudo el acero limpio.[437]

LEÓNIDO Yo, al irte a matar Eraclio,

              `le desnudé° en tu servicio.   *unsheathed my sword*

2940 ERACLIO Yo le saqué en tu defensa,

              al irte a matar Leónido.

    FOCAS (*a Eraclio*) ¡Mientes, mientes! ¡Porque ya

              que yo no pueda hacer juicio

              de la voz, ni de la acción,

2945   por el pavor° que—adivino   *terror*

              el corazón—desde el pecho

              me dice en callados gritos,

              tú eres el traidor. Sí, ¡tú!

              Pues en tu mano blandido°   *brandished*

2950   de esa cuchilla° el acero,°   *blade, sword*

              de aquese puñal° el filo,°   *dagger, edge*

              tanto me espeluza, tanto

              me sobresalta...[438] ¡Leónido!

              Defiéndeme de él, que todo

2955   mi valor estremecido°   *shaken*

              no basta contra el amago°   *threat*

---

437 **pues miro...***both men have their swords out* It was a crime to unsheathe a weapon in the presence of the king, this crime was known as *lèse-majesté* in French and *lesa majestad* in Spanish.

438 **tanto me...***so makes my hair stand on end, so startles me*

<table>
<tr><td></td><td></td><td>de haberle contra mí visto</td><td></td></tr>
<tr><td></td><td></td><td>tan `sañudamente fiero,°</td><td>wrathfully savage</td></tr>
<tr><td></td><td></td><td>tan ciegamente atrevido,°</td><td>daring</td></tr>
<tr><td>2960</td><td></td><td>tan sangrientamente osado,°</td><td>audacious</td></tr>
<tr><td></td><td></td><td>esgrimir° el rayo° altivo</td><td>wield, flash</td></tr>
<tr><td></td><td></td><td>de aquel `áspid de metal,°</td><td>metal snake (sword)</td></tr>
<tr><td></td><td></td><td>con señas de basilisco.[439]</td><td></td></tr>
<tr><td></td><td>ERACLIO</td><td>¿Por qué, señor, cuando yo,</td><td></td></tr>
<tr><td>2965</td><td></td><td>no solo `el acero rindo°</td><td>surrender my sword</td></tr>
<tr><td></td><td></td><td>a tus pies, pero la vida,</td><td></td></tr>
<tr><td></td><td></td><td>de mí te asombras?</td><td></td></tr>
<tr><td></td><td>FOCAS</td><td>¡Lisipo!</td><td></td></tr>
<tr><td></td><td></td><td>¡Cintia! ¡Libia! Pues que sois</td><td></td></tr>
<tr><td></td><td></td><td>familiares,[440] sed amigos,</td><td></td></tr>
<tr><td>2970</td><td></td><td>¡que me da la muerte Eraclio!</td><td></td></tr>
<tr><td></td><td>ERACLIO</td><td>(*Ap.*) (A esto una vez persuadidos,</td><td></td></tr>
<tr><td></td><td></td><td>me han de matar. ¿Dónde, cielos,</td><td></td></tr>
<tr><td></td><td></td><td>huiré de tanto peligro?) (*Vase*)</td><td></td></tr>
<tr><td></td><td>FOCAS</td><td>¡De él me amparad!</td><td></td></tr>
<tr><td></td><td>LEÓNIDO</td><td>Yo, señor,</td><td></td></tr>
<tr><td>2975</td><td></td><td>(*Ap.*) (pues tan bien ha sucedido,°</td><td>happened</td></tr>
<tr><td></td><td></td><td>`hacer la deshecha° importa)</td><td>to deceive</td></tr>
<tr><td></td><td></td><td>le seguiré, y en castigo</td><td></td></tr>
<tr><td></td><td></td><td>de igual traición, le daré</td><td></td></tr>
<tr><td></td><td></td><td>mil muertes.</td><td></td></tr>
<tr><td></td><td>FOCAS</td><td>Corre, Leónido,</td><td></td></tr>
<tr><td>2980</td><td></td><td>que del aleve la fuga</td><td></td></tr>
<tr><td></td><td></td><td>es el no menor indicio.[441]</td><td></td></tr>
</table>

Vase Leónido. Salen Lisipo y las mujeres.

<table>
<tr><td>TODOS</td><td>Señor, ¿qué es esto?</td></tr>
<tr><td>FOCAS</td><td>No sé,</td></tr>
</table>

---

439   **basilisco** *basilisk* (a lizard-like or dragon-like monster that could kill just by looking at its enemies or breathing on them)

440   **familiares** has many meanings ranging from *family members*, to *servants* to *spirits* and *demons.*

441   **que de aleve...***fleeing is no small indication of his betrayal*

un letargo, un parasismo,°   attack
un frenesí, una locura,
2985   un pasmo,° un ansia, un conflicto,   shock
que aunque no dudo el saberlo,
descansaré con decirlo.
Fingí el sueño, y él,[442] vengado
de ver que le había fingido,
2990   perturbadas las ideas,
verdadero hacerse quiso.[443]
Y en aquel pequeño espacio
que iba acechando resquicios,[444]
crepúsculo° de la vida,   twilight
2995   ni bien sombra ni bien viso,°   sparkle
a Leónido vi y a Eraclio,
sobre vuestros dos avisos
con dos puñales. Y aunque
cada uno se previno
3000   de que era suyo el amparo,
y era ajeno el homicidio.[445]
No sé con qué oculta causa,
sin asustarme en Leónido
el acero, vi el de Eraclio,
3005   jurara en mi sangre tinto.[446]
Con que infiero, que al oír
que era hijo de Mauricio,
reventó° la saña en él.   [Eraclio reventó]
Y pues que yo no me afirmo,°   I'm not certain
3010   decid vosotros, decid,
si bien o si mal colijo°   deduce
de sus acciones.

---

442   **él** *el sueño* Focas imagines sleep to be a god who is offended that Focas pretended to be asleep.

443   Sleep, offended that Focas had pretended to be asleep, avenged itself by making Focas truly fall asleep.

444   **iba acechando…***it (sueño) waited for a moment of weakness* This phrase has the connotation of an animal stalking its prey, waiting for the perfect moment to attack. See Cintia's use of the phrase in verse 1913.

445   **era suyo…***that he was the one trying to help and the other was the killer*

446   **jurara en…***I could have sworn it was stained with my blood*

CINTIA	Si ellos
	llegaron así escondidos,
	sus intentos no podemos
3015	explicarlos sin oírlos,
	que lo que no sale al labio,
	no lo alcanza nuestro arbitrio.[447]
FOCAS	¿Tú, qué infieres?
LISIPO	Si pudiera
	yo hablar, ya lo hubiera dicho,
3020	pero hay deidad, que mi vida
	amenaza, si lo digo.[448]
FOCAS	Pues oblígalos a que
	esos formados prodigios°
	lo digan.
LAS DAMAS	Ya mal podrá
3025	obligarnos, ni oprimirnos.
LISIPO y	
FOCAS	¿Por qué?
LIBIA	Porque ya fatal...
CINTIA	...cumplió el término preciso...[449]
ISMENIA	...el día en aquel instante...
LIBIA	...en que forzados venimos...
3030	TODAS	...a la fuerza de un conjuro,°
	y de un encanto al hechizo.°

esos formados prodigios° — [Cintia y Libia]

...a la fuerza de un conjuro,° — incantation

y de un encanto al hechizo.° — magic spell

Vanse las Damas.

FOCAS	¡Oíd! ¡Esperad!
LISIPO	Es en vano,
	y pues te dejo en el sitio

---

447   This reflects the notion that spirits and demons could not themselves acquire knowledge of the hearts of human beings. Human beings have to reveal their desires and thoughts to demons either through actions or words.

448   This is the explanation that Lisipo first gave Focas in verses 1461-1478.

449   **cumplió el...***the allotted time has ended.* It is now absolutely clear that the two figures who seemed to be Cintia and Libia were only magical apparitions.

3035	que te encontré,[450] lo que callo infiere de lo que has visto.

FOCAS   ¿También huyes tú?

UN HOMBRE   (*Dentro*) A la selva.

OTRO   (*Dentro*) Al monte.

OTRO   (*Dentro*) Al jaral.

OTRO   (*Dentro*) Al risco.

LIBIA   (*Dentro*) ¿Focas?

CINTIA   (*Dentro*) ¿Señor?

FOCAS   En la propia°   same

acción, `el propio distrito°,   the same area

3040   que perdido me dejaron

monteros y criados míos,

vuelvo a hallarme, sin que haya,

en tan `nunca usado° estilo,   extraordinary

que fue síncopa de un año[451]

3045   o paréntesis de un siglo,

ni sabido, ni alcanzado,°   grasped

ni rastreado,° ni inferido,   figured out

más de que en Eraclio fue

piedad todo, hasta haber visto

3050   blandir su mano el acero,

todo crueldad en Leónido,

hasta haber visto que él fue

—si he de creerme a mí mismo—

él que la vida me dio.

3055   ¡O mal explicado abismo!

¡Qué de cosas me has callado,

y qué de cosas me has dicho!

OTRO   (*Dentro*) El manchado bruto,[452] a quien

ayer Focas siguió, he visto

3060   calarse° otra vez al monte.   enter

---

450   Remember that Lisipo promised to show Focas in just an day what would happen over a long period of time. What Lisipo says here is that they are returning to where all of this started chronologically. So we have to imagine that only a day has passed in the experience of characters who were outside the magical palace.

451   **síncopa de...***the abbreviation or distillation of an entire year*

452   That is, the tiger, previously described as a "manchado galán." See verses 2073-2074.

CINTIA (*Dentro*) Pues acosadlo° y seguidlo,   hound, pursue
que sin duda, pues que Focas
desde ayer no ha parecido,
le dio muerte y vuelve hambriento.
3065 TODOS (*Dentro*) ¡A él Melampo! ¡A él Barcino!
FOCAS Porque el fin de tanto asombro
se enlace° con su principio,   is connected with
acosado de los canes
vuelve, sangriento° y herido°   bloody, wounded
3070 a mí el bruto, a tiempo que
no puedo acudir rendido
a mi defensa. ¿Ah del monte?[453]
¿Vasallos? ¿Criados míos?
¿No hay quien me socorra?

Salen Eraclio y Leónido, de pieles.[454]

LOS DOS   Sí,
3075 que habiendo tu voz oído...
ERACLIO ...vuelvo a saber, mas ¿qué veo?
LEÓNIDO ...vuelvo a ver, pero ¿qué miro?
ERACLIO ¿Esta no es mi antigua piel?
LEÓNIDO ¿Este no es mi traje antiguo?
ERACLIO ¿Este el monte?
3080 LEÓNIDO   ¿Esta la selva?
LOS DOS ¿Dónde...?
FOCAS   ¿Qué os ha suspendido?
ERACLIO ¡Si he visto lo que he soñado!
LEÓNIDO ¡Si he soñado lo que he visto!
ERACLIO ¿Qué se hizo[455] aquel alcázar
donde estaba?
3085 LEÓNIDO   ¿Qué se hizo
aquel edificio?
FOCAS   ¿Qué
alcázar, ni qué edificio?

---

453 **¿Ah del...** *Is anyone here (on the mountain)?*
454 **de pieles** *dressed in animal skins*
455 **¿Qué se hizo...** *What have they done with*

        Desde ayer a esta hora ando
        tras una fiera, perdido,
3090   donde hallándome anoche
        fueron mi lecho esos riscos.[456]
        Salió el Alba, procurando
        vencer deste entretejido°   dense underbrush
        seno el ceño,[457] no hallé senda°,   trail
3095   con que habiendo el aire oído
        de los monteros las voces,
        de los canes° los latidos,   dogs
        llamé, no tanto porque
        —yendo el bruto huyendo el ruido—
3100   me diesen socorro, cuanto
        porque deste laberinto
        me sacasen. Y supuesto
        que en mi busca habéis venido,
        debajo de aquel seguro[458]
3105   que Cintia y Libia habrán dicho,
        yendo de paz a buscaros
        con aparatos festivos
        de músicos instrumentos.
        Seáis los dos bienvenidos,
3110   id adonde a oírse vuelve
        el montaraz alarido°   shouting
        de la caza.
TODOS   (*Dentro*) ¡Llegad todos,
        que hacia allí los descubrimos!

Salen las Damas, Luquete, Sabañón y gente.

SABAÑÓN Bien puede ello ser verdad,
3115   mas yo he de perder mi juicio.
LUQUETE Yo no, que ya no le tengo.[459]

---

456 **fueron mi...** *these crags were my bed*

457 **vencer desde...** *to break through the dense underbrush of this valley (entretejido seno) with my anger (ceño)*

458 Focas makes this promise of safety in verse 1611.

459 **ya no...** *I've already lost my wits* (mi juicio)

ERACLIO   Cielos, ¿qué me ha sucedido?

LEÓNIDO   ¿Qué es lo que por mí ha pasado?

SABAÑÓN   ¿Hate tu amo despedido,[460]

3120   que te quitó la librea?°   uniform

LUQUETE   ¿Qué se hicieron los vestidos,
                    joyas y plumas?

LEÓNIDO   No sé.

CINTIA   (*a Focas*) Alegre, señor, te pido
                    la mano en albricias nobles

3125   de que con vida te miro,
                    después que en tu busca fui°   [hice]
                    tan `desvelado registro°   tireless search
                    del monte, que la esperanza
                    perdí de encontrarte vivo.

3130   LIBIA   A todos nos da tus plantas.

        FOCAS   Yo la fineza os estimo.

        CINTIA   Y yo estimo a mi fortuna
                    el que esté Eraclio contigo,
                    que habiéndole hallado yo,

3135   y habiendo él en tu peligro
                    sido el que llegó primero,
                    me persuado a que he tenido
                    alguna parte en su dicha,
                    y no pequeña en tu alivio.

3140   LIBIA   Lo mismo a mi me sucede
                    contigo, hallando a Leónido.

        FOCAS   Los dos llegaron agora.

        LUQUETE ¿Cómo agora? ¿No estuvimos
                    contigo en aquel palacio?

        FOCAS   ¿Qué palacio?

3145   SABAÑÓN   Aqueso es lindo.
                    Uno, que `a fuer de° pastel   [a manera de]
                    mandó alguien hacer hechizo,
                    donde cuántos aquí estamos
                    allá estábamos contigo,

3150   o díganlo Libia y Cintia.

        LAS DOS ¿Estáis, villanos, sin juicio?

---

460   **¿Hate tu amo…**¿*Te ha despedido tu amo?*

	LEÓNIDO	(*Ap.*) (Si yo convengo° con ellos[461] agree
		a mí me dirán lo mismo...)
	ERACLIO	(*Ap.*) (Que padezca la sospecha
3155		también de loco es preciso.[462])
	LEÓNIDO	(*Ap.*) (...y así disimule y calle.)
	ERACLIO	(*Ap.*) (...y así calle y finja.)
	FOCAS	Digo,
		que habiendo agora llegado,
		y habiéndoles las dos dicho
3160		que quiero más ser piadoso
		con los dos que vengativo
		con el uno, es bien que vamos
		donde sean recibidos
		en tu Corte con aplausos,
3165		festejos y regocijos,
		y donde muden el traje
		en adornos y vestidos
		en reales púrpuras.[463]
	LEÓNIDO	(*Ap.*) (Cielos,
		¿si será esto lo fingido,
3170		y lo otro lo verdadero?
		¿O si habrá al contrario sido
		esto lo cierto, y lo otro
		lo incierto?[464] Mas ¿qué averiguo?
		Vaya yo donde me vea
3175		de reales pompas vestido,[465]
		en palacios alojado,

---

461 *Tp* "Si yo no vengo con él"

462 **Que padezca...***It's inevitable that I'll be considered crazy (if I say something).*

463 **reales púrpuras** *royal purple* Purple was traditionally the color of royalty. The book of Judges (8:26) in the Bible, for example, speaks of the "purple garments worn by the kings of Midian."

464 This inability to discern what is real and what is illusion is not unlike Segismundo's confusion in *La vida es sueño*. Segismundo, echoing Leónido's doubts, wonders aloud:

¿Tan semejante es la copia
al original, que hay duda
en saber si es ella propia?

There are similar issues in Mira de Amescua's *La rueda de la fortuna*, in which Mauricio is unable to tell the difference between his dream of Focas and waking life.

465 **Vaya yo...***Let me go wherever I find myself dressed in royal clothing*

               de varias gentes servido,
               y sea cierto o no sea cierto,
               pues en los faustos° del siglo   incredible luxuries
3180   lo que se goza se goza,
               dure o no dure.) (*a Focas*) Rendido
               a tus pies beso tu mano,
               por el honor que recibo.
FOCAS   (*Ap.*) (Cuerdo anda Leónido, pues
3185   no se da por entendido.)
               Pues, Eraclio, ¿no me das
               las gracias de que te admito
               en mi Corte?
ERACLIO   No, señor.
FOCAS   ¿Cómo?
ERACLIO   Como cuando miro,
3190   que la púrpura real
               el polvo la esmalta en Tiro,
               y que no hay polvo que no
               se desvanezca en suspiros,[466]
               siendo tan leve° su pompa,   insubstantial
3195   que no hay humano sentido
               que ser mentira o verdad
               pueda afirmar, te suplico
               que más lustre no me des,
               que dejarme en mi retiro
3200   a vivir como viví:
               destas montañas vecino,
               destos brutos compañero,
               ciudadano destos riscos.
               Que no quiero oír aplausos
3205   de tan mañoso° artificio,   crafty
               que no sepa cuando son
               verdaderos o fingidos.

---

466 Enameled jewelry (esmaltes) was made by heating colored powders to make a coating of glass. Purple enamelwork was particularly associated with the Mediterranean city of Tyre (Tiro), south of Beirut. Eraclio says that this powder that is used to make symbols of royalty (purple enamels) is like all powder and dust: it disperses and vanishes in an instant. It is always a moment, a puff of breeze away from being nothing.

FOCAS   No te entiendo.
ERACLIO   Yo tampoco.

Sale Astolfo.

ASTOLFO   (*Ap.*) (Sabiendo que están Leónido
3210   y Eraclio con Focas ya,
a verlos vengo, movido
de mi amor. Mas no me atrevo
a llegar porque, ofendido
de que de la prisión salga,
3215   no se disguste conmigo.
Desde aquí me basta el verlos.)

Sale Lisipo.

LISIPO   (*Ap.*) (A qué se habrán persuadido
los dos deseo saber.
A esta parte me retiro,
hasta informarme.)
3220   FOCAS   En efeto,
ingrato, desconocido,
¿mi grandeza desprecias?°   scorn
ERACLIO   No
la desprecio, antes la estimo
tanto que no quiero verla
3225   aventurada° al peligro,   risked
y que una piedad padezca
escrúpulos de delito.
Y así, a tus pies arrojado,°   thrown
que me desvíes° te pido   send away
3230   de ti, porque a mí me basta
el reino de mi albedrío°   my own making
sin más ambición.
FOCAS   ¿Y eso
no es hacer, di, desperdicio°   refusal
y desaire° de mi honor?   snub
3235   ERACLIO   No, señor, sino del mío.

FOCAS   ¡No es sino hallarte tirano,
acusado y convencido
de tu traición (*ap.*) (mas, ¿qué hago?)
y no atreverte (*ap.*) (¿qué digo?)
3240   a ponérteme delante!
(*Ap.*) (Mal ˋla cólera reprimo.°   control my anger
Arrebatóme° la ira,   seized me
al ver que aun no le he perdido
aquel pasado pavor.)

3245 CINTIA   ¿Qué traición puede haber visto
en él, si agora ha llegado?

FOCAS   Y así, ingrato, por lo mismo
que mi favor aborreces,
has de estar siempre conmigo,
3250   que menos cuidado así
me darás, siendo registro
yo de todas tus acciones,
que si huyeres fugitivo
donde no sepa de ti,
3255   el día que persuadido,
no en vano estoy que tú eres
el hijo de mi enemigo.

ERACLIO   Es verdad, y pues tú rompes
el secreto de un prodigio,
3260   que yo ni alcanzo, ni entiendo,
o peligre o no mi juicio.
Hijo de Mauricio soy,
y estoy tan desvanecido°   proud
de serlo, que por lograr
3265   tan glorioso, tan invicto
blasón de mí, delatando°   revealing
una y mil veces lo afirmo.

FOCAS   Aunque ya, para saberlo,
me bastaba el inferirlo,
¿de qué lo sabes?

3270 ERACLIO   Lo sé
de tan superior testigo
que ˋno padece objeción°,   can't be refuted

          tu secreto, me he valido
          de medios que ser Eraclio
3335   me han dicho hijo de Mauricio.[472]
ASTOLFO   Será la primer verdad,
          que la mentira haya dicho.[473]
FOCAS   Pero para que no quede
          escrupuloso° en Leónido   uncertain
3340   el crédito,° dilo claro.   belief
ASTOLFO   Yo, señor, no he de decirlo.
          Sábelo tú, pero no
          de mí.
CINTIA   Tú, traidor Lisipo,
          andas por aquí.
LISIPO   Señor,
3345   airada contra mí miro
          la deidad por quien calló
          el labio y habló el indicio.
          Y puesto que me amenaza
          sañudo su ceño° esquivo,   scowl
3350   muera por todo, saneando
          lo inobediente lo fino:[474]
          Leónido es tu hijo, que casos
          en dos tiempos sucedidos,
          bien pude alcanzarlos yo,
3355   y baste que yo lo afirmo
          el que no lo niega Astolfo.
FOCAS   Es lo más. Vasallos míos,
          Leónido es mi hijo, y vuestro
          príncipe.
TODOS   ¡Viva Leónido!
FOCAS   ¡Viva! ¡Y muera Eraclio!
3360 CINTIA   Tente.
FOCAS   ¿Tú lo impides?
CINTIA   Yo lo impido.

---

472   **medios...***medios que me han dicho ser hijo de Mauricio Eraclio* These "medios" were Lisipo's
illusions.

473   **Será la...***It will be the first truth that lies have ever told*

474   **saneado...***my disobedience (to Cintia) made better by my service to you*

                        Debajo de tu palabra,

                        y de mi seguro vino,[475]

                        o has de cumplírsela o antes

3365   que muera, en el pecho mío,

                        has de ensangrentar tu acero.[476]

FOCAS   ¿Qué es lo que yo le he ofrecido?

CINTIA   Ni matarle, ni prenderle.°   imprison him

FOCAS   Por ti y por mí he de cumplirlo.

3370   Desamarrad aquel barco

                        que está orilla del marino,

                        dadle un barreno en entrando

                        en él.[477] Y ya le dejo vivo,

                        pues no le doy muerte, y ya

3375   no le prendo, pues le envío

                        donde pueda correr todo

                        ese `campo cristalino.°   shining sea

                        Ea, llevadle, pues.

ERACLIO   No, villanos,

                        con violencia, que yo mismo

3380   al sepulcro° por mi pie   my grave

                        iré, pues sepulcro mío

                        es ese barco, que agora

                        me recibe compasivo,

                        para que vuelta la quilla,°   keel

3385   en el primero desvío,°   turn

                        sea tumba el que fue albergue.[478]

                        (*a Cintia*) Adiós, hermoso prodigio,

                        primero que vi y postrero°   last, final

                        que veré. (*a Astolfo*) Adiós, padre mío,

3390   que solo siento dejarte

---

475   **Debajo de…***Eraclio came here with your promise not to harm him and is under my protection, as well*

476   **en el pecho…***you will have to bloody your steel in my breast*

477   **Desamarrad aquel…***Untie that boat and drill a hole in its hull (and set Eraclio adrift in it)* Focas will comply with the letter of his promise, he will neither kill Eraclio nor make him prisoner. Instead, Focas will set Eraclio adrift in a leaking ship.

478   It was common to liken a boat to a tomb during Calderón's lifetime. Artists depicted Noah's Ark in particular with the dimensions of a coffin.

en poder de mi enemigo,
que mintiendo en la verdad,
verdad la mentira dijo.
FOCAS   Espera, que porque veas,
3395   siendo piadoso contigo,
aun no te quiero quitar
aqueste pequeño alivio°,   comfort
llevad con él a ese anciano
caduco vil.°   worthless
ASTOLFO   Vamos, hijo,
3400   que yo no quiero más vida,
que el ir a morir contigo.
CINTIA   ¡Qué lástima!
LIBIA   ¡Qué desdicha°!   misfortune
LUQUETE   ¡Qué confusión!
SABAÑÓN   ¡Que conflicto!
FOCAS   Agora, porque no lleguen
3405   los ecos de sus gemidos°   groans, cries
a nosotros, empezad
desde aquí los regocijos,
con que es bien Leónido entre
en la corte. Ven conmigo,
3410   para que te reconozcan
todos, y todos rendidos
besen tu mano, diciendo
a voces:
TODOS   ¡Viva Leónido!
3415   ERACLIO   ¡Favor,° cielos divinos!   help
ASTOLFO   ¡Cielos, favor!
LOS DOS   ¡Piedad!

Vanse Astolfo y Eraclio.

MÚSICOS   ¡Viva Leónido!
LEÓNIDO   Sea mentira o sea verdad,
sea cierto o sea fingido,
o desvanézcase o no,
3420   ya por lo menos me miro

                    sin competencia, heredero
                    de un imperio, y aunque esquivo
                    el hado° quiera vengarse,   *fate*
                    no me quitará haber visto

3425   aquesta felicidad
                    a costa de aquel peligro.

Eraclio   *(Dentro)* ¡Favor, cielos divinos!

Astolfo   *(Dentro)*¡Cielos, favor!

Los dos   *(Dentro)*¡Piedad!

Músicos   ¡Viva Leónido!

           Dentro tiros[479] y cajas y trompetas.

Focas   Esperad. ¿Qué salva es

3430   la que a lo lejos se ha oído,
                 cuyas trompetas y cajas,
                 al son del bronce, han querido
                 trocar en toques de guerra
                 estos aplausos festivos?[480]

3435 **Cintia**   De compasiva, la vista
                 siguiendo iba el combatido
                 leño[481] de vientos y olas,
                 cuyo inútil desperdicio,
                 como jugando con él,

3440   conservaba en su bullicio°   *bobbing*
                 el inquieto afán de tanto
                 salobre campo de vidrio,
                 cuando afilada en los lejos
                 de aquel átomo de pino,

3445   descubrió en sus golfos una
                 vaga ciudad de navíos,[482]

---

479 **tiros** *gunshots ring out*

480 **trocar en toques...***replace this festive revelry with the sounds of war*

481 **el combatido leño...***the beleaguered bark (the ship that Eraclio and Astolfo were placed in, assaulted by wind and waves).* Cintia describes it getting smaller and smaller as it floats away until it becomes a tiny "átomo de pino."

482 **ciudad de navíos** *a multitude (a city) of ships on the horizon* This multitude of ships appears at the moment when Astolfo and Eraclio's doomed ship was about to disappear.

           que al reconocer el puerto,

           salva a sus murallas° hizo.   *walls*

FOCAS Tributo será de alguno

3450   de tantos reinos vecinos,

           como feudatarios son

           al Imperio.

LISIPO   Más me inclino

           yo, señor, que de más cerca

           las latinas[483] velas miro,

           a pensar...

FOCAS   ¿Qué?

3455 LISIPO   ...que es la armada

           del príncipe Federico

           de Calabria de quien ya

           noticias di.

FOCAS   `Por el mismo

           trance de° pensar que es él,   *despite the risk*

3460   no cesen los regocijos,

           que a mí no me asusta nada,

           y mientras la gente alisto,°   *I prepare*

           pues se repiten sus salvas,

           repítanse vuestros himnos.

3465 LEÓNIDO Tú verás, que `desempeño

           los créditos° de tu hijo.   *prove myself worthy*

CINTIA (*Ap.*) Y que (a pesar de mis penas)

           yo con mi gente te sigo.

ASTOLFO y

ERACLIO (*Dentro*) ¡Piedad, Dioses divinos!

FEDERICO (*Dentro*) ¡A tierra, a tierra!

OTRO   (*Dentro*) ¡Arma, arma!°   *to arms*

3470 OTRO   (*Dentro*)¡Guerra, guerra!

ASTOLFO y

ERACLIO (*Dentro*)¡Favor!

TODOS   ¡Viva Leónido!

---

483 *Tp* "hinchadas" Calderón's original says that the sails are "latinas" or lateen sails. This is a nautical term that refers to a boat with a short mast. The mast supported a pole or yard from which a triangular sail was strung. Lateen-rigged boats were common in the Mediterranean during Calderón's day.

Vanse todos y sale Federico.

FEDERICO ¡A tierra! Y tan brevemente
como la vaya tomando,
se vaya al punto doblando
3475 en escuadrones la gente,
porque más desprevenida°   unsuspecting
le coja[484] el susto sin que
nadie, sino es yo, les dé
la nueva° de mi venida.   news
3480 Ya que afables agua y viento
quieren, `franqueada la tierra,°   safely on land
que a fuego y sangre la guerra
les publique otro elemento.[485]
Príncipe me hizo heredero
3485 de Calabria mi destino,
de Mauricio soy sobrino.
Y pues por su muerte infiero,
que el sacro laurel es mío,
¿por qué tengo de pagar
3490 feudo de él y no vengar
la pérdida de mi tío?
Mayormente, cuando sé
que el día que se perdió,
el póstumo° que dejó   posthumous son
3495 humana víbora fue,
que reventando a su madre,[486]
en los montes se ocultó
donde fiel le retiró
un vasallo de su padre°   [i.e. Astolfo]
3500 de quien nunca se ha sabido.
Y siendo así, que me ha dado

---

484 The infinitive of "coja" is "coger."

485 A reference to the four elements: earth, air, fire, and water.

486 **que el día…**_The day Mauricio died, the heir that he left was a human snake, ripping apart his mother at childbirth…_ It was a common belief that snakes burst forth from their mothers causing the mother to die in childbirth, for that reason, children whose mothers die in childbirth are often compared to snakes.

esta embestidura° el hado,   *charge*
¿por qué el día que ha venido
con poca gente de guerra
3505   a Trinacria ese tirano,
no ha mi valor soberano
de infestarle mar y tierra
en su venganza[487] y la mía?
Pues cuando yo no tuviera
3510   más razón que me moviera
a tan gloriosa osadía
que el agüero de Lisipo,
a quien de Calabria eché,
ella bastara, porque
3515   vea el mundo que anticipo°   *outdo*
a su ciencia mi valor,
y mi ánimo a ʿsus recelos,°   *Lisipo's fears*
diciendo mi fama...

ASTOLFO   (*Dentro*) ¡Cielos,
amparo!

ERACLIO   (*Dentro*) ¡Cielos, favor!

3520   FEDERICO   ¿Qué voces en el mar oí,
que entre tanto horrible estruendo
lugar se hace? Aunque ya atiendo°   *concentrate*
a lo que ya desde aquí
mirar se deja, marino
3525   monstruo me parece que
arroja de sí, porque
sus ansias no determino.
Pues humano en la animada
voz, y bruto en lo que anhela°,   *gasps*
3530   no es ave, pues que no vuela,
y no es pez, pues que no nada.
Ya del quebrantado hielo,
a embates de la resaca,°   *undertow*
uno a la orilla° le saca.   *shore*

Salen Eraclio y Astolfo.

---

487 **en su venganza...***to seek vengeance for Mauricio*

ERACLIO ¡Cielos, piedad!

3535 ASTOLFO   ¡Favor, cielos!

FEDERICO El que parecía, abrazado,
uno en el mar, ya son dos
en tierra.[488]

ASTOLFO   Gracias a Dios,
que pude sacarte a nado.

3540 FEDERICO Prodigios—que entre crueles
`ovas, légamos[489] y lamas,°   kelp, muck and silt
en vez de armaros de escamas°   fish scales
el mar os vistió de pieles—
¿quién sois?

ASTOLFO   Dos tan desdichados
3545 que los hados han querido
matarnos y no han podido
aun conseguirlo los hados.

ERACLIO Tanto, que hijos de unas rocas,
aun el mar no nos sufrió°   couldn't bear us
3550 y a otros nos restituyó.
Si sois soldados de Focas,
usad,° pues tenéis por él   do your worst
poderes, de la fortuna
y en suerte tan oportuna,
3555 sea la piedad cruel.
Pues para que el beneficio
de matarnos mi voz hoy
os obligue, Eraclio soy,
hijo infausto° de Mauricio.   ill-fated
3560 Ese anciano, a quien destierra
la lealtad más singular,
y el que me ha dado en el mar
una vida, otra en la tierra,
Astolfo es. Por él os pido
3565 que, ya que a mí me matéis,

---

488 It appeared to Federico that he was seeing only one body when Eraclio and Astolfo were in the water, but once Eraclio and Astolfo are safely ashore, Federico realizes that there are actually two of them. Compare this to the changes in perspective ("pintura a dos visos") in verse 677.

489 *Tp* "ráfaga"

a él la vida reservéis.°	spare (his life)

      Y pues a esos pies rendido,

os ruego `abreviéis los plazos°` — cut the time short

de mi muerte. ¿Qué esperáis?

3570 ¿Por qué, pues, `me la negáis?°` — deny me death

FEDERICO   Por no negarte los brazos,

que al oírte agradecida

está el alma de manera,

que su misma vida diera

3575 en albricias de tu vida.

      Y aunque parezca hoy en mí

`sobrada facilidad°` — great gullibility

creer tan gran novedad

`en el punto°` que la oí, — the very second

3580 salvo la objeción⁴⁹⁰ que

el que la estime y la crea,

no es posible que no sea

causa superior°, en fe — i.e. divine

de que el cielo soberano

3585 quiere, contra una malicia,° — wrongdoing

volver hoy por su justicia,

y la de ese noble anciano,

a cuyas lealtades hoy

también los brazos aplico.

LOS DOS   ¿Quién eres? ¡Di!

3590 FEDERICO   Federico,

Duque de Calabria soy,

con que no en vano sospecho

que la pasada objeción

tiene `otra satisfacción°:` — another explanation

3595 pues la sangre de mi pecho

—tan tuya como ser hijo

de Casandra, hermana bella

de Mauricio—nuestra estrella

confronta.⁴⁹¹

---

490 *Tp* "obligación"

491 **la sangre…***la sangre de mi pecho confronta nuestra estrella* (The fact that we carry the same blood predisposes us to get along.) This use of "confrontar" (roughly, "to cause two people to get

	ERACLIO	Si bien colijo,	
3600		cobrado° el susto, tus señas,	recovered from
		ya me acuerdo que te vi.	
	FEDERICO	No es posible, porque a mí	
		nunca me vieron las peñas	
		que tú habitaste.	
	ERACLIO	Es verdad,	
3605		pero vite° a ti sin ti.⁴⁹²	[te vi]
	FEDERICO	¿A mí, sin verme a mí?	
	ERACLIO	Sí.	
	FEDERICO	Esa es otra novedad,	
		casi a la primera igual...	
		Mas, hasta descansar no	
3610		te la he de preguntar yo.	
		A la capitana° real	flagship
		le llevad, donde después	
		que te hayas reparado°	rested
		y vestido y adornado,	
3615		será justo que me deis	
		cuenta de todo, ya que hoy	
		vi noticias tan extrañas.	
	ERACLIO	Hijo soy de las montañas,	
		hecho a trabajos estoy,	
3620		y aunque es mi fatiga mucha,	
		contigo descansaré	
		más que conmigo.⁴⁹³	
	FEDERICO	Si fue	
		para ti alivio, di.	
	ERACLIO	Escucha:	
		aquella empinada° sierra,	steep
3625		a cuya atalaya° están	lookout
		de guarda el Etna y Volcán...⁴⁹⁴	

---

along") is obsolete.

492   For a similar misunderstanding, see *Sueños hay que verdad son* (938).

493   *Tp* "Mas, ven conmigo"

494   Calderón suggests that there are two volcanoes on the island of Sicily, one called Mount Etna, the other simply "Volcán." Cruickshank attests that this mistaken belief was fairly widespread in Spain (232).

HOMBRES	(*Dentro*) ¡Arma, arma, guerra, guerra!
FOCAS	(*Dentro*) Llegad, antes que formado
	en escuadrones esté.

Sale un Soldado.

3630	SOLDADO	Ya el ejército° se ve,	army
		con que Focas ha llegado	
		a tu opósito°, a impedir	defenses
		de la desembarcación°	disembarking
		la altiva resolución.°	resolve
3635	FEDERICO	Yo también le he de salir	
		al paso, porque el denuedo	
		dicen, que es al enemigo	
		primer batallón.[495]	
	ERACLIO	Contigo	
		yendo yo, verás que puedo	
3640		servirte de algo, una espada	
		solo en adorno me dad.	
	ASTOLFO	Aunque mi caduca edad	
		serviros no pueda en nada	
		más que en morir, moriré	
3645		a vuestro lado el primero.	
	FEDERICO	En los dos mi triunfo espero.	
		En cuya segura fe,	
		ya tocando al arma, cierra°	attack
		mi gente con saña altiva.	

Hácese la batalla dentro.

	UNOS	(*Dentro*) ¡Viva Federico!	
3650	OTROS	(*Dentro*) ¡Viva	
		Focas!	
	TODOS	(*Dentro*) ¡Arma, arma, guerra, guerra!	
	ERACLIO	¡Yo sé la senda, seguidme!	
		¡Por aquí podéis romper!°	break through

---

495 **el denuedo...***valor is the first blow to the enemy*

Vanse todos y salen Luquete y Sabañón de soldados.

	Luquete	Sabañón, ¿por qué no vas
3655		a pelear, pues que ya ves
		cuán trabada° anda la lid?°

hotly fought, battle

	Sabañón	Préstame tú un buen porqué°

reason why

y respondéréte° yo.

[te responderé]

Luquete   Vesle° allí: porque no me den

[Lo ves]

con algo.

3660   Sabañón   Pues, ¿verle allí?

que si a eso va, yo también...

Todos   (Dentro)¡Arma, arma, guerra, guerra!

Luquete   ¡El demonio que aquí esté!

Sabañón   ¡Belcebú° que aguarde aquí!

Beelzebub

Vanse Luquete y Sabañón. Salen Eraclio por una parte y Cintia por otra.

3665   Eraclio   ¡Por aquí podéis romper!⁴⁹⁶

Cintia   No podréis, porque es el puesto°

position

que me toca defender.

Eraclio   ¿Quién podrá contra mi saña?

Cintia   Yo.

Eraclio   ¿Qué es lo que llego a ver?

3670   Cintia   ¿Qué es lo que llego a mirar?

Eraclio   Trocarse la suerte, pues.

Yo un paso te defendía

al verte la primer vez,⁴⁹⁷

¿y ahora tú me le° defiendes?

[lo]

3675   Cintia   Mas `tan al contrario,° que

so reversed

yo fui allí tu admiración,°

amazement

y admirarte ahora fue

verte la admiración mía.

---

496   The entire passage composed of verses 3654-3665 does not appear in the *Tp* and other early printed versions of the play; however, this section is present in the original autograph.

497   **Yo un paso...***When I first saw you, I was defending a mountain pass against you (and now it's just the opposite).* See verses 836-839 for the previous encounter Eraclio mentions.

ERACLIO	No eso admiración te dé,[498]	
3680	que la farsa[499] de mi vida	
	toda es pasos al revés.	
	Dígalo,° al hallarte aquí,	take, for instance
	volverme huyendo, con que	
	huir yo, y huir de ti, serán	
3685	dos cosas al parecer	
	tan opuestas que ellas digan	
	que son sin que puedan ser.	
CINTIA	Dejando que de tu vida	
	me doy a mí el parabién,[500]	
3690	¿no será mejor que el paso	
	rompas, con que, roto él,	
	victorioso quedes?	
ERACLIO	No,	
	porque no quiero vencer	
	tan a toda costa.°	at such great cost
CINTIA	Lidia°	fight (command)
3695	y no huyas, porque aunque	
	estimo mi fama, estimo	
	también la tuya.	
ERACLIO	No sé	
	si te crea.	
CINTIA	¿Por qué no?	
ERACLIO	Porque aunque tan fina estés	
3700	conmigo agora, dirás	
	que no te acuerdas después.	
FEDERICO	(*Dentro*) Por aquí Eraclio subió.	
	Pues subid los dos tras él.	
ERACLIO	Mas, ¡ah infeliz! que ya,	
3705	aunque quiera huir, no podré.	

---

498 **No eso...***Don't let that (i.e. seeing me) amaze you...* Of course Cintia is amazed! She watched Eraclio's ship get smaller and smaller until—she thought—it disappeared into the sea. She thought Eraclio was drowned.

499 **farsa** *play or dramatic spectacle* (and in this play, as Eraclio explains, everything happens in reverse)

500 **me doy...***I congratulate myself* Cintia has done everything she could to spare Eraclio's life to this point.

        Mi gente llega, y la tuya,
        viendo el inmenso tropel°   mob
        que me sigue, desampara°   abandons
        la línea dese cuartel°   station

3710   que guardabas. Huye tú,
        que tampoco defender
        podré tu vida.
    Cintia   Eso no,
        de ti bien pudiera ser,
        si ser pudiera no de otros.[501]

                Sale Leónido.

3715   Leónido   ¡Volved, soldados, volved!
        que el puesto en que Cintia está
        han rompido, a defender
        su vida, en cuyo reparo,°   aid
        yo el primero moriré.
3720   Eraclio   Sí morirás, y a mis manos,[502]
        ¡ingrato, fiero, cruel!
    Leónido   Poco el mirarte me asombra
        vivo,[503] al persuadirme a que
        debió—porque no me falte
3725   este triunfo más—tener
        el mar lástima de ti.
    Eraclio   Agora lo verás.

                Riñen los dos.

    Cintia   (*Ap.*) (Pues
        no me puedo declarar
        por quien quisiera, al temer,
3730   si vence Eraclio, mi ruina,
        pues es contra mi poder,
        si Leónido, mi esperanza,

---

501   **de ti bien...***I would be willing to die at your hand (but not at the hand of another).*
502   This recalls Focas' account of killing Mauricio "murió en campaña a mis manos" (161).
503   **Poco el mirarte...***El mirarte vivo poco me asombra.* I am hardly surprised to see you alive.

pues es contra mi interés.
¿Qué he de hacer, cielos piadosos?)

Tocan la caja.

3735   FOCAS   (*Dentro*) Bruto, que a tu dueño infiel,[504]
el freno° rompiendo, rompes   bridle
con la obediencia y la ley,
ya que te desbocas,° sea   run wild
al enemigo no des
3740   al pensar que al desbocarte
es huir.[505]

FEDERICO   Cargad a aquel
grueso que gobierna Focas.[506]

Sale cayendo Focas.

FOCAS   ¡Cielos, mi vida valed!
ERACLIO   Mi enemigo es, ¡muera!
LEÓNIDO   ¡No
muera!
3745   FOCAS   ¡Ay de mí! ¿Qué escuché?
¿Qué vi? Otra vez de los dos,
equívoca llego a ver
voz y acción, "¡muera!" y "¡no muera!",[507]
porque quién me mata y quién
3750   me defiende confundido
vuelva a dudar otra vez.
ERACLIO   Pues no lo dudes agora,
que si allí quisiste hacer
ensayo° de tus tragedias,   rehearsal

---

504 **que a tu…**_que infiel a tu dueño_ Focas is shouting at his horse.

505 The "caballo desbocado" or runaway horse is one of Calderón's favorite images. It is often a way of talking about uncontrolled passions. In this case, you may want to look back to verses 93-104, where Focas explains that his first loyal subjects were wild animals. Now, even a domestic animal refuses to obey him.

506 **Cargad a aquel…**_Shoot that huge horse that Focas is riding._

507 Focas has, in fact, heard something very similar before. See verses 2918-2919.

3755	aquesta la verdad es	
	y solo mudó° un ensayo,	changed
	que se trocara un papel.[508]	
FOCAS	¿Qué papel?	
ERACLIO	El de Leónido,	
	que allí era el del cruel,	
3760	y el mío, que era el del piadoso,	
	y tan trocados° los ves,	switched
	que soy el que te da muerte,	
	aunque te defienda él.	
CINTIA	A tu lado, Eraclio, estoy.	
3765	FOCAS No en vano el presagio° fue	forewarning
	de ver sangriento tu acero...	
LEÓNIDO	Ni el temblar a la mujer	
	yo, aun antes de verla...[509]	

*Salen por un lado Libia y los soldados de Cintia
y por otro lado Federico con sus soldados.*[510]

LIBIA	Aquí	
	cayó Focas.	
FEDERICO	Aquí fue	
3770	donde le arrojó° el caballo.	threw
LEÓNIDO	(*Ap.*) (Perdido me llego a ver.)	
SOLDADO	¡Llegad todos! Mas, ¿qué es esto?	
ERACLIO	Ver un tirano a mis pies,	
	vengada casi en la misma	
3775	campaña la muerte infiel	
	de Mauricio por Eraclio	
	su hijo.	
FOCAS	No es eso.	
SOLDADO	¿Pues qué es?	
FOCAS	Un hidrópico de sangre,	
	que por no poder beber	
3780	la de todos, en la suya	

---

508   **trocara un...***changed roles (or played a new part)*
509   Leónido recalls the fear of women he expressed in verses 659-670.
510   They do not immediately see Focas, Eraclio, Cintia, and Leónido.

está apagando su sed.[511]

Muere Focas.

ERACLIO Retirad ese cadáver.
CINTIA Ya puesta en fuga se ve
toda su gente, y la mía
3785 sacudido el yugo° que	shook off the yoke
su tiranía le puso,
diciendo una, y otra vez...
TODOS ¡Viva Eraclio! ¡Eraclio viva!
UNO Ciña el sagrado laurel,[512]
3790 que por hijo de Mauricio
le toca.

Saquen una corona.

ERACLIO	Esperad, tened,
que ese honor es Federico
quien le llega a merecer,
pues es suya la vitoria.
3795 FEDERICO Solo pretendí° romper	planned
el yugo deste tirano,
y no quitarle a cuyo es,[513]
y más, `tocándote a ti.°	pertaining to you
Por mí le ciñe.
ERACLIO	No sé
si me atreva.
3800 FEDERICO	¿Por qué no?
ERACLIO Porque aun todavía dudo
si es mentira o si es verdad

---

511 Focas spoke of his "hidrópica sed de sangre" in verse 61.

512 **Ciña el...***crown yourself with the sacred laurels* Laurels were a symbol of victory and are here, figuratively, the crown.

513 **no quitarle...***not to deprive the rightful owner (of these laurels).* Federico only aspired to cast off the yoke of Focas' oppression, not to become emperor himself.

                    todo cuanto llego a ver.

FEDERICO   ¿Cómo?

ERACLIO   Como ya me vi

3805   en majestad otra vez,

         y otra vez en un instante,

         me volví a mi antigua piel.

LISIPO   Ese fue engaño que hizo

         aparente mi saber°,   wizardry

3810   y pues a ti te mintió

         y a Federico también,

         y a quien amenazó ruinas

         le dio vitorias después.

         Perdón a entrambos os pido.

3815   LIBIA   Y yo, puesta a vuestros pies,

         por él intercedo.[514]

ERACLIO   Viva,

         con el pretexto° de que   stipulation

         no use de sus ciencias más.

ASTOLFO   Yo, si puedo merecer

3820   algo contigo, el perdón

         de Leónido he de tener.

ERACLIO   Leónido fue hermano mío,

         y siempre en la antigua fe

         de nuestra crianza debo

         mantenerle.

3825   LEÓNIDO   Yo seré

         tu más leal y rendido

         vasallo.

ERACLIO   Pues yo, porque

         si acaso se desvanece

         este no esperado bien,

3830   me coja con una dicha

         imposible de perder:

         la mano a Cintia le doy.

CINTIA   Humilde estoy a tus pies.

TODOS   ¡Viva Eraclio! ¡Eraclio viva!

---

514 **por él...***I intercede on his behalf (I ask you for his life)*

3835 FEDERICO En cuyo aplauso se dé
fin a su historia...
ERACLIO Esperando
que sea felice° rey [feliz]
el que entra con desengaños
de que no hay `humano bien° worldly good
3840 que no parezca verdad
con duda de lo que es.

FIN

Appendix: History, Identity, and *En la vida...*

MOST SCHOLARS—INCLUDING CRUICKSHANK, the play's most important critic and editor—conclude that Eraclio truly is the son of Mauricio. A very good critic, William R. Blue, says that at the end of the play, "the rightful heir is brought to power" (145). His argument is reasonable: "As the action progresses, Leónido's growing drift toward tyranny and violence and Eraclio's movement toward compassion, self-governance, and *mesura* are stressed" (148). This logically leads Blue to believe that Eraclio is indeed the son of Mauricio and Leónido is the son of Focas. At the same time, Blue explains that "the audience is forced to weigh carefully a character's actions and statements to try to decide the rightful heir" (147). If this is true, then readers and audiences must decide which young man is Mauricio's son *by imitating Focas*. After all, Focas, too, must "weigh carefully" the actions of Eraclio and Leónido, and "try to decide the rightful heir." Astolfo, however, criticizes efforts to use behavior to determine paternity. As he says:

> No te creas de experiencias
> de hijo a quien otro crió,
> que apartadas crianzas tienen
> muy sin cariño el calor
> de los padres... (1197-1201)

According to Astolfo, nurture may trump nature; this would mean that Focas' attempt to determine which of the two young men is his son by observing them may be doomed. Building on this uncertainty, critics such as David J. Hildner have suggested that Focas' "experiment" proves very little and that *En la vida...* is about doubt rather than discovery; Hildner calls Calderón's play "un drama que recalca lo incognoscible de la realidad" (411). As the historian of science, Paul Forman, once remarked: people "not only tend to find what they are looking for, but also fail to recognize what they are not prepared to see" (11).

As you try to decide for yourself whether Eraclio or Leónido is the son of Mauricio, or whether we can know for sure at all, you should consider a number of things. First, you should follow Blue's advice and observe the two young men carefully. Keep in mind, however, that Eraclio tells us that "no hay humano sentido, / que ser mentira o verdad / pueda afirmar" (3195-3197). The paradoxical title of the play underscores this uncertainty. Second, you should weigh other sources of information: the one piece of concrete evidence (i.e. the *lámina* possessed by Astolfo); the magical divinations of Lisipo; the words and actions of Astolfo; and so on. Regarding Astolfo, a great deal depends on how you interpret the scene between Astolfo and Focas, when Focas announces that Eraclio is Mauricio's son. Astolfo responds, "Será la primer verdad, / que la mentira haya dicho" (3336-3337). If you believe that Astolfo says this sincerely, then it is fairly clear that Eraclio is, in fact, Mauricio's son. If he says this *ironically*, then there still may be doubts. (Focas himself still wants Astolfo to be explicit—"dilo claro"—but Astolfo refuses: "Sábelo tú, pero no / de mí.") Ultimately, you will have to decide whether this is a play about facts or a play about doubts. Careful readers of this play have come to both conclusions.

There are two more bits of information you might want to consider, information that you cannot figure out relying exclusively on the play. First, Calderón may have drawn on Mira de Amescua's play entitled *La rueda de la fortuna*. Both *En la vida...* and *La rueda de la fortuna* are about Mauricio's son; however, in *La rueda de la fortuna,* there is no doubt that Eraclio is the true son of Mauricio. In an 1879 reimagining of Calderón's play (i.e. a "refundición" of the original) one of the most significant changes the playwrights made is to clarify that Eraclio was truly the son of Mauricio and Leónido was truly Focas' son; in fact the 1879 version has Leónido fall on Focas' dead body and cry out "¡Padre!" at the end of the play. So there is a strong dramatic tradition in which Eraclio is unequivocally Mauricio's son.

The second bit of information is that, as we explain in the introduction, this play deals with historical characters from the seventh century. In English, their names are Phocas, Heraclius, and Maurice. All of them were emperors of the Byzantine Empire. Some details of Calderón's play mirror historical accounts: Phocas did overthrow Maurice, and Heraclius did overthrow Phocas. Phocas is sometimes described as a tyrant and a usurper in historical accounts, and Heraclius was admired as a champion of Christianity. There are many reasons why this period of Byzantine history might have interested Calderón; seventeenth-century Spain, like the seventh-century Byzantine Empire, was undergoing serious problems. And it would not be the first time that the island of Sicily, part of Spain during Calderón's lifetime, would have served as a way to speak about Spanish issues generally. It is important to note, however, that Heraclius was not, historically speaking, the son of Maurice. Neither was Heraclius the son of Phocas. There is no question about this, and there was no doubt about it in the seventeenth century. Cruickshank's edition explains that Heraclius was not "the long-lost son of Maurice, and Phocas had no heirs but a daughter" (lxix).

You may decide that Calderón followed Mira de Amescua's lead and that the Eraclio of *En la vida...* is definitely the son of Mauricio. Or, you may decide that Calderón leads us to think that the Eraclio of the play should not be definitively considered Mauricio's biological son. This is a debate waiting to be settled by readers like you.

PEDRO CALDERÓN DE LA BARCA

Sueños hay que verdad son

Personas:

LA CASTIDAD/ASENET[1]	RUBÉN	ZABULÓN
EL SUEÑO	JUDAS	JOSÉ
EL COPERO	GAD	BENJAMÍN
EL PANADERO	ASER	EL REY
SOMBRA 1	NEFTALÍ	JACOB
SOMBRA 2	MANASÉS	LA FE
ISACAR	SIMEÓN	BATO
EL ALCAIDE	LEVÍ	MÚSICOS y DAMAS

Sale la Castidad, dama, coronada de flores[2] y el Sueño.

SUEÑO	¿Dónde me llevas, hermosa
	virtud,[3] que entre los diversos
	coros° de cuantas virtudes *choirs*
	siguen al legal Cordero,[4]
5	tú sola los `crespos rizos° *curly hair*
	coronas de tus cabellos,

---

1 **Castidad** *Chastity* It will be revealed shortly that Asenet is the daughter of the high priest of the sun god, while Castidad is the embodiment of chastity (or more broadly, self-control). However, these two very different characters are played by the same actor. José will not be able to tell them apart.

2 **coronada de...***crowned with flowers*

3 **hermosa virtud** *lovely virtue* Sueño is speaking to Castidad and she is the virtue: chastity.

4 **legal Cordero** *lamb of God (Christ)*

191

       de cuantas vírgenes rosas

       guarnecen° los ˋrizos crespos°   adorn, wavy locks

       de todas las demás,° dando   [demás virtudes]

10   a entender que en tu obsequio

       todas se complacen?[5] ¿Dónde

       me llevas (a decir vuelvo)?[6]

       Porque siendo, como eres,

       en tantos sagrados Textos°   Holy Scriptures

15   ˋtriunfante laurel,° que arrastra°   crowning glory, pries

       los no fáciles trofeos

       de la lid de los sentidos,[7]

       ˋvencedores de sí mesmos,[8]

       parece que hace no poca

20   repugnancia a tu respecto[9]

       que la virtud° que es de todas   [i.e. Castidad]

---

5 **dando a entender...***making known that all [the other virtues] delight in complimenting or honoring you* The other, unspecified virtues honor Castidad by crowning her curls (crespos rizos) with the flowers they once wore in their own curly hair (rizos crespos). These opening verses provide a good illustration of how McGaha's edition clarifies problems in Pando y Mier's eighteenth-century edition. In verse 5, Pando y Mier's edition says "crespos rizas" which would make "rizas" a verb (from "rizar" to curl). "Rizas" makes it sound as if Castidad were *intentionally* curling her hair, which seems unlikely. McGaha's corrected edition (which we follow) reads "crespos rizos." This makes "rizos" an adjective and allows "coronas" to be more easily understood as a verb (from "coronar" to crown). We draw attention to these corrections because they illustrate that not only have interpretations of the play changed over time, *the words of the play* have changed from one printed edition to another, if ever so slightly. This indicates why the work of literary criticism is ongoing and why we need readers like you to keep improving everyone's understanding.

6 When Sueño asks Castidad where she is taking him, think of it this way: how might chastity lead or direct dreaming? We would expect a chaste dream to be pure, but that is not exactly what happens here.

7 **lid de...***the battle of the senses (or of sensuality)* It should be fairly clear how chastity might triumph in the battle against sensuality, but chastity is also a virtue that governs how characters interpret the sensory information they receive. Chastity is more than sexual abstinence, it is self control (and thus rational control of the senses).

8 **vencedores de...***the senses overcome (or subdue) themselves* It was commonly thought that the five senses were the cause of sensuality (the opposite of chastity). Chastity wins by helping the senses to control themselves, putting themselves in the service of something other than sensual pleasure. We often say that seeing is believing, implying that seeing is related to knowledge. For many intellectuals during Calderón's lifetime, the sense of sight only produces knowledge when one knows how to see correctly. The senses have to be controlled and put to proper use.

9 **no poca...***very contrary to (or repugnant to) your nature*

las virtudes ornamento°   added luster
me traiga a centro que es
de todos los vicios centro.¹⁰
25 Ésta es la cárcel° de Egipto.   jail
Bien claro te dice el serlo°   [ser cárcel]
que es la posada° que alberga°   inn, shelters
por huéspedes de aposento¹¹
al homicidio° y al robo,°   murder, robbery
30 al fraude° y al adulterio.°   fraud, adultery
Pues ¿`cómo cabe en razón°   how can it be?
—repito otra vez—que siendo
—si no lo han dicho las señas,°   traits
tu nombre lo diga excelso°—   magnificent
35 la Castidad, que es la suma°   utmost
pureza,° que vence a un tiempo,   purity
para los triunfos del alma,
las rebeliones del cuerpo,
y ella° la sentina° donde   [la cárcel], sewer
40 el político gobierno
de la república arroja
los perniciosos° desechos,¹²   destructive, evil
que son escorias° del siglo,°   garbage, age
tú te atreves° a entrar dentro,   you dare
45 sin temor° de que te empañe°   fear, sully
el vapor de sus alientos?°¹³   fumes
Y aun no cesa° aquí mi duda,   cease
sino en que para este efecto
aparentemente hayas
50 tomado el `semblante bello°   beautiful appearance
de Asenet,¹⁴ hermosa hija

---

10 **centro que es...**_the center of the vice that is the center of all vices (or, the very heart of all sin)_

11 **huéspedes de...**_members of the household_ Technically, a "huésped de aposento" was a member of the king's household who was given lodging. Sueño uses the term ironically.

12 **ella la sentina...** "Ella" still refers to "cárcel" (and _not_ to "alma"). The prison is the sewer or bilge where Egypt ("la república") throws its criminal, human waste ("los perniciosos desechos").

13 To reconstruct this very long question, start with the basic construction: "¿cómo cabe en razón... (que) tú te atreves en entrar dentro...?"

14 Remember that Castidad will play the role of Asenet in this play. You can imagine Sueño's confusion seeing Christian Chastity playing the part of the daughter of the high priest of the sun god.

	del sacerdote° del Templo	priest
	de Heliópoli, ciudad del sol,[15]	
	y aun ella es el sol mesmo.°	[mismo]
55	Sepa, pues, de estas dos dudas[16]	
	la causa, porque suspenso°	dumbstruck
	hasta oír tu voluntad	
	tendrás a mi entendimiento.[17]	
Castidad	Vaga° fantasía, que sabes	vague
60	hacer con tus devaneos°	deliriums
	la quietud° de los sentidos,°	tranquility, 5 senses
	de los sentidos estruendo,°	chaotic noises
	pues cuando para el descanso	
	te ha introducido el sosiego,	
65	traidoramente has sabido	
	sacar del descanso el riesgo,[18]	
	`fantástica aparición,°	untrue appearance
	que en imágenes `de viento,°	insubstantial
	bien como yo de° Asenet	in the guise of
70	—por complacerme° en objeto	delight
	tan gloriosamente amable,°	pleasant
	tan amablemente honesto—[19]	
	la forma° tomé, tomaste,	[de Asenet]
	por complacerte, en Morfeo[20]	
75	tú de su negro semblante	

Chastity herself is bringing Sueño to a sinful place: a prison.

15   Sueño explains the etymology or root of "Heliópoli", it means "ciudad del sol." The temple is dedicated to the worship of the sun as a divinity.

16   All of the first 55 verses have been a way to ask these two questions or express these two doubts: why are we in a disgusting prison and why are you, Castidad, dressed like Asenet?

17   **suspenso hasta…***tendrás a mi entendimiento suspenso hasta oír tu voluntad (I'll be silent until I hear your plan)*

18   **para el descanso…** This allegorical description can be a little tricky until you get the hang of it. You might imagine "sosiego" (i.e. calm or peace) to be much like another allegorical character. So Castidad says that "sosiego" introduces or brings "sueño" to people so that they can rest, but "sueño" traitorously disrupts our sleep instead of helping us rest.

19   **honesto** More than just honest, "honesto" implies innocence of any wrongdoing or base desire. You might think of "honestidad" as decency.

20   In other words, Castidad is dressed as Asenet, while Sueño is dressed as Morpheus, the god of sleep. Morpheus shares qualities with death (because sleep is a kind of image of death).

lo adusto,° pálido° y yerto.°   bleak, pale, stiff
Ya, `a la una° de las dudas   [a la primera]
te he respondido, supuesto
que el haber vestido tú
80   sombras y luces° yo, a efecto   lights
habrá sido de hacer más
representable un concepto[21]
en que importa que seamos
debajo de los dos velos°   disguises
85   de Morfeo y Asenet,
yo la Castidad, tú el Sueño.
Y aunque también a la otra
duda responderte puedo,
`en cuanto a° que sea una cárcel   regarding
90   campaña de nuestro duelo,[22]
no lo `he de° hacer hasta que   [tengo que]
te digan mis sentimientos
la razón con que quejarme°   denounce
de tu sinrazón° pretendo.°   injustice, try
95   Y, pues no tiene `el oírlo°   hearing it
la fuerza que tendrá `el verlo,°   seeing it
llega° conmigo.[23] ¿Qué escuchas?   [ven]

Dentro voces y cadenas.

SUEÑO   Lo que ves, escucho y veo,
de la cadena° el ruido   chain
100   y de la queja° el lamento.°   complaint, wail

---

21 **a efecto…***in order to make these concepts representable* Allegory is a way of making available to the senses what might otherwise be imperceptible. Castidad returns to this phrase in verse 295: "Hagamos representable / a los teatros del tiempo…" This is an important explanation of Calderón's literary theory.

22 **campaña de…***our place of combat (or our dueling ground)* Castidad suggests that an allegorical conflict in the play will be between Castidad (control of the senses and sensuality) and Sueño (described in the play as "sinrazón," "fantástica aparición," and "vaga fantasía").

23 What we see can be less trustworthy than what we hear, but what we hear (el oírlo) is not as convincing as what we see (no tiene…la fuerza que tendrá el verlo). The function of allegory is to make things properly visible or to present to our eyes reliable visual stimuli. So what we see in the play is more truthful and more reliable than what see in life.

Castidad	Retírate° ahora y atiende°	hide, pay attention
	a su pavoroso° acento.°	dreadful, cry
Uno	(*Dentro*) ¡Ah del calabozo![24]	
Todos	(*Dentro*) ¿Quién	
	es quien llama?	
Uno	Allá va un preso°	prisoner
105	que, esclavo,° para que sirva	slave
	a todos, envía° su dueño.°	sends, master

Salen el Copero[25] y el Panadero con prisiones.[26]

Castidad y	¿Esclavo, para que sirva	
Sueño	a todos, envía su dueño?	
Copero	¿Quién será este desdichado,[27]	
110	tan desdichado° que siendo	unfortunate
	esclavo a ser preso venga	
	dos veces cautivo,° puesto	captive
	que servidumbre° y prisión	bondage
	le están doblando° los hierros?[28]	doubling
115 Panadero	Será algún facineroso°	criminal
	que su amo° tenga por menos	master
	mal, darle a una cárcel que	
	sufrirle° en casa.	put up with, bear
Copero	¡Que luego	
	te has de ir hacia lo peor![29]	
120	¿No puede ser que sea—¡ay cielos!	

---

24 **¡Ah del...**_Is anyone in the dungeon? (Is anyone there?)_

25 **Copero** *cupbearer, butler* A "copero" is a personal servant, usually in a position of trust. (A cupbearer makes sure no one poisons or drugs your drink.) Between them, the Copero and the Panadero represent bread and wine.

26 **con prisiones** *bound or in chains*

27 The Copero is speaking about a new inmate (a "desdichado" or unfortunate person) being sent to the prison.

28 **hierros** *irons or chains (but figuratively, suffering)* His suffering is doubled because he is both a prisoner and a servant to other prisoners, the lowest of the low. This is another instance in which McGaha's corrections have been invaluable, Pando y Mier has "yerros" (errors) instead of "hierros" (chains). The change in emphasis is from a presumption of the prisoner's guilt (yerros) to a focus on his suffering (hierros).

29 **¡Que luego...**_You always have to think the worst!_

	—otro infeliz que `sin culpa°	innocently
	padezca,° cual° yo padezco?	suffers, [como]
Panadero	¡También padezco sin ella°	[culpa]
	yo! Mas° no he de creer por eso	but
125	que no padezcan culpados°	guilty
	los demás.	
Copero	A ver, lleguemos.°	let's draw closer
	¿Quién será este preso?	

Sale José de cautivo, con cadena.

José	Quien,[30]	
	por saber que aqueste seno°	hidden place
	es sepultura° de vivos,°	tomb, the living
130	penosamente° contento,	sadly
	tiene por buena fortuna	
	ser en él `esclavo vuestro.°	your slave
Copero	Alza del suelo. ¡Qué talle°	figure
	tan airoso° y `bien dispuesto!°	graceful, handsome
135 Panadero	Si tiene talle de dar	
	la patente, será bueno.[31]	
José	Un mísero° esclavo era	lowly
	en la casa de mi dueño.	
	Un mísero esclavo soy	
140	aquí, pues a servir vengo.	
	¿Qué puedo tener que dar?	
Panadero	Jaqueta y birrete.[32]	
Copero	(*Al Panadero*) Eso	
	no es justo que tú lo digas,	
	ni nadie, que no es bien hecho	
145	afligir° al afligido,	torment
	principalmente sujeto°	individual
	tan rendido.°	crushed

---

30 José here answers the question posed by the Copero and Panadero ("who might it be?" answering "it is he who...")

31 **Si tiene...***It would be great if he's got something extra to buy us a round.* A "patente" is the meal or drink that a new arrival buys for the old timers, usually in a work or school setting.

32 That is, the Panadero asks José for his clothes.

Panadero	¿Ya querrás	
	`de él compadecerte?°	feel sorry for him
Copero	Es cierto.	
	La `buena presencia° es	poise
150		el sobrescrito primero	
	de las cartas de favor[33]	
	que escribe piadoso° el cielo,°	devoutly, heavens
	encomendando° a quien quiere	entrusting
	que gane el primer afecto°	affection
	de los demás.	
155	Panadero	Ya eso es	
	filosofar y no quiero	
	estarte oyendo piedades°	pious talk
	toda la vida.	

Vase el Panadero.

Copero	¿Qué puedo	
	hacer mejor? Y más, cuando	
160		presumo que no vi aspecto°	appearance
	en mi vida más amable.	
	¿De dónde eres?	
José	Soy hebreo.°	Hebrew
Copero	¿De qué tierra?	
José	De Canaán.[34]	
Copero	¿Tu nombre?	
José	José.	
Copero	"Aumento°"	increase
	significa.	
165	José	Soylo[35] de ansias.°	worries
Copero	¿Qué derrotados° sucesos°	disastrous, events
	te han traído a Egipto?	

---

33 **sobrescrito primero...***the address on a letter of recommendation* It announces the good qualities contained within.

34 **Canaán** *Canaan (the Promised Land of the Israelites)* It is generally the land west of the Jordan River.

35 **Soylo** *Lo soy* The word play involves the Copero's explanation of the meaning or etymology of "José." José says, in effect, "I may be 'aumento' but 'soy aumento de ansias.'"

JOSÉ   Son tales,
tan tristes y tan adversos,°   unfortunate
que son más para sentidos°   lamented
que contados.°   told

170   COPERO   Pues no quiero
afligirte la memoria.³⁶
Este es mi albergue.° Copero   lodging
fui de Faraón, esotro°   [ese otro]
camarada,° Panadero.   companion

175   Indiciados° de un delito°   suspected, crime
estamos, pero yo espero
que presto° saldremos libres.   soon
He dicho `de paso° esto,   in passing
porque° sepas hasta entonces   [para que]

180   rancho y señas,³⁷ que es inmenso
el tráfago° de esta cárcel,   coming and going
y no será fácil luego
volver aquí sin noticias,°   knowledge
adonde que tengas, quiero,

185   algún abrigo.³⁸ Y ahora,
ve a otras partes discurriendo,°   passing through
que pues vienes a servir,
según entendí, no quiero
malquistarte,³⁹ con que sea

190   mi agrado° tu privilegio.⁴⁰ (*Yéndose*)   pleasure
JOSÉ   Perdóneme tu piedad,°   goodness, devotion
señor, si no la agradezco,°   thank
que es ésta la vez primera
en que obligado me veo

195   a agradecer, porque soy
tan desdichado en extremo

---

36   **afligirte...**_bring up painful memories_

37   **rancho y señas...**_(roughly) what you need to know to get back to this spot_ "Rancho" _generally_
refers to a place where people congregate to eat or make camp.

38   **adonde que...**_adonde quiero que tengas algún abrigo (where I want you to have some shelter)_

39   **no quiero...**_I don't want you to be hated (here in the prison on my account)_

40   **privilegio** _exclusion_ Calderón draws on the root of the word, which is like "deprive." The
Copero does not want to keep José from seeing the rest of the prison.

que nunca le vi la cara
al favor, y así, ˋno he puesto
cuidado° en aprender cómo   have not taken care
habla el agradecimiento.°   gratitude
COPERO Id con Dios. (*Ap.*) (ˋSobre galán,°   more than handsome
parece el joven discreto.°   intelligent
El corazón me ha quebrado°   broken
verle tan mísero.°)   downtrodden

Vase el Copero.

JOSÉ   ¡Cielos!
Si porque serví leal,
no supe agradar a ˋun dueño,°   i.e. only one
¿cómo he de agradar a tantos?⁴¹
¡Oh, nunca hubieran mis sueños
despertado aquella envidia⁴²
que en este estado me ha puesto!

Vase José.

CASTIDAD Cuanto pudiera decir
yo,⁴³ gastando mucho tiempo
en encarecer⁴⁴ sus penas,
ha dicho él en un momento.
De aquellos sueños se queja
en que le empeñaste,⁴⁵ viendo
los haces° de sus hermanos,   sheaves (of grain)
que sin impulsos del viento,
de sus doradas espigas°   golden stalks
doblaban° los rubios cuellos,   bent

---

41 **a tantos** *all of the inmates of the enormous prison*

42 **envidia** *envy* Although it is not entirely clear from the text of the play, those familiar with the Bible story know that José's dreams prompted other people to be envious of him.

43 **Cuanto pudiera…***Everything I could have said* Castidad is speaking now to Sueño.

44 **encarecer** Literally, "encarecer" means "hacer más caro" in the sense that Castidad is trying to get Sueño to see the significance of and feel for José's suffering.

45 **le empeñaste** *you insisted on giving him*

<table>
<tr><td></td><td>como obedeciendo al suyo,[46]</td><td></td></tr>
<tr><td></td><td>y añadiendo ʼempeño a empeño,°</td><td>labor upon labor</td></tr>
<tr><td></td><td>le hiciste también soñase°</td><td>[que soñara]</td></tr>
<tr><td></td><td>sol, luna y estrellas puestos</td><td></td></tr>
<tr><td>225</td><td>a sus pies. No sé si arguya°</td><td>indicates</td></tr>
<tr><td></td><td>si fue cuerdo° o no fue cuerdo</td><td>wise</td></tr>
<tr><td></td><td>en revelarlo,° porque</td><td>[a sus hermanos]</td></tr>
<tr><td></td><td>no hay error donde hay misterio.[47]</td><td></td></tr>
<tr><td></td><td>Y así, baste° por ahora</td><td>let it be enough</td></tr>
<tr><td>230</td><td>que por baldón° y desprecio°</td><td>insult, contempt</td></tr>
<tr><td></td><td>"el soñador°" le llamaron,</td><td>the dreamer</td></tr>
<tr><td></td><td>cuya envidia fue creciendo</td><td></td></tr>
<tr><td></td><td>tanto, que desde el cariño°</td><td>tenderness</td></tr>
<tr><td></td><td>de hermano se pasó a ceño°</td><td>menace</td></tr>
<tr><td>235</td><td>de enemigo, de enemigo</td><td></td></tr>
<tr><td></td><td>a empozado.[48] Y no contentos,</td><td></td></tr>
<tr><td></td><td>desde empozado a vendido,°</td><td>sold (into slavery)</td></tr>
<tr><td></td><td>y desde vendido a preso.</td><td></td></tr>
<tr><td></td><td>Dirásme° que ¿por qué yo</td><td>me dirás</td></tr>
<tr><td>240</td><td>tanto sus favores siento?</td><td></td></tr>
<tr><td></td><td>Y responderéte, que es</td><td></td></tr>
<tr><td></td><td>porque en el mundo no tengo</td><td></td></tr>
<tr><td></td><td>otro alguno que venere°</td><td>venerates</td></tr>
<tr><td></td><td>más mi alto merecimiento.°</td><td>merit</td></tr>
<tr><td>245</td><td>Por no empañar mi pureza,[49]</td><td></td></tr>
<tr><td></td><td>por no ofender a su dueño,</td><td></td></tr>
<tr><td></td><td>atento° a la religión</td><td>mindful</td></tr>
<tr><td></td><td>cuanto a la lealtad atento,</td><td></td></tr>
</table>

---

46 **como obedeciendo…***as if their sheaves of wheat were bowing down in obedience to his sheaf of wheat* This, as well as the dream described in the next two verses, is an allusion to the book of Genesis (37:7-9). José's dreams enraged his brothers because he dreamed that he was in a position of power over them.

47 **misterio** *secrecy* Castidad is wondering whether José made a mistake by telling his brothers about his dream. "Misterio" is a key word in this play. As a theological term, it refers to the things that we cannot know directly—a mystery is a secret. The real presence of Christ in the Eucharist, for example, is a mystery.

48 **empozado** *thrown in a well* Because the brothers threw José in a "pozo" or dry cistern.

49 Castidad now explains all of the things José did to preserve his chastity.

a la más blanda sirena,[50]	
250 al áspid° más halagüeño,°	viper, flattering
al más traidor cocodrilo,°	crocodile
al más incauto[51] veneno,°	poison
y a la más incauta hiena,°	hyena
sordo° a la voz, mudo° al ruego,°	deaf, silent, plea
255 inmoble° al llanto° y veloz°	unmoved, cry, quick
a la fuga, venció huyendo.[52]	
¿Pero, qué mucho,[53] qué mucho	
si al lunado° monstruo fiero°	horned, wild
supo dejarle la capa?[54]	
260 Siendo así, que algún ingenio°	wise man
—no menos que iluminado—	
dijo que si desde el cielo	
una piedra se arrojara,°	threw
detenerse° fuera menos	stopping it (midair)
265 prodigio° en el aire que	wonder
un hombre en la ocasión puesto.[55]	
Pues siendo así que tú fuiste	
a sus ruinas fundamento°	cause
y yo estoy de sus victorias	
270 obligada a ser el premio,°	prize
¿qué extrañas que aquí te traiga,	
a que° veas el extremo	[para que]
en que tus sueños le tienen,	
por si pudiesen tus sueños,	
275 ya que acarrearon° el daño,°	they led to, harm
solicitarle el remedio?[56]	
Bien sé que Dios es `primera	

---

50   **más blanda sirena** *sweetest singer* Sirens or "sirenas" were mythical creatures that lured sailors to their doom with beautiful songs.

51   "Incauto" generally means "lacking prudence" or "unsuspecting." In this instance, however, it means something closer to "seemingly harmless." It only seems as though we don't need to take precautions against the "incauto veneno" and the "incauta hiena."

52   **veloz a...***quick to run away (from temptation) he triumphed by fleeing*

53   **¿qué mucho?** *why should that be surprising?*

54   **dejarle la capa...***to sacrifice one thing to avoid a greater loss*

55   **que un hombre...***than a man resisting temptation when given the opportunity (ocasión)*

56   **solicitarle...***to work diligently for (or in the service of) the solution*

	venderle en traje de siervo°	slave

venderle en traje de siervo°   *slave*
y estar preso, que hay en él
340   ` sobrenaturales hechos.°   *supernatural actions*
Mírale siempre a dos luces,[65]
y verás que todo esto
va encaminado° a que anda   *directed*
aquí oculto° y encubierto°   *hidden, shrouded*
345   algún misterio, que venga
a ser en los venideros
siglos,[66] venciendo las sombras,
misterio de los misterios,
milagro° de los milagros,   *miracle*
350   portento de los portentos,
y en fin, luz, verdad y vida
del más alto sacramento.

Vase la Castidad.

SUEÑO   ¡Oye, aguarda!° No tan solo   *wait*
confuso, absorto° y suspenso°   *astonished, awestruck*
355   mi entendimiento ha dejado
—que esto no es mucho, supuesto
que el sueño siempre fue obscuro
pasmo[67] del entendimiento—
sino también convencido,[68]
360   que es más. ¿De cuándo acá suelo
dejarme yo convencer[69]
de la razón? Pero miento,

---

65 **a dos luces** *from two perspectives* Castidad returns to the language of painting. Compare her ideas here (330-341) to Astolfo's reference to anamorphic paintings in *En la vida...* (676-693).

66 **venideros siglos** *future ages* This may refer either to New Testament times or the audience's present. One of the fascinating possibilities that Calderón exploits with allegory is that allegory can work in multiple timeframes at once. So, this play is both the history of something that happened in Genesis (i.e. a *long* time ago), but something that is happening now.

67 **pasmo** *shock (in the sense that it leaves one without the ability to reason)*

68 **confuso, absorto...**ha dejado mi entendimiento (no solo) confuso, absorto y suspenso...sino también convencido

69 **¿De cuándo...**Since when do I tend to let myself be convinced... "Suelo" (i.e. "yo suelo") is from the verb "soler" and means "to be accustomed to" or "to tend to."

que en sueños ha revelado
Dios infinitos secretos,
365 y cuando no hubiera otros,°   [otros sueños]
bastara a suplir por ellos
el de su padre° en la escala°   Jacob, ladder
que abrazaba tierra y cielo.⁷⁰
Luego, sí hay aquí virtud
370 que ruega,° y yo me convenzo   begs
aquí hay Dios que manda. Pues,
¿qué aguardo que no obedezco?
(*Canta*) *Dormid, dormid, mortales,*
que el grande y el pequeño
375 *iguales son lo que les dura el sueño.*
Mortales, que en la cárcel
del mundo vivís presos,
no tan sólo los hierros arrastrando,
mas también arrastrándoos los yerros.
380 *Dormid, dormid, al son°*   sound
de mi músico acento,°   voice
que mudas° consonancias de la vida   silent
son también las quietudes del silencio.
Dormid, dormid, no sólo
385 *hoy al descanso atentos°*   attentive
pero atentos a ver qué es lo que quiere
en vuestras sombras revelar el cielo.
Y vosotras, ideas,
que en fantásticos° cuerpos   unreal
390 *representáis como retratos° vivos*   portraits
ansias° y gozos° a sentidos muertos,⁷¹   worries, pleasures
ved que Dios, conmovido°   moved to pity
de una virtud al ruego,
en términos nos manda que las ruinas
395 *que el sueño destruyó,° restaure° el sueño.*   destroyed, restore

Salen el Copero y el Panadero.

70 A reference to Jacob's dream in Genesis 28, commonly known as "Jacob's Ladder." In the
dream Jacob sees a ladder that extends all the way to the heavens; angels ascend and descend the ladder.
71 **sentidos muertos** *senses that are dead to the world (because the dreamer is asleep)*

TODOS   *Dormid, dormid, mortales,*
que el grande y el pequeño
iguales son lo que les dura el sueño.

Vase el Sueño.

COPERO   ¡Qué `perezoso letargo°   lazy stupor
400   es el que sobre mí tengo!
PANADERO   Parece que hubo patente[72]
          según que todo me duermo.
COPERO   ¿Qué haré yo para vencer
          esta pesadez° que tengo?   heaviness
405 PANADERO   Lo que yo, `echarse a dormir.°   take a nap
COPERO   ¿A esta hora?
PANADERO   Eso es lo mesmo
          que comer, porque el `reloj
          da° cuando gana no tengo,   clock strikes
          y `cuando tengo la gana,°   when I feel like it
410   esperar a que dé.° Necios,°   it strikes, idiots
          comer cuando hubiere° hambre,   [tenga]
          dormir cuando hubiere sueño,
          que no han de ser nuestras tripas
          las cuerdas de su instrumento.[73]
415 COPERO   Deja locuras. Aquí,
          a mi pesar, me recuesto.[74]
PANADERO   Yo `a mi placer,° que dormido   happily
          no sé si estoy libre o preso.
          O dígalo aquel cantar
420   que dijo en no sé qué versos:
MÚSICA   *Dormid, dormid, mortales,*
que el grande y el pequeño
iguales son lo que les dura el sueño.

---

72 **patente** The Panadero refers to the drinks he wanted José to buy (136). He feels so sluggish that it is as if he went out drinking the night before.

73 **nuestras tripas...***our guts don't have to be tuned like musical instruments* The joke here is that musical instruments were often strung with strings (*cuerdas*) made of catgut or the guts (*tripas*) of other animals.

74 **a mi pesar...***with a heavy heart, I lie down*

Con esta repetición van saliendo los dos bofetones.⁷⁵ Recuéstanse los dos,
divididos,⁷⁶ el Copero en el carro⁷⁷ donde está el bofetón en que ha de salir la
Sombra que ha de venir debajo de la vid, y el Panadero debajo del que ha de
traer la Sombra de las aves y canastillos de pan, y dando vuelta ambos bofe-
tones encontrados, cantan:

SOMBRA 1	*(Canta) El pan que del rocío°*	dew
425	*se amasó° de los cielos*	kneaded
	cuando en hermosa aurora,° blanda nube	dawn
	trujo la luz, la sombra y el sustento...°	nourishment
SOMBRA 2	*(Canta) El generoso vino*	
	que dio racimo° bello	bunch of grapes
430	*cuando de promisión la fértil tierra*	
	sucedió a la aspereza del desierto...⁷⁸	
SOMBRA 1	*...con permisión de Dios*	
	al hombre se le llevo.	
	Mas, ¡ay de aquel que en culpa se le roban	
435	*funestas° aves, que le° dan al viento!*	ill-fated, the bread
SOMBRA 2	*...con permisión de Dios*	
	al hombre le prevengo,	
	feliz en gracia, aquel para quien sabia°	wisely
	le exprimo,° le recojo° y le conservo.	crush, harvest
440	SOMBRA 1	*De pájaros nocturnos*
	en vano le defiendo.	
	SOMBRA 2	*En vano intentan malograr° los frutos*
	ni el granizo,° ni el ábrego, ni el cierzo.⁷⁹	hail

---

75 A "bofetón" in this case is a stage contrivance or a piece of scenery set on a turntable so that
it can spin to reveal a character. In this instance there are two "bofetones" that reveal the two Sombras.
Sombra 2 appears with "la vid" or grapevine (symbolic of wine and the Copero) while Sombra 1 appears
with "aves y canastillos" or birds and baskets of bread (symbolizing the Panadero). These two Sombras
are the dreams of the Copero and Panadero described in Genesis 40:9-19.

76 **Recuéstanse...** The Copero and the Panadero lie down separately.

77 *Autos sacramentales* were performed on movable stages elaborately constructed on carts or
carros. For this play, four *carros* were attached to a temporary stage. The *carros* came complete with
props, scenery, and large enclosures (often towers or globes) that could open to reveal action inside.

78 **de promisión...** *as was promised, the fertile Promised Land followed after the harshness of the*
desert

79 "Ábrego" is a hot south wind that brings drought; "cierzo" is a freezing north wind.

Sombra 1	*¡Ay de quien no le adore...*	
445 Sombra 2	*¡Feliz quien sea su dueño...*	
Sombra 1	*...pues si le come en culpa, es pan de muerte!*[80]	
Sombra 2	*...pues si en gracia le bebe, es de los cielos!*	
Sombras y	*Dormid, dormid, mortales,*	
Música	*que el grande y el pequeño*	
450	*iguales son lo que les dura el sueño.*	

El Panadero y el Copero despiertan despavoridos.[81]

Panadero	¡Huye,° infausta° sombra horrible!	go away, infamous
Copero	¡No huyas, dulce asombro bello![82]	
Panadero	Mas, yo iré huyendo de ti...	
Copero	Mas, yo iré en tu seguimiento°...	pursuit
455 Panadero	...que hasta perderte de vista...	
Copero	...que hasta alcanzarte°...	reaching you

José, saliendo.

José	¿Qué es esto?	
	¿Tan asustados° los dos,	startled
	despavoridos e inquietos,°	unsettled
	cuando yo con alborozo°	joy
460	de que ya serviros vuelvo?	
Panadero	`No te admires.°	Don't be surprised.
Copero	No te espantes.°	Don't fear.
Panadero	Que una pena...	
Copero	Que un contento...	
Panadero	...aun es de dolor soñada.[83]	

---

80   Sombra 1 is talking about bread and the Eucharist at the same time. The idea contained in "come en culpa" (or eating in sin) is a theological point that was important for Calderón: receiving the Eucharist without the proper attitude (which could mean going to Confession first) was a grave sin. For Roman Catholics, the bread of Communion physically becomes the body of Christ (although it retains the appearance of a wafer of bread). To mistreat the Eucharist is to disrespect the physical body of Christ. To eat in sin or "comer en culpa" is sacrilege.

81   **despavoridos** *petrified*

82   **dulce...** *sweet, beautiful, astonishing dream*

83   The Panadero's whole thought is "aun una pena soñada es de dolor": even pain in a dream hurts (in real life).

Copero   ...aun soñado se huye presto.

465   José   Si yo tuviera licencia°   permission
          para preguntar, bien creo
          que me moviera la justa
          curiosidad de saberlo.°   [saber lo soñado]

Copero   Aunque de los sueños no
470   hay que `hacer caso,° confieso   pay any mind
          que la viva aprehensión° de éste   perception
          me obliga a `hacer más aprecio°   esteem
          de él° que de otros sueños.   [el sueño]

Panadero   Yo
          puedo asegurar lo mesmo,
475   y por deshacerme° de él,   forget, get over
          le he de decir. Oye atento:
          como en nuestra fantasía°   imagination
          siempre el sueño nos retrata°   portrays
          aquello que más `se trata°   is dealt with
480   en `los discursos del día,°   daily activities
          fue fácil° que yo soñase   likely
          —que al fin panadero soy—
          que del floreado[84] pan que hoy
          dispuse° que se amasase°   arrange, kneaded
485   para el Rey, tres canastillos,°   baskets
          blanco y sabroso° llevaba,   tasty
          y vi que, cuando esperaba
          en la real° mesa servillos,°   royal, [servirlos]
          en el camino embestían°   attacked
490   tropas de funestas aves
          que, nocturnamente graves,
          cebadas en él,[85] hacían
          tales presas° que mis gozos°   thefts, joys
          murieron `a breves plazos,°   right away

---

84   "Floreado" here refers to "pan de flor" or bread made with "la flor de la harina." It is the most refined and generally the whitest bread, made with the finest flour. It was highly prized and often reserved for the nobility.

85   **cebadas en él** *drawn to the bread (or madly feeding on the bread)* "Cebadas" is from the verb "cebar" (not the noun "cebada," or barley). Varey suggests that the "funestas aves...nocturnamente graves" are owls (*Cosmovisión* 347).

495	pues, devorado a pedazos
	y `desmenuzado a trozos,° — crumbling into pieces
	aun migajas° no dejaron, — crumbs
	y si las dejaron, fue
	para el viento, puesto que,
500	hechas átomos,° volaron — tiny pieces
	de suerte que aquel contento
	en que esmeraba mi oficio,[86]
	después de ser desperdicio° — waste
	de aves, fue estrago° del viento. — destruction

505   COPERO   Yo soñé—porque también

sean especies° del día   images

las que hoy en mi fantasía

señas de mi oficio den—

que veía en un `prado ameno°   pleasant meadow

510   una vid hermosa y bella

y de los pámpanos° de ella   small bunches

todo su follaje° lleno   foliage

de tan dulce fruto opimo°   abundant

que, fértilmente lozano,°   vigorous

515   era un rubí° cada grano°   ruby, grape

y un ámbar° cada racimo.   fragrant liqueur

De uno, que entre dos pendía°   dangled

del `sarmiento superior,°   upper vine

soñé que el blanco licor°   liquor

520   con una mano exprimía,°   squeezed

cuyo líquido tesoro

nada se desperdiciaba,°   was wasted

porque al exprimirle estaba

yo con una copa de oro

525   en la otra mano, de modo

que un átomo no perdía,

pues todo lo recogía,°   harvested

con que se lograba° todo.   obtained

     JOSÉ   (*Ap.*)° (¡Oh, válgame el cielo![87] ¡Cuánto   an aside (aparte)

---

86   **esmeraba…** *I worked so hard at my job*

87   **válgame…** *Lord help me!* "Válgame" is the imperative of the verb "valer" and the phrase "válgame el cielo" is often used colloquially as one might say "¡Por Dios!" or "Good God!" Here, however,

530   campo la imaginación
               con una y otra visión
               corre! ¿Desperdicio tanto
               en pan? ¿Tanto logro en vino?
               ¿Allí ruina y aquí aumento?°   *increase*
535   De algún alto sacramento,
               de algún misterio divino,
               luces uno y otro dan,
               pero tan en sombras hoy
               que pienso que viendo estoy
540   vida y muerte en vino y pan.)
     COPERO   ¿Cómo habiéndonos oído
               mudo, absorto y elevado
               parece que te has quedado
               sin habernos respondido?
545   JOSÉ   Como cuando a ambos escucho,
               me ofuscan° vuestros diseños,°   *blur, designs*
               que entiendo mucho de sueños,
               porque ha que me cuestan mucho.
               Y así, no sé si me obliga
550   más el que aquí al discurrir,
               calle lo que he de decir,
               que lo que he de callar diga.
 PANADERO y   En tal duda es—`a mi ver°—   *in my eyes*
    COPERO   mejor decir que callar.
      JOSÉ   ¿Si es pesar?°   *bad news*
555 PANADERO   Porque es pesar.
      JOSÉ   ¿Si es placer?
    COPERO   Porque es placer.
 PANADERO   Porque al que pesar tocó
               pueda resguardarse° de él.   *protect oneself*
    COPERO   Y al que el placer, es cruel
               cosa ocultársele.°   *hide it from him*
560   JOSÉ   Yo,
               aunque bien quisiera aquí...
 PANADERO y
    COPERO   ¡Habla!

José is actually requesting help from above.

JOSÉ	...por no dar dolor,		
	no dar gusto, hay superior		
	causa. En fin, ¿`he de° hablar?		[tengo que]

PANADERO y
COPERO   Sí.

565   JOSÉ   Pues en acción tan unida
que una en otra se convierte,
hay pan, que es vida y es muerte,
hay vino, que es muerte y vida.
Libre tú en tu indicio° estás,   suspicion
570   tú convencido° en tu indicio.   convicted
(*Al Copero*) Tú volverás a tu oficio
(*Al Panadero*) y tú presto morirás.

PANADERO   Mucho cuidado° me diera   concern
interpretación tan rara,
575   si de ti no imaginara
que inútil venganza° era   revenge
de aquel primer lance,° en quien   situation
te pedí.[88]

COPERO   `Ten acción tal,°   Stop that
y no aprecio hagas del mal,[89]
580   pues yo no le hago del bien.

PANADERO   ¿Cómo no? Pues, aunque digo
que no he de creer su agüero,°   omen, prophecy
no por eso de embustero°   fraud
he de excusar° el castigo.[90]   forego

585   COPERO   Mira que en su amparo° puesto   defense
estoy yo.

PANADERO   También estoy
yo en su ofensa.

JOSÉ   (*Ap.*) ¡Entre ambos hoy
tengo de morir!

---

88   The Panadero refers to his attempt to bully José in verse 132.

89   **no aprecio...** *no hagas aprecio del mal* (don't put too much stock in the bad prediction)

90   In other words, even though the Panadero doesn't believe José's interpretation of the dream, he's going to punish José for being a swindler.

Al irse a embestir, se pone José en medio, deteniendo al uno
con una mano y al otro con la otra, se retienen los dos, mirándole suspensos.

	Panadero y		
	Copero	¿Qué es esto?	
	Panadero	¿Quién me pudo suspender?°	stop
590	Copero	¿Quién me ciega° en nueva luz?	blinds
	José	Cuando, a manera de cruz,[91]	
		entre ambos `me llego a ver,°	I find myself
		segundo misterio muestra	
		ver que su furor impida	
595		a la diestra el que es de vida,	
		y el de muerte a la siniestra.	

El Panadero vuelve a querer embestirle.

	Panadero	¿Mas quién me podrá impedir	
		muerte a un vil esclavo dar?°	[dar muerte a...]

Sale el Alcaide.

	Alcaide	(*Al Panadero*) Mal hace en querer matar	
600		quien tiene `por qué° morir,	a reason
		pues habiendo ya salido	
		—conforme a justicia y ley—	
		la sentencia, manda el Rey	
		que tú que estás convencido	
		en tu culpa, mueras.	
605	Panadero	¡Cielos!	
		¿Qué escucho?	
	Alcaide	(*Al Copero*) Y que tú, que estás	
		sin culpa—porque jamás	
		te obsten° pasados recelos°—	block, suspicions
		a servir su copa vuelvas,	

---

91 José is standing between the Copero and the Panadero with his arms outstretched (forming a cross with his body). The Copero is on his right hand (symbolizing good fortune) and the Panadero is on his left hand (symbolizing bad fortune or evil omens). From the word "siniestro" (left hand) we get the word sinister.

610 restituido° a tu honor,   restored
    a su° gracia y su favor.   [del Rey]
    (*Al Panadero*) Y pues es bien te resuelvas°   resign yourself
    tú a obedecer a tu suerte°   fortune
    con este negro cendal°   veil
615 cubro tu rostro,° en señal°   face, signal
    de estar condenado a muerte.

Échale un velo negro por el rostro.

PANADERO   `¡Ay, infelice de mí!°   woe is me!
    En fin, mi culpa pagué.
COPERO   ¡Felice yo, que llegué
    a ver este día!
620 ALCAIDE   De aquí
    ven tú, y tú, cuando quisieres,
    podrás salir, que ya abierta
    y franca° tienes la puerta.   unbarred

Vanse el Alcaide y el Panadero.

COPERO   Abrázame tú, que eres
625   a quien debo las albricias°   rejoicing
    de esta dicha,° pues tú fuiste   happiness
    quien primero la previste.
JOSÉ   Si es que pagarlas codicias,[92]
    con una cosa podrás.
COPERO   ¿Qué es?
630 JOSÉ   Que `te acuerdes de mí.°   you remember me
    Y puesto que desde aquí
    a servir a tu Rey vas,
    le digas el duro exceso
    con que yo padezco,° y pues   I suffer
635 sabes `cuán penoso° es   how terrible
    estar inocente y preso,
    duélete,° por Dios, de mí,   have pity
    que es mi mal tan infinito

---

92 **Si es...***If you really want to repay your joy*

	que si cometí delito,°	crime
640	es que no le cometí.	
	Copero Tan compadecido° voy	moved to pity
	de dejarte... Mas no quiero	
	—sin merecerlas° primero—	deserve them
	gracias.[93] Palabra te doy	
645	y con fe° y mano prometo	good faith
	el que he de volver por ti.	
	José ¿Palabra, fe y mano?	
	Copero Sí.	
	Yo la doy.	
	José Y yo la acepto.	

Vase el Copero.

	Hermosas luces, en quien miro atento,[94]	
650	con rasgos° y bosquejos° desiguales,[95]	features
	el número infinito de mis males	
	y la esfera° capaz de mi tormento.	sphere
	¿Cuál de vosotras,° cuál desde su asiento	[luces]
	es la que influye[96] en mis desdichas° tales?	misfortunes
655	¿Cuál de vosotros, astros° desiguales,	stars
	a su cargo° tomó mi sufrimiento?	responsibility
	Tú me parece que serás ¡oh estrella!	
	`la más pobre de luz,° la más obscura.	faintest
	Óyeme tú, que para ti prevengo.°	speak
660	Ya pensarás que digo una querella,°	grievance
	no, sino un galardón° por la ventura°	prize, fortune

---

93 **Mas no quiero...***Mas no quiero gracias sin merecerlas primero* (I don't want thanks until I've earned it)

94 José expresses his deep emotions here in the form of a sonnet (649-662). The use of sonnets for soliloquies was very common in seventeenth-century drama. Taking a step back, verses 641-670 provide a good opportunity to examine how Calderón shifts the tone of a scene or passage by changing poetic meters from *redondilla* to *soneto* to *romance*. See the section of the Introduction on "Versification and Metrification."

95 **desiguales** *uncertain, vague, erratic*

96 The idea that a star might influence life on earth is a basic astrological concept widely believed during Calderón's time. According to the astrology of the time, stars can influence us but they cannot control us. See *En la vida...*, verses 443-444.

que no me has de quitar, pues no la tengo.
Y ya que mis dichas hoy
todo su consuelo° fundan   consolation
665 en que, faltándome todas,°   [dichas]
no puedo perder ninguna.
Hidrópico° de desdichas,   greedy
ahora al contrario arguya
en que, pues todas las tengo,
670 ¿por qué ha de faltarme una?
Ésta° es—no habiendo podido   [desdicha]
saber de mi padre nunca—
saber de una vez que yace°   lies flat
muerto a manos de mi injuria,[97]
675 porque no `acierto a encontrar,°   manage to find
por más que en ello discurra,°   think it over
qué habrán dicho mis hermanos[98]
para salvarse en disculpa
de mi venta.[99] Pero no
680 se la habrán dicho. Es sin duda
que la traición° siempre viste°   betrayal, wears
los disfraces° de la astucia.°   disguises, cunning
Mas ¡ay de mí! que no pueden
haber hallado ninguna,°   [disculpa]
685 que ya que encubra su error,
mi falta a mi padre encubra.[100]
¡Ay, anciano padre mío!
¿Quién duda ¡ay de mí! ¿quién duda
que ella habrá acabado° ya   finished
690 contigo, según la suma°   utmost
terneza° con que, por hijo   tenderness
de Raquel, cuya hermosura

---

97   **mi injuria** *the wrong (done to me)* José's "muerto a manos de mi injuria" inverts Libia's phrase
in *En la vida...* (380-381): "¡Muera / a manos de mi desdicha!"

98   **qué habrán...***what my brothers might have said*

99   **mi venta** *when they sold me into slavery*

100   **ya que encubra...***and since they cover up their crime, my absence will be the end of father*

                tanto te costó,[101] me amabas?
                Y aunque sé que no me escuchas,
695   `te suplico° ¡oh padre mío!   I beg of you
                Benjamín mi falta supla.[102]
                Más parecido es° que yo   [es Benjamín]
                a la hermosa madre suya.
                y pues tienes el espejo°   mirror
700   en él de aquella difunta°   deceased
                hermosa beldad,° que el fértil   loveliness
                campo de Belén° sepulta,°   Bethlehem, entombs
                `no me eches menos a mí.°   don't miss me
                Y tú, Benjamín, procura
705   que se consuele° contigo,   finds consolation
                hazle amorosas ternuras,°   tenderness
                que `caduca edad° renace   old age
                cuando en los hijos caduca.°   passes away
                Mas ¡ay! que en vano este ruego
710   será, si vuelvo a la angustia°   anguish
                de que el pesar° le habrá muerto   sadness
                con el dolor de mi fuga,°   disappearance
                que la `más fácil razón°   likeliest explanation
                que habrá encontrado la industria°   craftiness
715   de mis hermanos será
                que no saben de mí. ¡Oh, suba°   may it rise
                mi llanto° al cielo! Quizá   cry
                entre sus virtudes puras
                habrá alguna que, piadosa,°   merciful
720   no porque de mí presuma°   assumes
                que merezco° su favor   I deserve
                sino por la piedad° suya,   mercy
                haciéndome saber cómo

---

101   José's parents were Jacob and Raquel. They fell in love at first sight. When Jacob asked Raquel's father, Labán, for her hand in marriage, Labán proposed a deal: Jacob could marry Raquel, but only if he first worked 7 years for Labán. Jacob toiled away for 7 years and was married. It was not until the next morning that Jacob realized that Labán had substituted his less desirable daughter Leah at the altar! Labán forced Jacob to work 7 more years to marry Raquel. So, Raquel's beauty cost Jacob dearly.

102   **Benjamín mi...***may the fact that you have another son by Raquel, Benjamín, make up for my loss* Benjamín looks more like Raquel than José does.

cover up

725 la traición le disimulan,°

y qué hizo él, mi duda venza.°   *resolve*

Sale la Castidad, atravesando el tablado[103] por delante de él.

Castidad   Sí habrá,[104] que hasta que una duda

vehementemente aprehendida°   *grasped*

forme fantasmas confusas,[105]

es tan piadosa licencia°   *permission*

730 que `no ha menester° disculpa.   *it's not necessary*

Juzga° tú cómo sería,   *think*

quizá verás lo que juzgas.

Vase la Castidad.

José   ¡Oye, aguarda, escucha, espera!

Mas ¡ay cielos, qué locura!

735 Jurara° que la beldad   *I could swear*

de una divina hermosura

se me había puesto delante.

¡Cuánto una aprehensión° perturba   *vision*

los sentidos! Y aun `no cesa°   *doesn't stop*

740 en que ella aparezca y huya,

sino que también jurara

que veo[106] que en la espesura°   *dense woods*

de Canaán, con Benjamín

anda mi padre en mi busca,

745 en cuyo pasmo° el sentido   *shock*

absorto atender procura,[107]

`por si° ilusión que se ve   *in case*

---

103   **atravesando...**_crossing the stage_

104   This is a reference back to José's plea in 717-719: "Quizá / entre sus virtudes puras / habrá alguna..." Castidad essentially answers, "Sí habrá virtudes puras..." What José sees before him is an allegorical virtue (chastity) that has taken on the form of Asenet.

105   **fantasmas confusas** _ambiguous or confused ideas in the imagination_

106   The audience will see this vision, too, in just a moment.

107   **el sentido...**_I am straining to hear_ At this moment, José can see a dreamlike vision of his brother, Benjamín, and father but he has not yet heard their voices. He is trying to hear.

es ilusión que se escucha.

Ábrese el carro, y haciendo en el aire tablado y vestuario,[108]
sale Jacob, viejo venerable, con Benjamín, de zagal.[109]

JACOB	¡Cuánto, hermoso Benjamín,	
750	cuidados° de amor madrugan!°	worries, don't rest
	Desde que envié° a José	I sent
	a ver si crecen fecundas	
	las crías° y en lo que entienden°	lambs, manage
	tus hermanos, con ser suma	
755	siempre[110] su presteza,° no	speediness
	ha vuelto, pues aunque suban°	travel up
	de Siquén a Dotaín[111]	
	buscando pastos,° ya acusa	pasture
	su tardanza° mi amor.	lateness
BENJAMÍN	¿Cuándo	
760	tardanza de amor no es mucha?	
JACOB	¿Son celos,° Benjamín?	jealousy
BENJAMÍN	¿Yo?	
	¿Celos de José? ¡Qué injusta	
	sospecha! Que yo y José	
	somos dos cuerpos con una	
765	alma,[112] un alma con dos cuerpos,	
	\`estrecho lazo° nos junta,	a close bond
	como, en fin, hijos los dos	
	de Raquel.	

---

108   Part of the movable stage opens up, revealing a second, raised stage. What José sees in verses 749-861 is actually a vision of the past, back to Genesis 37 (when José's brothers sold him into slavery).

109   **zagal** *young shepherd, youth*

110   **siempre** José is "always" very quick, in the sense that he is normally very quick to return (but not this time).

111   These are Biblical place names, which in English are Shechem and Dothan. So Jacob reasons that even if the brothers have brought the flocks up from Shechem to Dothan (farther away), José is taking a long time in returning home.

112   **una alma** *one soul* Usually, we say "un alma" even though "alma" is a feminine noun, just as we would "el agua." Here, however, to maintain the u/a assonant rhyme of the *romance* (injusta...una...junta), Calderón uses "una." (When he does not need to maintain the rhyme scheme, he goes back to "un alma" in 765.

JACOB   ¡Cuánto me gusta
que tanto os améis! Y pues
770   mi amor y tu amor `se aúnan,°   unite you
y es ya interés° de `los dos°   concern, [nosotros]
buscarle, a subir me ayuda
a aquel ribazo,° de donde   hillside
más el camino descubra,
775   por si adelanta° la vista   hasten
el gozo de verle.
BENJAMÍN   Excusa
la diligencia,[113] que allí
vienen ya Rubén y Judas,
Isacar y Manasés,
que dirán de él.

Salen los dichos, de pastores, hablando aparte.[114]
Traen envuelto en un tafetán una tunicela roja.[115]

780   RUBÉN   Pena dura
es, que queráis que yo sea
el que tal dolor le anuncia.
JUDAS   Tú has de ser, pues por mayor[116]
tendrás, Rubén, más cordura,
785   no sólo en `fingir el hecho°   sell the lie
pero en `suavizar la angustia.°   soften the blow
JACOB   ¿Cómo, cuando a mi presencia
llegáis nadie me saluda,
y para no hablar, parece
790   que andáis conciliando° excusas?   agreeing to
¿Cómo mi José no viene

---

113   **Excusa la…** *The effort is unnecessary* (you can spare yourself the trouble)

114   **los dichos…** *the aforementioned brothers, dressed as shepherds, talking among themselves* Benjamín has just spoken of four of his brothers: Rubén, Judas, Isacar, and Manasés. Rubén's first lines will be addressed only to those brothers; Jacob and Benjamín do not overhear them. José, however, can hear everything in this flashback.

115   **Traen envuelto…** *They carry wrapped up in a light cloth (taffeta) a red tunic.* A "tunicela" was also a ceremonial robe worn by priests.

116   Ruben was Leah's son and the first born of all Jacob's children.

　　　　con vosotros? ¡Pena injusta!
　　　　¿No merece más respuesta
　　　　que lágrimas mi pregunta?
795　　　¿Qué es esto? ¿Todos calláis
　　　　y todos lloráis?

RUBÉN　　　　　　　Si apuras°　　　　　　　press
　　　　tanto nuestro dolor, `fuerza
　　　　será,° ya que `no articula　　　　　　it will be necessary
　　　　el labio,° que hable esta vez　　　　　my lips don't speak
800　　　más retórica° y más muda.°　　　　　eloquently, silently
　　　　¿Conoces...

　　　　　　　　Descubre° el tafetán.　　　　uncovers

JACOB　　　　　　　¡Ay, infelice!
RUBÉN　　...esta talar[117] vestidura°　　　　garment
　　　　que a José hiciste?
JACOB　　　　　　　　No,
　　　　que son cifras° muy obscuras[118]　　　signs, figures
805　　　que yo se la° diese a él blanca　　　　[la vestidura]
　　　　y él me la vuelva purpúrea.
　　　　¿Qué ha sido esto?
RUBÉN　　　　　　　Una fiera°　　　　　　wild beast
　　　　—la más fiera y más sañuda°　　　　　furious
　　　　de cuantas aborta el monte,[119]
810　　　parto° horrible de sus grutas°—　　　offspring, caverns
　　　　al pasar de Dotaín
　　　　el valle, de entre sus rudas°　　　　　rough
　　　　quiebras° salió, ensangrentando°　　　chasms, bloodying
　　　　en su tierna sangre pura
815　　　de sus colmillos° las presas　　　　　fangs, prey
　　　　y de sus garras° las uñas.°　　　　　claws, nails
　　　　Despedazado° el cadáver　　　　　　torn to pieces
　　　　hallamos,° y en mil menudas°　　　　　we found, tiny

117　"Talar" here is an adjective, describing a cloak or robe that covers the entire body.

118　**obscuras** *difficult to make out or to see*

119　**aborta el monte** *that the mountain gives birth to* In this passage, phrases like "aborta el monte" recall the language of *En la vida...*: "aborto destos montes..." (verse 73).

		partes la túnica° y...	tunic
	Jacob	¡Calla,	
820		calla! Que es tu lengua aguda°	sharp
		flecha° avenenada,° que	arrow, poisoned
		en mil repetidas puntas	
		el corazón me penetra	
		con cada voz° que pronuncia.	word
825		(*Toma la túnica.*) ¡Ay, José del alma mía!	
	Benjamín	¿Cómo esto mi amor escucha	
		y no muere de dolor?	
	Jacob	¡Funestas,° tristes, impuras°	baleful, stained
		prendas,° por mi mal halladas![120]	garment
830		¿Qué os hizo esta edad caduca	
		para que de mi `mejor	
		espejo° eclipséis la luna?	[José]
		Si era la luz de mis ojos,	
		¿por qué me dejáis `a escuras,°	in the dark
835		viendo `la flor de sus años°	[la juventud]
		en su primavera mustia?°	withered
		En el cristal que bebía	
		el licor de sus dulzuras,°	sweetness
		¿por qué con sangre queréis	
840		que beba ponzoña° turbia° ?	venom, dark
		¡Ay, José! Pésima° fiera	dreadful
		te dio muerte. ¿Quién lo duda?	
		Pésima fiera sería.	
		Señor—antes que discurra°	ponder
845		en que a la envidia la dieron	
		ese apellido mil plumas°—	writers
		permitid que este dolor	
		dé conmigo en las obscuras	
		mansiones que a tantos padres	
850		depositados sepultan.[121] (*Vase*)	
	Benjamín	¡Ay de mí! Que de mi padre	

---

120 This is an allusion to a famous sonnet: Garcilaso de la Vega's "Soneto X," which begins "Dulces prendas por mi mal halladas."

121 **permitid que...***permit, O Lord, that this pain send me to those dark dwellings that serve as tombs to so many fathers (i.e. let me die)*

    la pena aunque es grande es una,

    pero en mí son dos,° que siento   [dos penas]

    la de José y la suya. (*Vase*)

855   RUBÉN   En fin, que quisisteis ver,

    sin darme lugar° que acuda   time

    de la cisterna a sacarle,°   [sacar a José]

    esta lástima.

  ISACAR   Hizo Judas

    tan presto la venta.°   the sale (of José)

  JUDAS   Eso

    no es de aquí.[122]

  LOS CUATRO   ¿Qué? ¿Nos acusas?[123]

860   HERMANOS   No soñara él[124] y no viera

    tan deshecha° su fortuna.   ruined, undone

        Vanse, y ciérrase° el carro.   [se cierra]

  JOSÉ   ¡Aguarda, detente,° espera!   halt

    ¡No huyas, ilusión! ¡No huyas

865   hasta que sepa mi padre

    que vivo y...

        Sale el Copero.

  COPERO   ¿Dónde apresuras

    el paso?[125]

  JOSÉ   No sé, no sé...

  COPERO   No dirás que mis venturas°   good fortune

    me olvidan° de ti.   makes me forget

  JOSÉ   Ya veo

870   la gran piedad° que te ilustra.[126]   goodness

---

122 **Eso no es...** *That's neither here nor there.* Judas is saying, in effect, "Don't blame me!"

123 Although it might seem at this moment that Isacar, Rubén, and Manasés are reacting to Judas, all four brothers feel accused by the others.

124 **No soñara...** *Would that he never dreamed (or, It would have been better if he had never dreamed)*

125 **¿Dónde apresuras...** *Where are you rushing off to?*

126 **que te ilustra** *that typifies you (that characterizes you)*

COPERO	Pues no sólo vengo a verte,	
	que `vengo por ti.° ¿Qué dudas?[127]	I've come for you
JOSÉ	Si es dicha, ¿no he de dudarla?	
COPERO	Pues aun es mayor `que juzgas.°	than you think
875	Este el anillo° del Rey	ring
	es, que tu libertad jura,°	proclaims
	y el Rey es quien por ti envía.	
JOSÉ	¿Por mí el Rey?	
COPERO	Sí.	
JOSÉ	¿Cómo?	
COPERO	Escucha.	
	Soñó° el Rey... Pero mejor	dreamed
880	el camino lo descubra.[128]	
	No perdamos tiempo. Ven	
	donde te aguarda.° (*Vase*)	awaits
JOSÉ	Fortuna,[129]	
	no sea esto ilusión también.	
	Mira si de mí te burlas,	
885	que para ilusión es poca	
	y para verdad es mucha.	

*Vase, y sale por una parte Asenet,[130] dama, y todos (músicos, hombres
y mujeres) con ella, y empezando a cantar, sale el Rey por
otra parte, paseándose, suspenso.[131]*

ASENET	*¿Quién es aquel que, cabiendo°*	fitting
	en corta,° abreviada° esfera,	small, reduced
	quiere que quepa° en él todo	[from caber]
890	*el ámbito° de la tierra?*	circumference
MÚSICA	*¿Y no por eso deja°*	ceases

---

127 Everything in the play up to now that concerns the Biblical characters has followed the account in Genesis very closely. However, Genesis 40:23 is very clear about the fact that after promising to remember José, the Copero forgot him.

128 **Pero mejor...***It might be better if I just tell you along the way*

129 José speaks directly to his "fortuna" in an apostrophe, still uncertain whether good fortune or ill fortune awaits him.

130 Remember that the part of Asenet is being played by Castidad.

131 **paseándose, suspenso** *pacing, lost in thought*

	de haber lugar en que caber la queja?	
DAMA 1	*El humano corazón,*	
	que vive en cárcel estrecha°	narrow
895	*y el mayor° reino,° por más*	greatest, kingdom
	que le ocupe, no le llena.	
	Y no por eso deja	
	de haber lugar en que caber la queja.	
DAMA 2	*El gran Faraón° de Egipto*	Pharaoh
900	*lo diga, puesto que reina*	
	en cuantos cotos° el Nilo	territories
	baña, fertiliza y riega.°	irrigates
MÚSICA	*Y no por eso deja*	
	de haber lugar en qué caber la queja.	
905	REY Suspended,° suspended de vuestras voces	stop
	los ecos, que aunque dulces y veloces	
	pueblan° el aire en métrica armonía,	populate
	no son remedio° a la tristeza mía.[132]	remedy
ASENET	Viendo, señor, que todos	
910	cuantos te aclaman solicitan° modos°	seek out, measures
	contra esa melancólica tristeza,	
	el coro°—cuya `métrica destreza°	chorus, poetic skill
	al Templo° de Heliópoli servía	temple
	cuando su sacerdote me vivía,	
915	mi padre y yo en él° era	[el templo]
	de sus sacerdotisas° la primera—	priestesses
	de tonos e instrumentos prevenida,	
	quise hoy `tenerte al paso°	stop your pacing
	por si lograse, acaso,°	by chance
920	la dicha yo de haberte divertido.[133]	
REY	¡Ay, hermosa Asenet! En vano ha sido,	
	que aunque yo la fineza° te agradezco,	show of concern
	la pena que padezco°	I suffer
	es tal que, porque° más su dolor sienta,	[para que]

---

132   The mysterious melancholy of the king is a feature of a number of *autos sacramentales* by Calderón, such as *La cena del rey Baltasar*.

133   This is a wildly complicated sentence in which we learn three things. First, Asenet's father was priest of the temple, but he is dead. Second, Asenet was herself a priestess in the temple. Third, she has brought a choir to entertain the melancholy king.

925 lo mismo que la alivia, la acrecienta.[134]
Y hasta saber qué es lo que quiso el cielo
en mis sueños decir, no habrá consuelo
para mí. Y ya es en vano el esperalle,°   [esperarle]
puesto que no es posible que le halle
930 el número infinito
de tantos `sabios mágicos° de Egipto,   wise sorcerers
pues ninguno me quieta° mi deseo.   calms

Salen Copero y José.

COPERO Este es José, aquel esclavo hebreo
que te dije que había interpretado
el sueño de los dos.[135]
935 JOSÉ   Y el que postrado°   kneeling
logra primero y último consuelo
hoy a tus reales° pies.   royal
REY   Alza° del suelo.   arise
JOSÉ (*Ap.*) ¡Cielos! ¿Qué es lo que miro?[136] ¿No es aquella
la divina beldad que vi, sin vella?
REY ¿De dónde eres?
940 JOSÉ   De tierra
de Canaán.
REY Pues no habiendo habido guerra
en tu edad entre hebreos y gitanos,[137]
¿a dónde cautivaste°?   become a prisoner
JOSÉ   (*Ap.*) (Tan tiranos
mis casos son, que con contarlos muero
945 por no infamar° las cosas que más quiero.)   defame
(*Al Rey*) Quien pudo me vendió, ismaelitas[138] fueron,

---

134 **lo mismo que...**the same thing that alleviates this pain, intensifies it

135 **los dos** the Copero and the Panadero

136 **vella** verla (ver + la) Asenet is seeing José for the first time, but he mistakenly thinks he has seen her before. Castidad appeared to him in the form of Asenet in in verses 726-732. Compare this to Eraclio's reaction to Federico in *En la vida...* (3601-3607).

137 "Gitano" often meant "Egyptian" during the seventeenth century.

138 **ismaelitas** *Arabs (literally, the descendants of Ishmael)* José is technically telling the truth, his brothers sold him to "Ishmaelites" who brought José to Egypt to be a slave. See Genesis 37.

	señor, los que mi compra y venta hicieron.	
REY	¿Y por qué estabas preso	
	despúes de ser esclavo?	
JOSÉ	Menos eso	
950	puedo decir, muriendo consolado	
	de padecer sin culpa ni culpado	
	al precio de que quede de mí honrada	
	una mujer con culpa y disculpada.[139]	
	Y pues mi propia pena	
955	no he de honestar a costa de honra ajena,[140]	
	y nada te ha importado	
	que otro sea ruin° para que yo sea honrado,	vile
	de mí te sirve en esta corta esfera	
	en cuanto Dios iluminarme quiera.	
960 ASENET	¡Qué `cuerdamente atento°	wisely courteous
	calló el cómplice° y dijo el sentimiento!	guilty party
REY	Aunque a lo que has venido	
	no dudo que lo traigas ya sabido,	
	con todo, he de decirlo, por si acaso	
965	no lo contaron bien. Este es el caso:	
	Yo soñé[141] que de un río a la ribera°	shore
	siete vacas bellísimas salían,	
	y cuando de sus márgenes° pacían°	riverside, grazed
	las `esmeraldas de la primavera,°	green plants
970	vi que otras siete° de la `undosa esfera,°	[vacas], water

---

139 This is a reference to how José ended up in jail. Potiphar's wife tried to seduce José. José—very chastely—resisted. So she accused *José* of trying to seduce *her*. What José says here is that Potiphar's wife is guilty of bearing false witness against him (this is her "culpa"), but thanks to José, she is not guilty of adultery (so she is "disculpada"). However, he does so without revealing her identity. This episode is key to understanding why José is so closely associated with chastity, as well as discretion.

140 **mi propia pena...***I don't have to defend my honor by dishonoring someone else*

141 This verse begins a pair of sonnets. The king recounts his two dreams (one about "vacas" and the other about "espigas") in the first sonnet, which is based on Genesis 41. This sonnet uses highly conventional poetic images such as "esmeraldas de la primavera" (springtime emeralds) for plants. José answers with a sonnet that is not quite so weighed down with familiar images, but he interprets the king's dream precisely in terms of its conventionality: "el río jeroglífico ha sido / del tiempo" (980-981). The explanation that José gives here regarding *how* he interpreted the dream is very different than how the Biblical Joseph explains his thinking in Genesis 41. In the Bible, Joseph says that it is the doubling of the dream (the fact that Pharaoh has two related dreams) that is the key to the interpretation.

	tan flacas° que esqueletos parecían,	skinny
	saliendo contra ellas,° consumían	[bellísimas vacas]
	la lozanía° de su edad primera.	freshness
	Después vi siete fértiles espigas,°	stalks of grain
975	lágrima cada grano del rocío,[142]	
	y otras siete,° que en áridas fatigas°	[espigas], labors
	sin granarlas abril, taló el estío,[143]	
	y lidiando° unas y otras enemigas,	fighting
	venció lo seco con llevarlo el río.	
JOSÉ	Que el río jeroglífico[144] haya sido	
	del tiempo, gran señor, prueba° es bastante,	evidence
	que siempre corre y siempre va adelante,	
	sin que nunca haya atrás retrocedido.°	gone backward
	Luego° es el tiempo de quien ha nacido	therefore
985	en espigas y vacas lo abundante,	
	y es el tiempo también el que, inconstante,°	fickle
	todo lo deja a nada reducido.	
	Siete fértiles años imagina	
	en espigas y vacas, cuyo halago°	pleasure
990	en `otros siete estériles° termina,	seven sterile years
	y pues te avisa el golpe en el amago,[145]	
	la abundancia prevén contra la ruina	
	y la felicidad contra el estrago.[146]	
REY	Dame los brazos, que nadie	
995	de cuantos en esto hablaron	
	quietaron mi corazón	
	sino tú. Dame los brazos,	
	digo otra vez, y pues habla,	

---

142   **lágrima cada...***dripping with dew*

143   **sin granarlas...***without forming grains (on the stalks) in April, summer cut them down* The image is of dry stalks of wheat that never had a chance to grow strong before summer heat mowed down the crop. These are the dry ears of wheat that fight against the fertile ears.

144   It was common during the seventeenth century to use "jeroglífico" to refer broadly to visual symbols. So although the context here is specifically Egyptian, audiences would have understood the word to mean something like "emblem" or "symbol." What the king says, in effect, is that "río" is a well-known symbol for "tiempo." José's explanation of the dream is characterized as a logical explanation of the symbols it contains.

145   **te avisa...***the sign (your dream) warns you of the blow (or the coming difficulty)*

146   **la abundancia...***use abundance to avert disaster and ruin, use happy times to prepare for havoc*

según el sumo descanso
1000 que en mí introducen tus voces,
en ti, tu Dios, y veo cuánto
tu infusa divina ciencia[147]
excede a todos los sabios°   wise men
que tiene Egipto, has de ser,
1005 ya que preveniste° el daño,   you prevented
el que el remedio prevenga,[148]
para cuyo efecto mando
que a tu obediencia estén todos,
desde el más noble vasallo°   vassal
1010 al más humilde, porque
no esté el puesto° desairado°   job, snubbed
sin autoridad,[149] que el lustre°   luster
hace respetuoso al cargo:°   position
comprometiéndome° en ti,   committing myself
1015 virrey[150] de Egipto te hago,
de mi púrpura[151] te viste,
toma mi anillo, y en tanto
que, con mi collar al cuello,
en el más triunfante carro
1020 salgas en público, donde
cuantos te encuentren al paso
`doblen la rodilla,° ven   kneel
ahora a mi diestro° lado,   right-hand
y venid delante todos,
1025 dándole común aplauso.
Unos   ¡Viva José!
Otros   ¡José viva!
Rey   Oíd, escuchad, qué extraño
ese nombre a nuestro idioma,

---

147 **tu infusa...**_your divinely inspired knowledge_

148 **has de ser...**_you must be, because you averted harm (through the interpretation of the dream), the one who implements the remedy (by implementing my plan)_

149 **porque no esté...**_so that no one disregards or snubs the authority of this position_

150 **virrey** _viceroy_ A viceroy is to the king as a vice-president is to the president: second in command.

151 Purple was a color reserved for royalty.

		y pues traducirse es claro	
1030		en la siríaca[152] lengua	
		José, "Salvador,°" en altos	Savior
		ecos: "¡Viva el Salvador!"	
		decid, pues viene a salvarnos	
		el amenazado° riesgo°	threatened, risk
1035		a que fuimos condenados.°	condemned
	TODOS	¡Viva el Salvador de Egipto![153]	
	JOSÉ	¿Quién creerá, oh piadosos astros,°	stars
		que sean otros los que duermen	
		y sea yo el que estoy soñando?	
1040	REY	Tú, bellísima Asenet,	
		pues preveniste,° no acaso,°	prepared, by chance
		tus coros para otro efecto,	
		mejore asumptos° el canto[154]	[asuntos], subjects
		en su alabanza.°	praise
	ASENET	Sí hará,	
1045		que aunque no me debió agrado	
		ningún hombre[155] hasta hoy y fue	
		siempre mi ceño° su agravio,°	glare, insult
		no sé qué tiene este joven,	
		que sin violencia el recato°	modesty
1050		me inclina a su obsequio,° ella	deference
		sin duda fue, con que en cuantos	
		milagros viendo estoy, es	
		éste el más bello milagro.	
	REY	¿Qué esperáis? Todos venid.	

---

152 **siríaca** *Syriac* This is another word for the Aramaic language, spoken in Syria and the Middle East. It was common in Calderón's lifetime to say that ancient Egyptians spoke Syriac or Chaldean. McGaha points out in his critical edition that "Salvador" is not an accurate translation of "José."

153 The king describes José in terms often associated with Jesus: as a savior come to rescue humankind from damnation. While Christians have always understood Jesus' ministry as a fulfillment of Old Testament prophecy, during the seventeenth century it was very common to interpret almost *all* of the Old Testament (and not just the prophesies) as a symbolic foreshadowing of the coming of Christ. This kind of Biblical interpretation or allegorical reading (seeing the stories of the Old Testament as foreshadowing of the New Testament) is called typological interpretation.

154 **mejore asumptos...**(*que*) *el canto mejore asuntos en su alabanza* Pharaoh requests that the song be turned to the praises of José.

155 **no me debió...**_no man has pleased me (caught my eye)_

1055		Decid conmigo, cantando:
		Puesto que ser salvador...
	MÚSICA	*Puesto que ser salvador...*
	REY	*...de Egipto, José previene,...*
	MÚSICA	*...de Egipto, José previene,...*
1060	REY	*...diga el popular clamor...*
	MÚSICA	*...diga el popular clamor...*
	REY	*...bendito° sea el que viene*
		en el nombre del Señor.[156]
	MÚSICA	*...bendito sea el que viene*
1065		*en el nombre del Señor.*[157]

	REY	Pues de sus \`iras esquivas°	unpredictable rage
		por él° nos rescata° el cielo,	[José], rescues
		aclamaciones° festivas°	applause, festive
		echen las capas al suelo,[158]	
1070		y de palmas y de olivas[159]	
		corone° el fértil verdor°	crown, green
		sus sienes,° que bien conviene	temples (head)
		decir todos en su loor:°	praise
	TODOS y	*Bendito sea el que viene*	
1075	MÚSICA	*en el nombre del Señor.*	

*Éntranse todos, llevándose al Rey en medio José y Asenet, y todos echan
los mantos en el suelo al pasar, y sale por otra parte el Sueño.*

	SUEÑO	¿Bendito sea el que viene
		en el nombre del Señor?
		No en vano aquella divina
		hermosa virtud,° que tanto [Castidad]

---

156 This verse—"Blessed is he who comes in the name of the Lord"— appears in the Old Testament (Psalm 118), the New Testament (Luke 13) and the Sanctus, or prayer of consecration spoken or sung during Mass. This is indicative of Calderón's carefully stitching together of the Old and New Testaments and the Eucharist (the bread and wine that become the body and blood of Christ).

157 This verse, like a number of sung verses, is not present in Pando y Mier's edition, the text simply indicates that the musicians would repeat the king's song: "Bendito sea, &c." (290). We have followed McGaha's edition here (verses 1056-1075) and below (e.g. verse 1248).

158 **echen las...**Capes, or other articles of clothing, would be spread out so that José's feet would not touch the ground.

159 **palmas...**palm and olive branches

1080 le favorece, me dijo
que, sus acciones notando,
vería en él lejanas° luces   distant
de asuntos que hoy embozado°   hidden
hasta destinado tiempo,
1085 anda en sombras, y no en vano
yo la obedecí. Mas ¿qué
logro, consigo,° ni alcanzo,[160]   [from conseguir]
si no alcanzo ni consigo,
ni logro, por más que hago
1090 en su favor, luz ni seña°   sign
de aquel inmenso, aquel alto
sacramento[161] que me dijo
que de todo este aparato°   earthly world
había de ser cumplimiento?°   fulfillment
1095 Y así, he de apurar si salgo
de esta duda. Nueva hermosa
deidad,[162] que excedes al ampo°   snowflake
de la nieve en la pureza,
pues yo acudí° a tu mandato,   heeded
1100 acude° a mi ruego tú.   come
Vuelve, vuelve al soberano°   supreme
disfraz,° que en forma visible   disguise
quiso hacer a los teatros
del mundo representable
1105 tu amor y mi desagravio.[163]

Sale la Castidad.

CASTIDAD ¿Qué es lo que me quieres?
SUEÑO Que veas que arguye° a contrario   indicates

---

160 **¿qué logro…** *what do I accomplish, achieve, reach….?*

161 Because this play was staged for Corpus Christi, the Feast of the Eucharist, audiences would have understood that the sacrament referred to was the Eucharist. Sueño mentions one of the central mysteries of the Eucharist in Roman Catholic teaching: that Christ's body is fully present in the consecrated bread of Communion (the Host) although human beings cannot perceive Christ's presence.

162 Sueño begins addressing Castidad, calling on her to appear.

163 **mi desagravio** *my making amends (or restitution)*

	mi advocación° a la tuya.	request
CASTIDAD	¿Cómo?	
SUEÑO	Como si guiaron	
1110	tus voces a un calabozo,	
	las mías guían a un palacio.[164]	
	Tú me llevaste a que viese	
	ansias, penas y trabajos,	
	y yo a que veas trofeos,	
1115	dichas y glorias te traigo.	

Chirimías y atabalillos.[165]

VOCES	(*Dentro*) ¡El gran Salvador de Egipto viva!	
SUEÑO	Mira en triunfal carro[166]	
	cómo salvador le aclama	
	el pueblo, y cómo los varios	
1120	males que causaron sueños	
	`en términos° satisfago[167]	bit by bit
	con las ventajas° que hay	advantages
	desde el baldón° al aplauso,	insult
	desde la miseria al triunfo,	
1125	y desde la ruina al lauro.°	victory
	Y pues que ya obedecida	
	de mí te miras, en cuanto	
	a causa segunda[168]—puesto	
	que es de la primera el mando°—	command
1130	en premio de mi obediencia,	

---

164   At the beginning of the play Castidad led Sueño into the prison where José was being held. Now Sueño leads Castidad into a palace.

165   **Chirimías...***Clarinets and small kettle drums* "Chirimías" are similar to clarinets in appearance, but are actually double-reed woodwinds, called shawms in English.

166   **triunfal carro** *grand chariot or open carriage* In some Corpus Christi celebrations there were "carros triunfales," somewhat like parade floats, that were used in processions.

167   **satisfago** *make restitution, repay the debt* It was José's interpretation of dreams that got him in trouble in the first place.

168   Once again, Calderón adapts the notion of God as first cause or cause of all other causes. Castidad is not God, but as a divine virtue she embodies a quality that exists perfectly in God. She is described in 1129 as first cause and sets things in motion, Sueño— the "causa segunda"—is subject to Castidad's influence. See also verses 277-238.

	salir de una duda aguardo.	
	Tú me dijiste que anda	
	en estos visibles rasgos	
	de embozo° un misterio, que es	disguise
1135	milagro de los milagros,[169]	
	y así, humilde te suplico	
	me le adelantes° en algo	inform
	que pueda ser de mi duda	
	arrimo,° si no descanso.	small comfort
1140	CASTIDAD Sí haré, mas con una salva.°	condition
	SUEÑO ¿Qué es?	
	CASTIDAD Que los dos parezcamos	
	lo que somos, esto es,	
	como personas tratarnos	
	alegóricas y no	
1145	reales.[170] Pues con eso es llano	
	que no habiendo en los dos tiempo	
	ni lugar,[171] daremos paso	
	a que la interpolación[172]	
	—como si acabara un acto	
1150	y empezara otro—nos supla°	make up for
	la síncopa° de los años,	abridgment
	dando por vividos siete	
	fértiles,[173] con que empezando	
	los estériles, verás	
1155	en el pósito o erario[174]	
	del trigo, que ha recogido°	harvested

---

169   Sueño refers to Castidad's lines in 341-352.

170   That is, Castidad will stop appearing in the form of Asenet and will appear as simply the embodiment of chastity.

171   As allegorical concepts, Sueño and Castidad occupy neither time nor space.

172   **interpolación** *the insertion of something new or extraneous* A later chapter in José's life will be inserted into the story now.

173   **dando por...***declaring the fertile years already lived (or passed)* We now leap ahead in time. The seven years of abundance that the king dreamed of have passed and the seven lean years have begun. Genesis chapters 41 and 42 narrate the events much the same way: skipping over the years of plenty and going directly to the years of famine. Compare "síncopa de los años" (1151) to the way *En la vida...* condenses a year into a day or a few hours—"síncopa de un año" (3044)—thanks to Lisipo's magic.

174   **pósito...***the public granary or bank where grain would be stored*

		de la abundancia el espacio,°	7 plentiful years
		cómo le reparte° a pobres	distribute
		y ricos, no exceptuando	
		personas.	
1160	SUEÑO	Eso deseo.	
	CASTIDAD	Pues ven conmigo a lo alto	
		del Monte de la Visión,	
		`patrimonio hereditario°	inheritance
		de José, pues si en él fue	
1165		Isaac, su abuelo, retrato°	portrait
		de quien también él lo ha sido,	
		justo es que convenga en ambos[175]	
		el mirar desde su cumbre°	peak
		cómo se pueblan los campos	
1170		de racionales hormigas°	ants
		que próvidas,° tras el rastro°	diligent, trail
		de la paja° que se lleva	straw
		el Nilo,° buscan el grano,°	Nile River, grain
		en cuya distribución	
1175		verás que hasta a sus hermanos	
		socorre,° sin acordarse	helps
		de que le fueron ingratos,°	ungrateful
		pues subiendo de Canaán	
		a Egipto... Mas, no perdamos	
		tiempo. Ven conmigo. (*Vase*)	
1180	SUEÑO	Ya	
		me parece que mirando	
		estoy, que en su busca llegan	
		diciendo...[176]	

Vase el Sueño, y salen Rubén, Judas, Isacar, Zabulón, Gad,
Aser, Neftalí, Manasés, Simeón y Leví, de pastores.[177]

| | RUBÉN | Pues ya miramos | |
| | | desde aquí las altas torres | |

---

175 **convenga...***it is important to both José and his grandfather Isaac*
176 Sueño perceives or makes out the brothers from afar and seems to hear them speaking.
177 **de pastores** *dressed as shepherds*

<table>
<tr><td>1185</td><td></td><td>del suntuoso° palacio</td><td>luxurious</td></tr>
<tr><td></td><td></td><td>del gobernador de Egipto,</td><td></td></tr>
<tr><td></td><td></td><td>lleguemos a él, confiados</td><td></td></tr>
<tr><td></td><td></td><td>en que su gran providencia[178]</td><td></td></tr>
<tr><td></td><td></td><td>no dejará, por extraños,°</td><td>foreigners</td></tr>
<tr><td>1190</td><td></td><td>de socorrernos, supuesto</td><td></td></tr>
<tr><td></td><td></td><td>que a todos socorre.</td><td></td></tr>
</table>

JUDAS   Es tanto,
según dicen, liberal,°   *generous*
piadoso, apacible° y blando°   *serene*
que lo será con nosotros.

1195   ISACAR   Pues a buen tiempo llegamos.

ZABULÓN   ¿Cómo?

NEFTALÍ   Como me parece,
según el séquito° y fausto°   *entourage, pomp*
que le acompaña, que es él
el que sale.

MANASÉS   No es engaño,
1200   pues lo asegura el que todos
a él se arrodillan.°   *kneel*

SIMEÓN   Hagamos
nosotros lo mesmo.

LEVÍ   Y sea,
porque se mueva a escucharnos,
hablándole `a nuestro modo°   *in our language*
1205   desde luego, con el canto
de que usan nuestros mendigos.°   *beggars*

GAD   Si lo somos,° pues llegamos   *[somos mendigos]*
limosna° a pedir, ¿qué haremos   *charity*
en parecerlo?

ASER   Postrados
le esperemos.

1210   RUBÉN   Va de voces,
que mezclen música y llanto.°   *cries*

---

178 **providencia** *preparation for the future or readiness to provide*

Salen José y el Copero. Unos hermanos de José representan[179]
y otros hermanos cantan.

UNOS Ya que del cielo el favor
   para consuelo te envía,
   con nombre de Salvador.

1215 OTROS *El pan nuestro de cada día,*
   dánosle hoy, señor.[180]

  JOSÉ (*Ap.*) (Este tono y este idioma,
   ¿no es hebreo? ¡Cielos santos!
   ¿Aquí hebreo idioma y tono?

1220   Mas ya lo que estoy mirando
   vence° a lo que vine oyendo.   trumps
   ¿No son estos mis hermanos?
   No con poca admiración
   de oírlos y verlos me espanto.

1225   Pero infórmense mejor
   oídos y ojos.)

 UNOS   La agonía
   nuestra goce tu favor.

  OTROS *El pan nuestro de cada día,*
   dánosle hoy, señor.

1230 JOSÉ (*Ap.*) (Ellos son, con que ya el cielo
   el primer sueño ha explicado,
   de que habían de adorar
   sus haces al mío. ¡Oh presagio°   prophecy
   inescrutable,° que el trigo   indecipherable

1235   aquí y allá, todo es pasmo!
   Pues ellos no me conocen.
   ¿Qué mucho, si es el estado
   mío feliz? Disimule,
   mas, ¿cómo he de poder, cuando

1240   me están instando° alma y vida   prompting
   a que `me arroje° a abrazarlos?   throw myself
   Mayormente,° cuando escucho   even more so

---

179 **representan** *speaking* (as opposed to singing)

180 This is an allusion to the Lord's Prayer: "Give us this day our daily bread." The passage is found in the New Testament (Matthew 6 and Luke 11).

	que me dice su quebranto°	distress
	en el mísero clamor	
1245	con que moverme porfía,°	persevere
	procurando° mi favor.)	trying to gain
Todos	*El pan nuestro de cada día,*	
	dánosle hoy, señor.	
José	A pesar del corazón	
1250	—que por salir a los labios[181]	
	me está latiendo° en el pecho,	beating
	aun más que a golpes,° a saltos°—	thumps, jumps
	disimular me conviene	
	hasta saber más despacio	
1255	—sin saber que hablan conmigo—	
	de mi padre y de mi amado	
	Benjamín. `No sea° que haya	may it not be
	mis desdichas heredado,°	inherited
	que es el aborrecimiento	
1260	infelice mayorazgo°	estate, legacy
	con herederos forzosos.°	unwilling
	(*A todos*) ¡Alzaos[182] de la tierra! Alzaos,	
	y decid quién sois, de dónde	
	venís y a qué.	
Rubén	Soberano	
1265	príncipe de Egipto, a quien	
	puso el cielo en este cargo	
	para redentor,° no sólo	savior
	suyo,° mas también de cuantos	[de Egipto]
	convecinos° reinos vienen	neighboring
1270	tu providencia buscando:	
	hebreos somos de nación,	
	aunque hoy en tierra habitamos	
	de Canaán, desde que Dios	
	mandó por sus juicios altos	
1275	a nuestro abuelo Abrahán	
	que, casa y patria dejando,	

---

181 José longs to speak aloud what he feels in his heart.

182 "Alzaos" (or "alzad" + "os") is the *vosotros* command of "alzar," to rise. As with many *vosotros* commands, the "d" in "alzad" is not pronounced.

	a peregrinar° saliese,	wander
	huyendo los simulacros°	statues
	idólatras° de Caldea.	pagan
1280	Pero esto aquí no es del caso.[183]	
	La grande esterilidad°	sterility
	que ha que padecen siete años	
	estos orientales climas,[184]	
	a tanto extremo ha llegado	
1285	en Canaán que hoja ni flor,	
	hierba ni planta ha quedado	
	que arista° no sea o espina.°	stubble, thorn
	Fuentes° y arroyos° negaron	sources, streams
	manantiales° y corrientes,°	springs, currents
1290	con tal sequedad° avaros°	dryness, miserly
	que aun mueren de sed los ríos,	
	y de hambre y sed los ganados,°	livestock
	pues en la más fértil dehesa,°	pasture
	y en el más puro remanso,°	pool of water
1295	al triste, inútil° y estéril	useless
	malogro° de siete años,	crop failure
	hallan catorce febreros,	
	sin ver en balsa° ni prado°	pond, meadow
	más que guijas° por bebida,	pebbles
1300	ni más que terrón° por pasto.°	lumps of earth, feed
	Pero, qué mucho, señor,	
	si al inclemente fracaso°	failure
	perecen las gentes, siendo	
	solo consuelo en su estrago	
1305	ver que, abierta en duras grietas,°	cracks
	la tierra está bostezando°	gaping
	horrores, como quien dice.[185]	

---

183   **Pero esto...***But that's neither here nor there* Rubén realizes that he has just inadvertently insulted the Egyptian religion while asking for help from Egyptians.

184   **que ha que...***ha (hace) siete años que padecen estos orientales climas*

185   **bostezando horrores...**This is an obscure reference, perhaps to Gabriel del Corral's *comedia* entitled *Dos flechas a un corazón*. The passage from Corral's play that uses the phrase "bostezando horrores" is:

El bruto entonces bostezando horrores,

Piedad es que, si el poblado
todo es cadáveres, sea
1310   todo sepulcros° el campo.   graves
Bien pudiéramos nosotros,
pues jóvenes nos hallamos,
peregrinar a otras tierras,
pero tenemos un lazo°   tether
1315   tan estrecho° que nos tiene   tight
atados de pies y manos.
Hermanos somos los diez,
y un venerable, un anciano
padre que no ha de seguirnos
1320   —que pesan mucho los años—
nos detiene, y nos obliga
a que para él vengamos
—aun más que para nosotros—
el trigo, señor, buscando.
1325   Que quisiere concedernos
tu piedad, para pagarlo
traemos dineros. Y pues
cuando está el cielo cerrado,
en tu mano ha puesto Dios
1330   la llave de sus candados,°   locks
no por nosotros, por nuestro
viejo padre...

                    José 'vuelve la espalda.°   turns his back

                    ¡Ay de mí! Cuando
más pensaba enternecerte,°   move you to pity
¿vuelves la espalda, mostrando
que `no me atiendes?°   not listening to me
1335   UNOS   ¡Señor!
OTROS   ¡Señor!

---

marchitando la yerba con espuma,
degollando las flores, dando en suma
con pestífero aliento
denso veneno al viento.

JOSÉ   (*Ap.*) (Ellos han pensado
que es sequedad° y es terneza,   lack of emotion
que es descariño° y es llanto.   disregard
Pero cobrarme° me importa,   pull myself together
1340   hasta ver si es fino o falso
este afecto, y el contraste
ha de ser mi desagrado.°)   displeasure
(*A todos*) ¿Hermanos sois?

TODOS   Sí, señor.

JOSÉ   ¡Lucida° tropa de hermanos!   splendid
Y ¿fuisteis más?

1345   RUBÉN   Otros dos.°   [dos hermanos]

JOSÉ   ¿Pues cómo allá se quedaron,
y no vienen con vosotros?

RUBÉN   Como el uno murió a manos
de una fiera.

JOSÉ   Bien. ¿Y el otro?

1350   RUBÉN   Le excusan sus pocos años
de caminos.

JOSÉ   (*Ap.*) (¡Oh, no sea
que le hayan muerto!) (*A todos*) Ahora acabo
de saber que sois espías,
y que venís a engañarnos°   deceive us
1355   con los pretextos° del trigo,   ploy
para saber de este estado°   country
las defensas, por el odio
que siempre con los gitanos
tenéis los hebreos, y hacernos
1360   guerra después. (*Ap.*) (Esto hago,
no viniendo Benjamín,
por el temor que me ha dado
que, por hijo de Raquel,
de él no hayan hecho otro tanto
como de mí.[186])

1365   TODOS   No presumas,
señor, que...

JOSÉ   Basta, que en vano

---

186   **de él no hayan...***that they haven't done to Benjamín something like what they did to me*

es persuadirme a que crea
que no es traidor° vuestro trato,°   *traitorous, dealings*
y mientras no me traigáis
1370   a esotro° menor hermano,   *[ese otro]*
a que yo vivo le vea,
ningún crédito° he de daros,   *credibility*
sino en vez... (*Ap.*) (¿Quién vio jamás
dos afectos° tan contrarios   *emotions*
1375   como severo° el amor   *harsh*
y enternecido el agravio?)
(*A todos*) ...sino en vez de hallar en mí
piedad, que todos hallaron,
castigo hallaréis.

TODOS   ¿Qué es esto?[187]

1380   RUBÉN   ¿Qué ha de ser? Es que pagamos
de un hermano en el amor
el odio del otro.

JUDAS   Es claro.

GAD   En términos nos castiga
el cielo.

JOSÉ   ¿Qué estáis hablando
1385   entre vosotros? ¿Es `veros
convencidos?°   *confess your guilt*

RUBÉN   Lo que hablamos
no es, señor, sino pensar
que si por Benjamín vamos
(que éste es del muchacho el nombre),
1390   será `arrancarle un pedazo°   *tear out a piece*
del corazón al buen viejo.°   *[Jacob]*

JUDAS   Y quizá su amor fiarlo°   *entrust him*
de nosotros no querrá.

JOSÉ   ¿Por qué, siendo sus hermanos?
1395   ¿Habéis de echarle en un pozo,°   *pit*
o venderle a los extraños,
o darle a las fieras?

RUBÉN   (*A sus hermanos*) ¿Qué hombre
es éste, que penetrando

---

187   The brothers begin to speak among themselves.

está nuestros corazones?

1400   TODOS   (*Ap.*) (Si nuestra culpa acordamos,
justamente padecemos.[188])

JOSÉ   (*Ap.*) (El ver que lo estén rehusando°   refusing
me ha puesto en mayor sospecha.)
(*A sus hermanos*) En efecto, ese muchacho°   [Benjamín]

1405   ha de venir a mis ojos,
o a todos diez he de daros,
por exploradores,° muerte.   spies
Y para que veáis que parto°   I divide
términos entre justicia

1410   y piedad, he de entregaros°   present you
el trigo que me pedís,
sólo con que por resguardo°   guarantee
de que volveréis con él,
quede preso y aherrojado°   in chains
uno de vosotros.

1415   RUBÉN   Puesto
que fuerza es que obedezcamos,
mirad cuál queréis que quede.

JOSÉ   (*Ap.*) Simeón fue el que más tirano
en mi venta se mostró,

1420   no es venganza sino halago
el darle con que merezca,
para que pueda, purgando°   atoning
más quien más pecó, alcanzar
el perdón de su pecado.°   sin

TODOS   A todos mira.

1425   JOSÉ   A éste elijo.

Señala° a Simeón   points, indicates

SIMEÓN   ¡Ay de mí!

RUBÉN   (*Ap.*) 'Como pecamos,°   as we sinned
padecemos. Simeón fue
el que primero la mano

---

188 **Si nuestra...***We all agree that we're guilty, and we deserve to suffer for what we did*

		puso en él,[189] y así el primero	
1430		padece el primero daño.	
	JOSÉ	Siquén.	
	COPERO	Señor.	
	JOSÉ	Ve con ellos,	
		y di que yo darles mando[190]	
		todo el trigo que pidieren,°	they might ask for
		y al que ves que yo he nombrado	
1435		para que se quede en prendas,[191]	
		lleva a una prisión.	
	RUBÉN	Postrados	
		a tus pies, señor, verás	
		que obedecemos con tanto	
		afecto que haya quien culpe	
1440		más la priesa° con que vamos	[prisa]
		y volvemos, que pudiera	
		la tardanza, no mirando	
		que aquí es preciso lo presto,°	speed
		y fuera culpa lo tardo.° (*Vanse*)	tardiness
	COPERO	Venid, pues.	
	JOSÉ	Siquén.	
1445	COPERO	Señor.	
	JOSÉ	En habiendo ellos pagado	
		el trigo, harás que les pongan	
		en las bocas de los sacos	
		el dinero a cada uno	
1450		que diere.[192] Y luego en llevando	
		a la prisión al que elijo,	
		haz que no como a ordinario	
		preso le traten y ya	
		que no sea con regalo,°	comfort

---

189 Rubén is thinking back to the terrible way they treated José, but he still does not recognize José.

190 **yo darles...***yo les mando dar (I command they be given)*

191 **se quede...**This is an idiomatic use of the phrase "en prendas." It means "remain as a deposit," but essentially Simeón is a hostage. Pando y Mier's edition uses "en rehenes" (as a hostage) instead of "en prendas."

192 The money with which they bought the grain will be returned to them in secret.

1455	sea con estimación.°	respect
	Copero En todo servirte aguardo. (*Vase*)	
	José ¿Cómo es posible, ¡ay amor!,	
	que haya yo podido tanto	
	conmigo,[193] que haya podido	
1460	no admitirlos en mis brazos?	
	Mas, hasta saber si es cierto	
	que a Benjamín no ha alcanzado	
	su rencor°... Pero esto quede	hatred
	suspenso° por este rato,	paused
1465	que Asenet, deidad hermosa,[194]	
	a quien debí el agasajo,°	honor
	sin saber cómo, de aquel	
	delirio, éxtasis o rapto,°	rapture
	si no me engaña el deseo,	
1470	que para hablarla obligado°	grateful
	otra ocasión no he tenido,	
	entrando viene en palacio.	

Sale Asenet.

	Asenet Quedaos todos.[195] (*Ap.*) De esta vez	
	he de hablar al Rey tan claro	
1475	que sepa si de mi padre...	
	Mas, ¿quién es quien está al paso?	
	José `Quien viéndoos,° divina aurora	He who, seeing you
	del sol que buscando vais,	
	teme que os desvanezcáis,[196]	
1480	como otras veces, ahora.	
	Y así, os suplico, señora,	
	no en esta ocasión paséis	

---

193 **que haya...***that I've been able to control myself*
194 José only refers figuratively to Asenet as a deity.
195 She commands her entourage offstage to remain where they are.
196 Asenet is looking for the king. José describes Asenet as the "aurora" or dawn searching for the sun. However, dawn and the sun are never fully present together, when the sun rises, dawn disappears. So José is he who fears (teme) that dawn will dissipate (desvanecer) or disappear, just as Castidad in the form of Asenet disappeared in 732.

tan veloz `como soléis.°   as you tend to
Ved que es piadoso rigor
1485   el que, si hacéis un favor,
con iros° le° deshacéis.¹⁹⁷   leaving, [el favor]
ASENET   Si yo, José, entendiera
lo que me decís, bien creo
que a vuestro cortés deseo
1490   cortés agrado siguiera,
pero extraño de manera
la voz "favor" en el labio
de un hombre tan cuerdo y sabio,
que me hace el sonido horror.
1495   ¿Qué quiere decir "favor"?
Que me suena como agravio...
JOSÉ   Si es dejaros ver y no
dejaros agradecer,¹⁹⁸
querer ser noble y querer
1500   que no lo parezca yo,
y si es que a lo que os debió
el alma no ha respondido,¹⁹⁹
es que ocasión° no he tenido,   opportunity
y así, achacad lo tardado
1505   a culpa de desdichado,
no de desagradecido.²⁰⁰
ASENET   Pues, ¿cuándo me dejé ver
yo de vos, ni cuándo yo
con vos hice acción que no
1510   pudisteis agradecer?
JOSÉ   Cuando al verme padecer
una duda que tenía,
que juzgase que la veía,

---

197   **es piadoso rigor...***you are cruel to do a favor and then undo it by leaving*

198   **dejaros ver...***allow yourself to be seen, but not allow yourself to be thanked*

199   **si es que** *si es que el alma (de José) no ha respondido a lo que os debió (i.e. what José's soul owed Asenet)*

200   **achacad lo...***lay the blame for my delay (in thanking you) on my misfortune and not on my ingratitude*

		dijisteis.²⁰¹ Ya lo juzgué
		y lo vi.
	ASENET	Pues pensad.
1515	JOSÉ	¿Qué?
	ASENET	Que alguna ilusión sería,

dijisteis.²⁰¹ Ya lo juzgué
y lo vi.

ASENET   Pues pensad.

1515   JOSÉ   ¿Qué?

ASENET   Que alguna ilusión sería,
y pues en sueños estáis
tan maestro° que os enseñan   masterful
a explicar lo que otros sueñan,

1520   explicaos lo que soñáis.²⁰²

JOSÉ   Aun no me desconfiáis
con todo aquese baldón.

ASENET   ¿Cómo?

JOSÉ   Como la razón
publica° en mis desempeños°   [publicar], tasks

1525   que aunque los sueños son sueños,
sueños hay que verdad son.²⁰³

ASENET   ¿Cómo puede ser verdad
que yo os hablase, ni viese,
ni que favor os hiciese,

1530   cuando es tal mi vanidad
que si la hermosa deidad
de la Castidad hubiera
de tomar forma, no fuera
posible que otra tomara

1535   que la mía, pues no hallara
quien más se la pareciera?
Ella y yo somos tan una
que nuestra gentilidad,°   pagan religion
si retrata° su deidad,°   portray, chastity

---

201   **juzgase que...***dijisteis que juzgase que la veía* José, still thinking he saw Asenet in the prison, refers to Castidad's words: "verás lo que juzgas" (732).

202   **explicaos...***explain yourself what you dreamed (or what you think you saw)*

203   This recalls the last lines in a powerful soliloquy in Calderón's *La vida es sueño*: "que toda la vida es sueño y los sueños sueños son" (2186-2187). As in the soliloquy from *La vida es sueño*, José's declaration about dreaming comes in the final lines of a *décima*. Ángel Valbuena Prat, in his edition of *Sueños hay que verdad son*, calls attention to these and other inversions of the ideas about dreaming found in *La vida es sueño* (Calderón, *Obras completas* 1209).

1540	es de mí espejo en la luna.[204]	
	Apenas veréis alguna	
	estatua suya° que no	[de la Castidad]
	se me parezca, y si vio	
	de paso la fantasía	
1545	vuestra alguna, ella sería,	
	porque no pude ser yo.	

JOSÉ   No sólo desengañado
      (para no ser atrevido)
      quedo, pero agradecido.

ASENET   ¿De qué?

JOSÉ   De que mi cuidado
1550   se tiene más bien hallado
      después que sé que ilusión
      fue, que si en mi religión
      por virtud la Castidad
      adoro, la paridad°   *similarity*
1555   disculpa° la adoración.   *excuses*

ASENET   No disculpa, que el desdén°   *disdain*
      mío hará... (*Ap.*) Mas no hará tal,
      que no me parece mal
      el que `le parezca° bien.   [yo le parezca]
1560   (*A José*) ...que escarmentados° estén   *taught a lesson*
      todos, en el que primero°   *first suitor*
      se atreva.°   *dare*

JOSÉ   Aun bien, que no espero
      serlo yo.

ASENET   ¿Por qué?

JOSÉ   Porque
1565   nunca yo me atreveré,
      señora, a decir que os quiero
      porque, como la voz mía,
      ya ilusión, ya estatua sea
      la que dio cuerpo a la idea
1570   de mi ciega° fantasía,   *blind*
      a decir tendría osadía°   *audacity*

---

204   **espejo en...** As the moon reflects the rays of the sun (acting as a mirror), Asenet is the reflection or the image of chastity.

                que desde aquel punto fue
                desde el que yo os adoré.
ASENET Pues...
JOSÉ   Suspended° el castigo,   desist
1575   que yo, en decir lo que digo,
              digo lo que no diré.
ASENET Ya en no decirlo incluyó
              por lo menos el saberlo.
JOSÉ Si quisisteis entenderlo
1580   vos, ¿qué culpa tengo yo?
ASENET ¿Eso no es decirlo?
JOSÉ   No.
ASENET ¿Pues qué? El `darlo a entender° es.   imply
JOSÉ ¿Daisme licencia?²⁰⁵
ASENET   Sí.
JOSÉ   Pues
              oíd atenta. Nadie ignora...
              ¡Pero el Rey...!

Sale el Rey.

1585 ASENET   (*A José*) Callad ahora,
              mas decídmelo después.
REY ¿Asenet? ¿José? ¡Oh, cuánto²⁰⁶
              de ver a los dos `me huelgo!°   I am glad
              Que sois los dos mi mayor
1590   cuidado, de quien deseo
              desempeñarme.²⁰⁷
ASENET   A tus pies
              humilde...
JOSÉ   A tus plantas puesto...
ASENET ...siempre a tu obediencia estoy.
JOSÉ ...y yo a tu servicio atento.

---

205 **¿Daisme...***Do you give me permission (to declare my love plainly?)*

206 After the stately *décimas* used in verses 1477-1586, the king makes his entrance speaking in a much more familiar style (all the characters will now speak to one another using *tú*), and shifting from *décimas* to *romance*.

207 **desempeñarme** *unburden my conscience*

1595	REY Tú, Asenet, habrás venido,	
	como otras veces, a efecto,	
	claro está, de que en ti premie	
	los servicios que confieso	
	deber a tu padre. (*A José*) Tú,	
1600	acreedor° de mis afectos	worthy
	también estás, por haberme	
	no solamente mi reino	
	restaurado pero el mundo	
	puedo decir, cuando veo	
1605	que a todo el mundo le alcanza	
	tu gran providencia, siendo	
	en tres idiomas tus nombres	
	José, Salvador y Aumento,[208]	
	con que viéndome obligado	
1610	a dos deudas,° no me atrevo	debts
	a resolver cuál será	
	de ambos el más digno premio.	
	Y así, para que no yerre°	[from errar]
	la elección,° consultar quiero	decision
1615	primero, José, contigo	
	el° de Asenet. Y luego	[el premio]
	contigo, hermosa Asenet,	
	el de José, pues con eso,	
	siendo vuestro el parecer,°	opinion
1620	vendrá a ser mío el acierto.°	wise decision
	(*a José*) Oye, pues, José. Yo estimo	
	tu persona `con extremo	
	tal,° que asegurar quisiera	to such a degree
	el que no como extranjero	
1625	`de paso° en Egipto vivas,	temporarily
	para esto es el mejor medio	
	tomar estado.° Asenet	get married
	es...	
	JOSÉ Sin decirlo, te beso	
	una y mil veces la mano	
1630	por tal honra, bien que temo,	

---

208 These previous explanations of José's name were in verses 164 and 1030-1031.

         si la merezco de ti,
         que de ella no la merezco.

REY Eso sabré yo. (*A Asenet*) Asenet,
         cuanto de José aprecio°   *appreciate*

1635   la persona, pues que todos
         lo saben, `fuerza es saberlo°   *you must know it*
         tú también, si en él te diere
         otro yo, pues yo no puedo
         darme a mí...

ASENET   Que no prosigas

1640   `te suplico,° pues es cierto   *I beg of you*
         que yo no tengo elección,
         que sólo obediencia tengo.

REY Pues ya que `uno y otro° sabe   *[José y Asenet]*
         la merced° que le prevengo,   *gift*

1645   particípela° uno a otro,   *confer*
         que yo, a dos deudas atento,
         ni puedo pagar con más
         ni puedo cumplir° con menos.   *do my duty*

                 Vase el Rey.

JOSÉ ¿Atreveréme° a saber   *do I dare*

1650   de ti, divino portento°   *wonder*
         —(*Ap.*) que hasta oírlo de tus labios,
         no me persuado a creerlo—
         lo que el Rey te dijo?

ASENET   Nada
         me dijo a mí.

JOSÉ   Según eso,

1655   a mí me lo dijo todo.

ASENET Pues dítelo tú a ti mesmo,
         sin que a mí me lo preguntes,
         que entre cariño y respecto,
         ni me está bien el decirlo

1660   ni me está bien el saberlo.

                Vase Asenet.

José Embarazóla el recato.[209]
      ¿Cuándo, oh infinito, oh inmenso
      Dios de Abrahán, Dios de Isaac,
      y Dios de Jacob, pudieron
1665 lograr tan altas fortunas
      tan cortos merecimientos?

Sale Copero.

Copero ¡Albricias,° señor!   joyful news
José   ¿De qué?
Copero De que, apresurando° el tiempo,   hurrying
        que vuela más cuando vuela
1670   con las alas del deseo,
        ya a tus umbrales° están   doorstep
        los diez hermanos hebreos.[210]
José   Diles que entren, y ve tú
        a hacer que traigan el preso.

Vase el Copero.

1675   Aquí del segundo amor,
        y no sé si del primero,
        que entre amor que todo es sangre
        y entre amor que todo es fuego,
        a fuego y sangre es forzoso
1680   lidiar con ambos afectos.

Salen los hermanos, Benjamín con ellos, y Bato, villano[211] rústico.

Todos   Danos, gran señor, tus plantas.
José   Alzad, levantad del suelo.
Rubén   Ya, señor, a Benjamín,

---

209 **Embarazóla...***Her modesty kept her from speaking*

210 José has eleven brothers, but Simeón is still José's hostage. The remaining ten—including Benjamín—now arrive.

211 **villano** *villager, person of humble origins*

1685		a pesar del sentimiento°	hurt
		y dolor de nuestro padre,	
		como mandaste, traemos	
		a tu presencia.	
	JUDAS	(*A Benjamín*) ¿Qué aguardas?	
		Llega a sus pies.	
	BENJAMÍN	Si merezco	
		besar tu mano, será	
1690		la dicha mayor que puedo	
		desear.	
	JOSÉ	Por las noticias	
		que tus hermanos me dieron	
		de ti, quise verte, seas	
		bien venido. (*Ap.*) (¿Cómo puedo	
1695		resistirme a no entrañarle	
		dentro del corazón?[212] Pero	
		aun me falta otra experiencia.°)	test
		(*A Benjamín*) ¡Cuánto de verte me huelgo!°	I am glad
		¿Cómo dejas a tu padre?[213]	
1700	BENJAMÍN	Con el sumo desconsuelo°	sorrow
		de quedar sin mí.	
	JOSÉ	¿Que tanto	
		te ama?	
	BENJAMÍN	Soy hijo postrero,°	youngest
		y quieren° mucho a los hijos	[los padres quieren]
		los que los consiguen viejos,[214]	
1705		y no sólo esto, ni el ser	
		hijo de Raquel me ha puesto	
		en tanto grado de amor,	
		bien que sin merecimiento,	
		sino que tuve otro hermano,	
1710		de ella también hijo, y siendo	
		así que faltó,° el amor	went missing
		que en dos partido° era medio,	divided, shared
		todo `se redujo a mí.°	fell to me

---

212 **entrañarle...***press him to my heart*

213 **¿Cómo dejas...***How was your father when you left him?*

214 **los que los...***the children born to their fathers in old age*

JOSÉ   ¿De qué murió esotro?

BENJAMÍN   Eso,

1715   te suplico no preguntes.

JOSÉ   ¿Por qué?

BENJAMÍN   Porque me enternezco

tanto que hablar no podré

si de mi José me acuerdo.°   remember

Baste° saber que murió,   it is enough

1720   sin que `refiera el suceso°   recount the event

tan trágico, (*Llora*) como a manos

de una fiera.

JOSÉ   (*Ap.*) (¿Cómo, cielos,

sus lágrimas y las mías

no están `a voces° diciendo   out loud

quién es y quién soy?)

1725   BENJAMÍN   En fin,

pues que no es del caso esto,

mi anciano padre, señor,

agradecido en extremo

a tu liberalidad,°   generosity

1730   conmigo te envía un pequeño

regalo, porque no da

más de sí estéril el tiempo:

unos recentales,° unos   lambs or calves

panales,° mantecas,° quesos,   honeycomb, butter

1735   pobre don° de pastor° pobre,   gift, shepherd

pero en `rendidos obsequios°   gifts offered up

más que lo que brilla° el oro   glitters

vale lo que ahúma el incienso.²¹⁵

Sale Copero y Simeón.

COPERO   Ya, señor, tienes aquí

1740   el que `en rehenes° quedó preso.   as a hostage

SIMEÓN   Todos los brazos me dad.

JUDAS   No dirás que no volvemos

---

215   **ahúma...***what is bathed in the smoke of incense* It is not the value of the gift, but the spirit of
devotion with which the gift is given that matters.

presto por ti, Simeón.
  SIMEÓN La fineza° os agradezco.   effort
1745 RUBÉN (*A Benjamín*) Pues te escucha con agrado,
          di que nos despache presto.
  BENJAMÍN (*A José*) Ya, señor, que ves cumplido°   completed
          tu mandato, y que el deseo
          de nuestro padre estará
1750   tan cuidadoso° hasta vernos,   worried
          te suplicamos nos vuelvas
          a dar licencia y sustento.²¹⁶
  RUBÉN Del trigo que mandes darnos
          traemos doblados los precios,²¹⁷
1755   porque allá tus cobradores,²¹⁸
          o por olvido o por yerro,
          en los costales° dejaron   bags of grain
          la cantidad del dinero
          del que llevamos entonces.
1760   JOSÉ Está bien, pero primero
          que os despache ni que os vais,²¹⁹
          en justo agradecimiento
          del regalo de Jacob,
          que comáis conmigo quiero.
1765   (*Al Copero*) Haz tú prevenir las mesas,
          y mira lo que te advierto:°   notify, alert
          sirvan siempre a Benjamín
          doblada porción. (*Ap.*) (En esto
          he de preferirle, hijo
1770   de la hermosa Raquel.) (*Al Copero*) Luego,
          al entregarles° el trigo,   deliver them
          vuelve a poner los dineros
          como antes, pero añade°   include, add
          la copa de oro en que bebo

---

216 **nos vuelvas...**_that you once again give us permission to leave and provide us with grain_

217 **traemos doblados...**_we're ready to pay twice the price_ The first time his brothers departed, José instructed the Copero to place their money in their bags of grain (1450). In essence, José charged them nothing. Rubén is willing to square the debt.

218 **cobradores** _those who were supposed to collect payment_

219 **primero que os...**_before we take care of that (settling accounts) and before you're on your way_

1775   al costal de Benjamín.
    COPERO   Verás que en todo obedezco.
              (*Ap.*) (¿Qué misterios estos son
              que yo ni alcanzo ni entiendo?) (*Vase*)
      JOSÉ   Entrad, pues, entrad conmigo,
1780   que éste es mi cuarto, en que quiero
              que a mi mesa os sentéis todos.
              ¿Qué `os detiene?°   stopping you
    TODOS   `Tu respeto.°   respect for you
    RUBÉN   Señor, humildes pastores
              ¿con tan alto, tan supremo
1785   gobernador, que es segunda
              persona del Rey excelso,°   magnificent
              sentarse a comer? Ved que es
              humanaros° mucho.   humble yourself
      JOSÉ   En eso
              de ser segunda persona,
1790   humanarme y dar sustento
              a todos los peregrinos°   pilgrims, wanderers
              que a mí vienen, quizá el cielo
              de otro pósito de pan
              anda rastreando° el misterio.[220]   hinting at

                 Vanse, y queda solo Bato.

1795   BATO Todo el tiempo que han habrado[221]

---

220   In this passage, José hints at a mystical significance to three otherwise unremarkable concepts. He is "segunda persona" or second-in-command to the king, but this is also an allusion to the
Trinity, the Christian idea that God exists in three persons: Father, Son, and Holy Spirit. Next, José
calls attention to the verb "humanar," which generally means to lower or humble. Here, however, it also
points toward Jesus as the Incarnation, or human person of the Trinity. Lastly, José speaks about giving
sustenance or food to all those who seek it, this alludes to the Eucharist, the Bread of Life that is Christ's
body. Whether or not these ideas are meaningful to you, the concision is marvelous: José describes the
divinity of Jesus (in the Trinity), the humanity of Jesus (in the Incarnation), and the abiding presence
of Jesus (in the Eucharist). See also Castidad's discussion of this mystery in 348.

221   **habrado** *hablado* Bato's speech is comically full of mispronunciations and rustic errors. In
particular, Bato mixes up r's and l's (so, "prato" is "plato"). McGaha's edition demonstrates that many
manuscripts exaggerated the comical and rustic aspects of Bato's speech. But the importance of this
passage should not be overlooked. Bato narrates what happens during the sumptuous feast offstage.

me he estado un pazguato° hecho,	rube, simpleton
la boca abierta. ¿Quién vio	
abrirla° para el silencio?	[la boca]
A que sirva en el camino	
1800 a Benjamín, mi amo° el viejo°	boss, [Jacob]
me envió, porque él° no cuide[222]	Benjamín, bother
de aparejarse° el jumento,°	saddle up, donkey
y ve aquí que de su padre	
toma a la letra el consejo,°	advice
1805 pues ni del jumento cuida	
ni de mí, que so° lo mesmo.°	[soy], donkey
`¿Tanto hiciera° de acordarse,	Would it kill him
ya que sentado le veo	
a tal mesa, de decir:	
1810 "lleven a aquel majadero°	dolt, fool
este prato?" ¡Cuántos amos	
se sientan a comer ellos,	
sin saber si los criados°	servants
comen, o no comen! Pero	
1815 yo le quiero disculpar,	
pues reclinado en el pecho[223]	
del Virrey, como muchacho	
se duerme, quizá suspenso	
de verse en tanta grandeza.	
1820 ¡Qué aparadores° tan bellos!	serving tables
¡Qué viandas!° ¡Qué bebidas!	foods, dishes
¡Qué lucidos escuderos,°	squires
y qué pajes° tan golosos![224]	pages, servants
Y deben de ser muy necios,°	stupid
1825 pues apenas° a un rincón°	scarcely, corner
hablan a un prato en secreto	
natural, cuando le dejan	
brumados° todos los huesos.	beat to a pulp

222 **porque él...**so that Benjamín doesn't have to bother

223 **reclinando en...**Audiences in 1670 would immediately have recognized this phrase as language used to describe the Last Supper, shortly before the crucifixion of Jesus. John, known as "the beloved disciple," spent part of the evening "leaning on Jesus' bosom" (John 13:23).

224 **golosos** *gluttonous (eating for pleasure rather than from need)*

Mas ya las mesas levantan,
y despedidos, es cierto
que hacia el pósito del trigo
irán. A él seguirlos quiero,
para ayudar a cargar°   load
los costales. Que no tengo
hartos° amos que servir,   more than enough
nadie lo dirá, supuesto
que estamos aquestas horas,
ellos hartos° y yo hambriento.°   full, starving
¡Ay, que es tan grande el palacio
que no sé si salgo o entro,
ni donde vengo ni voy!
Mas ¿cuándo yo voy ni vengo?
Hacia aquí el Gobernador°   [José]
viene.

Sale José.

JOSÉ   ¿Quién sois?
BATO   Si me acuerdo,
        lo diré.
JOSÉ   ¿Pues de quién sois
        os olvidáis?
BATO   No es muy nuevo,
        que muchos se han olvidado
        de quién son.
JOSÉ   ¿Cómo aquí dentro
        entrasteis?
BATO   (*Anda Bato*) Así.
JOSÉ   ¿Quién sois?
BATO   Soy, ahora que `caigo en ello,°   I think about it
        de Benjamín jomentizo.
JOSÉ   ¿Qué queréis decir en eso?
BATO   ¿Caballerizo no llaman
        el que acá en casa del dueño
        cuida los caballos?
JOSÉ   Sí.

	Bato	Luego será allá lo mesmo,
		pues será allá jomentizo
		quien cuida de los jomentos.[225]
	José	¿De Benjamín sois criado?
	Bato	Sí, señor.
1860	José	No sólo quiero
		enojarme ya con vos,
		sino antes favoreceros.°
		Tomad aqueste diamante.
	Bato	Y ¿para qué es, señor, bueno,
1865		metido en este latón
		este pedazo de espejo?[226]
	Copero	(*Dentro*) Todos habéis de pagar
		su culpa.
	Todos	(*Dentro*) Mirad primero...
	Benjamín	(*Dentro*) ¡Ay, infelice de mí!
	Todos	(*Dentro*) ...que, aunque pastores...

Salen el Copero y Todos, sacan como preso a Benjamín,
que traerá en la mano un cáliz dorado.

1870	José	¿Qué es eso?
	Copero	Es, señor, una osadía
		tan vil, un atrevimiento°
		tan bajo, como después
		de honrarlos con tanto exceso
1875		tú, y entregarles yo todo
		el trigo que me pidieron,
		llevarse hurtada° esta copa
		de oro, que es el cáliz° bello
		de tu más precioso vino,
1880		y habiéndole `echado menos,°
		los he seguido, y hallado
		en el costal más pequeño
		del menor hermano, a quien

show you favor

outrage

stolen

chalice

noted it missing

---

225   **jomentizo...** This is a long, if uncomplicated joke. Bato says that a "caballerizo" cares for horses, making Bato a "jomentizo" or someone who cares for "jumentos" (donkeys).

226   **metido en...** *this bit of mirror stuck in brass* Brass, is an alloy of copper and zinc.

1885	no se le he quitado, atento a que viéndole° en su mano, él diga su error.	[viendo el cáliz]

JOSÉ   Por cierto,
que habéis tenido muy poca
atención. Pues ¿mi festejo°   celebration
y mi agasajo?°   warm welcome

TODOS   ¡Señor!

JOSÉ Callad.

1890 BENJAMÍN   Que me oigas te ruego.

BATO ¡Miren el Benjaminito
la maña° que ha descubierto!   deviousness

BENJAMÍN Si el dinero que llevaron
mis hermanos te volvieron,
1895 sin saber ellos quién fuese
quien allí le hubiese puesto,
¿no es más fácil creer que a mí
me ha sucedido lo mesmo,
que no creer que hay aquí hurto,°   theft
1900 que es humano sacrilegio°   sacrilege
contra la sangre más noble?
Pues ya que no descendemos
de reyes, descenderán
reyes de nosotros.[227]

JOSÉ   ¡Menos
1905 arrogancia, rapaz!° ¿Cómo   delinquent
habláis así, cuando veo
tan claro vuestro delito?
Y aunque de uno y otro, es cierto
que todos cómplices° sois,   accomplices
1910 éste° castigar pretendo,   [Benjamín]
no más. La ley al que hurta
bienes de otro, en este reino
`dispone que° quede esclavo   provides that
el vil agresor del dueño°   rightful owner
1915 a quien los hurta. Y así,

---

227 **Pues ya no…**Benjamín refers to Genesis 35:11 in which God tells Jacob that his descendants will be kings.

bien podéis todos volveros,
porque Benjamín esclavo
mío ha de quedar.

BENJAMÍN   `No siento°   I'm not sorry

quedar tu esclavo, señor,

1920   que ese no es castigo, es premio.

La nota,° sí, y el dolor   notoriety

de un anciano padre viejo,

que por mí te representa

que nunca tuvo consuelo

1925   en la pérdida de un hijo,

desdichadamente° muerto.   unfortunately

Pues, ¿qué será la de otro,

muerto infamemente?° Habiendo   shamefully

de la desdicha a la culpa

1930   (cuando en mí la hubiera) extremos

tales como hay de morir

honrado a vivir sin serlo.

Duélete° de él, no de mí,   Take pity

que yo...

JOSÉ   ¡No más! Ea,[228] volveos°   [volved + os]

1935   vosotros sin él, pues él

mi esclavo queda.

TODOS   Primero°   before

que sin Benjamín volvamos

a vista, señor, de nuestro

venerable anciano padre,

`las vidas nos quita.°   take our lives

1940   RUBÉN   Y si eso

—que morir el desdichado

ya es dicha[229]—no merecemos,

mejor para esclavo yo,

de más servicio y provecho,°   benefit

1945   seré, truécale° por mí.   exchange him

MANASÉS Yo también por él me ofrezco.

SIMEÓN   ¡Vuélveme a mí a mis prisiones!

---

228 **Ea** An exclamation expressing resolve or determination. José has made up his mind.

229 **que morir...** *for the unfortunate, dying is good fortune (because their suffering ends)*

	JUDAS	¡Sellen° mi rostro tus hierros!²³⁰	brand

JUDAS ¡Sellen° mi rostro tus hierros!²³⁰ — brand

LEVÍ ¡Arrastre yo tus cadenas!

1950 ISACAR ¡Ponme a mí una argolla° al cuello! — shackle

NEFTALÍ ¡A mí el yugo° de tu carro! — yoke (for animals)

RUBÉN Que todos beber queremos...

GAD ...confesando que esto es
pena de un delito nuestro...

1955 RUBÉN ...nuestra muerte en este cáliz
que está de amargura° lleno... — bitterness

TODOS ...antes que sin Benjamín
volver.

JOSÉ ¿Qué aguardo, qué espero,
si confesando el delito

1960 con tan llorosos° extremos, — sorrowful
en mi cáliz de amarguras
bebe su arrepentimiento?° — repentance
Dame, Benjamín, los brazos,
que ya no cabe en el pecho

1965 roto el corazón. Rubén,
llega tú también a ellos.

RUBÉN Sin haberte dicho nunca,
¿mi nombre sabes?

JOSÉ No eso
te admire. Llega, tú, Judas,
Simeón, Leví, Gad...

1970 SIMEÓN, GAD,
JUDAS y LEVÍ ¿Qué es esto?

JOSÉ ...Isacar y Zabulón,
Manasés y Aser, abiertos° — [los brazos]
para todos están, ya
que arrepentidos° os veo. — repentant

1975 ¿Qué os admira, qué os espanta
en mí este conocimiento
si soy José, vuestro hermano?
No 'os turbe° verme en tal puesto, — upset you

---

230 **hierros** Slaves were marked with "hierros," which means they were branded on the face with a symbol indicating that they were slaves. In a kind of gruesome humor, they were branded with a visual pun: the letter "s" and the form of a nail (clavo). Together "s+clavo" visually symbolized "esclavo."

1980		que de culpas, ya una vez confesadas, no me acuerdo.
	Unos	¡De confusos...
	Otros	¡De turbados...
	Otros	¡De absortos...
	Otros	...y de suspensos,
	Todos	...no sabemos qué decirte!
	José	Ni yo sé qué responderos,°

Ni yo sé qué responderos,°   *answer you*

1985   y más cuando de estas sombras
al ver la luz me enternezco.

Bato   ¿Qué hago yo aquí, que no voy
con estas nuevas° al viejo?°   *news, [Jacob]*
¿Cuánto° ha que con sus años   *[Cuánto tiempo]*
1990   a cuestas[231] viene corriendo
a verle? Que un poco antes
o después, todo es del texto.[232]

Vase, y sale el Rey, Asenet y Músicos.

Rey   ¿Qué es esto, José, pues cuando
yo mismo a tu cuarto vengo
1995   con Asenet, a lograr
tu mayor merecimiento,
llorando estás?

José   Sí, señor,
que ˋtal vez° llora el contento.[233]   *sometimes*
Los que ves son mis hermanos,
2000   y no solamente el verlos
me arrebató° el corazón,   *enraptured*
sino el pensar que anda entre ellos
y entre mí un misterio.

Rey   ¿Cómo?

José   Como estar ˋcerrado el cielo,[234]

---

231   **con sus años...***with many years at his back (i.e. elderly)*

232   Bato hints that we are about to experience big changes in the way that time behaves; the temporal frames of the play that delineate what is past and future dissolve.

233   **el contento** *one who is happy*

234   **cerrado...***the sky closed up (in other words, it stopped raining)*

2005	necesitada° la tierra,	in need

2005   necesitada° la tierra,   in need
        venir ansiosos pidiendo
        pan mis hermanos, y hallarle
        del pósito que he dispuesto°   got ready
        encerrado en la custodia,[235]
2010   sentarse a mi mesa, y luego
        ver el cáliz de ella° en manos   [la mesa]
        del que se durmió en mi pecho,
        que es el menor de los doce,[236]
        ser él en su sentimiento
2015   el áspid° de su delito,   snake
        llorarle a voces, diciendo
        que es pena de su pecado:
        visos son, sombras y lejos[237]
        del prometido Mesías°   Messiah
2020   que a nuestros padres y abuelos
        en vino y pan han previsto
        el más alto sacramento.
REY   ¿Qué sacramento haber puede
        en el pan y el vino?

Descúbrese un monte, y en él al Sueño en un carro triunfal.

SUEÑO   Eso
2025   dirán mis ideas.[238] Yo,
        que desde este monte excelso,[239]
        adonde la Castidad

---

235   **custodia** One meaning of "custodia" that José implies here is a granary or silo for storing grain. The other meaning of "custodia" is an object made of gold in which the Eucharistic bread would be displayed (called a monstrance in English). The monstrance containing the Eucharist was often the most lavish part of Corpus Christi processions.

236   José is reframing the meaning of the meal he shared with his brothers in terms that again recall the Last Supper. You may want to look back at Bato's description of the feast in verses 1795-1843. The Last Supper is when Jesus explains to the disciples the meaning of the bread and wine of Communion, making it the Biblical source for most Eucharistic theology.

237   **visos son...***as if seen in a painting* Compare this to verse 330 above.

238   **ideas** Often an idea is a picture in the mind; the word frequently implies mental visualization (as opposed to "concept" or "notion").

239   The "Monte de la Visión," see 1162.

me dejó, por irse al pecho
de Asenet, estoy mirando,
no solo qué quiere el cielo
que a quien venció un torpe° amor,   sinful
corone un amor honesto,
pero en cuatro sueños míos,
las señas deste misterio.

REY ¿En cuatro sueños?

SUEÑO   Sí.

REY   ¿Cuáles
son esos cuatro?

SUEÑO   El primero,
el de Jacob, cuando llegue
a ver a José, diciendo:

Salen Jacob y Bato.

JACOB Dame, mi José, los brazos.
¿Es posible que te veo
vivo, al fin de tantos días
como te he llorado muerto?

JOSÉ Habla al Rey y a Asenet, antes
que a mí.[240]

JACOB   Perdone el respecto,
señor, que no estoy en mí,°   I'm distraught
que me parece que sueño,
como cuando vi una escala[241]
en que los cielos abiertos
se abrazaban con la tierra,
explicando ángeles bellos
al hombre cuándo subían,
cuándo bajaban, al Verbo.[242]

---

240 This was the protocol and custom of the court. It was proper to speak first to the king, before addressing any other people present.

241 This is another reference to the dream of Jacob's Ladder in Genesis 28. In other words, Sueño is showing us a dream in which characters talk about other dreams.

242 **al Verbo** *to The Word* An allusion to the opening of the Gospel of John: "In the beginning was the Word, and the Word was with God, and the Word was God."

SUEÑO   Ese el primer sueño es
de los cuatro, a quien siguieron
2055   después del Verbo Encarnado,[243]
el segundo y el tercero,
que al propósito de hoy
son los del pan y el sarmiento°   grapevine
en quien muerte y vida da,
2060   se explicarán, repitiendo:

*Aparecen las dos primeras Sombras, de gala, en el
carro del abanico,[244] elevadas en el aire.*

SOMBRA 1   El pan, a quien devoraron
las aves, para que el reo°   the convict
coma en él su juicio...
SOMBRA 2   El vino,
que exprimió racimo bello
para dar la vida...
2065 SOMBRA 1   ...ya
es pan que baja del cielo,
como se mira en aquel
sacrificio que incruento°   bloodless
es divina carne.
SOMBRA 2   ...ya
2070   es la sangre del cordero,
sacrificado en el ara°   altar
de la cruz, de cuyo pecho
se recogió° el cáliz.   was collected
ASENET   ¿Quién
asegura todo eso?

---

243 **Verbo Encarnado** *the Word made flesh* A reference to John 1:14 ("And the Word was made flesh, and dwelt among us").

244 **carro del abanico** In the staging for 1670, this was the cart all the way to the audience's right (McGaha, "Introducción" 58).

Descúbrese en un carro un altar, con sacrificio de panes, y al decir los versos de arriba, da vuelta el escotillón,²⁴⁵ y se ve una Forma²⁴⁶ grande, y en otro carro, un sacrificio de vino, y dando vuelta, se descubre un cáliz, y la Fe elevada entre las dos Sombras.

2075	FE	Yo lo aseguro, que soy
		la Fe, que interior lo veo,
		teniendo por el oído²⁴⁷
		cautivo el entendimiento.
	REY	Y el cuarto sueño que falta,
		¿cuál es?

2075   FE   Yo lo aseguro, que soy
       la Fe, que interior lo veo,
       teniendo por el oído²⁴⁷
       cautivo el entendimiento.
   REY   Y el cuarto sueño que falta,
       ¿cuál es?

2080   SUEÑO   Es tu mismo sueño,
       pues a la grande abundancia
       en cuyo siglo primero
       gozó° la naturaleza   *experienced*
       descanso,° paz y sosiego,°   *ease, calm*
2085   sucedió° (por sus pecados)   *it happened that*
       la esterilidad del tiempo,
       y pudo la Providencia
       reparar sus daños, siendo
       la Iglesia la troj° del pan   *storehouse*
2090   que en general alimento°   *nourishment*
       de los hermanos de Cristo,
       hizo la gracia herederos,°   *heirs*
       explicada en Asenet,
       que es de Castidad ejemplo.
   REY   ¿Cuándo aqueso ha de ser?
2095   SUEÑO   Cuando
       descendiendo de uno de esos
       doce linajes o tribus,²⁴⁸

---

245   **escotillón** *trapdoor*

246   This "Forma" is essentially a prop representing the Eucharist. What, exactly, it means to theatrically represent a sacrament—or to reenact the rituals of religious devotion in a dramatic setting—is a question that has never been fully answered by theologians. One of the questions you might ask is, "What is the power of this play?"

247   **por el oído** *through the sense of hearing* What one sees with one's own eyes is not a question of faith, but of knowledge. Faith is what one believes without seeing, only hearing.

248   **doce linajes...** *the twelve tribes of Israel (of which José and his brothers are the twelve founders)*

             hombre y Dios en alma y cuerpo,
             y en cuerpo y alma se dé
2100   en tan alto sacramento.

REY A tanto prodigio yo,
con ser gentil,° me convierto.   *gentile*

JOSÉ Eso es la gentilidad
ser de la viña heredero.[249]

2105 ASENET Yo, a tanto pasmo vencida,°   *overcome*
ofrezco ser tuya.

JOSÉ   Eso
es, con cada virtud Cristo
celebrar su casamiento.[250]

UNOS Todos a tan grande asombro...

2110 OTROS Todos a tan gran portento,
por convencidos nos damos.

SUEÑO Pues sea, todos diciendo:

MÚSICOS *Albricias, mortal, albricias,*
que aunque los sueños son sueños,
2115 *sueños hay que verdad son.*

TODOS Perdonad sus muchos yerros.

Tocan chirimías, y cerrándose los carros se da fin al auto.

---

249 José explains the allegorical significance of the conversion of Asenet from "gentilidad"—roughly paganism, but more properly any non-Judeo-Christian religion—to José's religion. She symbolizes pagans receiving Christianity.

250 Now José explains the significance of his wedding to Asenet: the marriage of José and Asenet is an allegory of the marriage of Christ and the virtues.

Spanish-English Glossary

THIS LIST CONTAINS WORDS that are glossed in the margins of the plays or explained in footnotes, as well as other words you may not know. At times, Calderón uses words in ways that are rare or unusual. He also loves the flexibility of language and often exploits all of the possible definitions of a word. We have defined the words as Calderón used them. That means that these definitions do not always correspond perfectly to modern usage.

a fuer de by means of
a sus solas by themselves
abatido low
abismo abyss
aborrecer to hate
aborrecimiento hatred, loathing
aborto monstrous or extraordinary birth
abrazar embrace
ábrego hot south wind
abreviar shorten, abbreviate
abrigo shelter, protection
absorto dumfounded, astonished
acabado finished
acaecimiento occurrence, event
acarrear to lead to, give way to
acaso chance, accident, luck
acechar to stalk, search, seek out
acecho ambush
acento voice
acero steel

acertar to hit (the mark), manage to
achacar to lay the blame
acierto wise decision
aclamación applause
aclamar to proclaim, hail
acobardar to intimidate, make fearful
acordarse to remember
acosado besieged, pursued, harassed
acrecentar to intensify
acreedor (n.) creditor, (adj.) worthy
acudir to come to the rescue, show up, to heed
adelantar to advance, forward, to announce or give advance notice
adivinar to guess
admiración amazement, wonder
adorno adornment

adulterio adultery

adusto bleak

adverso unfortunate

advertir to see, perceive, to notify, warn

advocación request, entreaty

afable affable, friendly

afán eagerness

afecto affection, emotion request

afilado sharpened

afirmar to be certain, affirm

afligir to upset, agitate, to afflict, torment

agasajo honor, regard, warm welcome

agora ahora

agradar to please

agradecer to thank

agradecido grateful, thankful

agrado pleasantness, pleasure

agraviar to cause harm

agravio insult, harm

aguardar to wait

agudo sharp

agüero omen, prophecy

aguja needle

aherrojado in irons, chains

ahumar to apply smoke to, to bathe in smoke

airado angry

airoso graceful

ajeno (adj.) alien, not pertaining to

ala wing

alabanza praise

alarido shouting, screams

alba dawn

albedrío will

albergar to shelter

albergue lodging

albor perfect whiteness, first light of day

alborozo rejoicing exultation

albricias an exclamation of joy, **dar albricias** give glad tidings

alcanzar to reach, grasp

alcázar fortress, palace

aldea village

aldeano villager

alentar to embolden, encourage

aleve treacherous

alhaja finery

aliento breath, exhalation, fume

alimentar to nourish, feed

alimento nourishment, sustenance

alistar to prepare

aliviar to alleviate, ease

alivio comfort, relief

aljaba quiver

alma soul

alojar to give shelter, house

alterar to disturb, rile

altivo haughty

alzar arise

amable endearing, congenial, amiable

amago threat, sign, hint

amargura bitterness

amasar to knead

ámbar fragrant liqueur

ámbito circumference

amedrentar to terrify, frighten

amenazar to threaten

amenidad pleasantness

ameno pleasant

amo person in charge, boss, master

amotinar to stir up

amparar to aid, help, protect

amparo (n.) protection, succor, defense

ampo snowflake, whiteness

añadir to include, add

anciano (n.) elderly person, (adj.) elderly

angustia anguish, torment

anhelar to long for

anillo ring

animoso eager, game, brave

ansia anxiety, craving

anticipar to anticipate, get a jump on, to outdo, exceed

antojo craving

apacible gentle, peaceful, serene

apagar to turn off, snuff out

aparador serving table, buffet

aparato device, apparatus (figuratively, earthly world), spectacle

aparatoso spectacular, marvelous

aparecer to appear

aparejar to saddle or care for an animal

aparición appearance

aparte aside (words spoken by a character that others cannot hear)

apenas scarcely

aplauso praise, applause

aprecio esteem, value

apreciar to value, appreciate

aprehender to grasp, to understand

aprehensión perception, the object of perception (i.e. what is seen, understood, or grasped)

apresurar to rush

apuntar to point, aim

apurar to insist, press, rush

aquilatado assayed, appraised

ara altar

arbitrio decision

árbitro mediator, arbiter

arco bow (e.g. bow and arrow)

arder to burn

ardor fiery passion, burning

argolla metal ring, shackle

argüir to indicate, to show, to argue

árido arid

arista stubble, spines

armada navy, ships

armonía harmony

armonioso harmonious

arpón arrow

arraigado ingrained, rooted

arrancar to tear out, pull up

arrastrar to drag, to grovel, to hold sway over, to pry

arrebatar to seize, take, to work up

arrepentimiento repentance

arrepentir to repent, regret

arrimo comfort

arrodillarse to kneel

arrojar to throw, cast down

arroyo stream, streambed

ascendencia lineage, ancestry

asegurar to assure, secure

asentar to suit, to settle

asir to grab

asistir to accompany, attend

asombrar to amaze

asombro astonishment, amazement

aspecto appearance
aspereza harshness
áspid snake, viper
astro star
astucia cunning
asumpto (asunto) matter, issue, subject
asustar to startle, scare
atabalillo small kettle drum
atajar to deter
atalaya lookout, watchtower
atar to tie
atender to concentrate, focus, to pay attention
atento attentive, mindful
átomo atom, smallest part
atraillar to leash, chain
atravesar to cross
atrever to dare to
atrevido daring, bold
atrevimiento insolence, daring
aumento increase
aunar to unite
auras breezes
aurora dawn
auxiliar assistant, **auxiliares** reinforcements
avaro miserly
avasallar to obey, submit to, to overwhelm
ave bird
avenenado poisoned
avenirse to move closer, come together
aventurar to risk, hazard
averiguar to learn, find out
avisar to warn
aviso warning, notice
azucena lily

bala bullet
balanza scale, balance
baldón insult, affront, reproach
balsa pond
bandido (adj.) banded together
barbero barber, surgeon
barreno bore, auger, drill
barrio neighborhood
basilisco basilisk (a lizard-like or dragon-like monster that can kill with a glance)
bastar to be enough
basto rough
batallón first blow of the battle, opening salvo
beldad beauty
Belén Bethlehem
belleza beauty
bendito blessed
beneficio benefit
blandir to brandish, wield
blando gentle, soft
blasón honor, acclaim
blasonar to flatter
bofetón stage machinery that turns or spins
boreal northern
boscaje grove
bosquejo outline
bostezar to yawn, gape open
breña scrubland, rough country
brevemente briefly
brillar to glitter, shine
brío spirit, verve
brioso spirited
bronce bronze
brumar to bruise, beat to a pulp
bruto brutish, uncivilized, gross
bullicio boiling, bustle

burlar to joke or prank

caballerizo one who cares for horses, stable boy

cabello hair

caber to fit

cadena chain

caducar to pass away, expire

caduco expired, dead

caja drum, box (often used for sweets)

calabozo dungeon, prison

calarse to enter, tear into

cáliz chalice

camarada companion

campaña campaign

can dog

canas gray hairs

canastillo basket

cancel screen

candado lock

cantidad quantity

canto song

capaz capable, informed (obsolete)

capitana flagship, lead ship

capitular to capitulate, give in

cárcel jail

cargar to charge, to load

cargo position, responsibility

caricia deep regard, caress

cariño affection, tenderness

carro cart

carta de favor letter of recommendation

castidad chastity

castigar punish

castigo punishment

caterva pack, bunch

caudal resources, flow, (figuratively, understanding)

caudillo leader

cautivar to capture, to become a prisoner

cautivo captive, prisoner

caza hunt

cebar to lure, bait

cebarse to vent

cegar blind

celos jealousy

cenador bower, enclosure

cendal cloth, veil

ceñir to gird

ceño anger menace, threat, scowl, frown

cercano near, impending, close

cercar to surround

ceremonioso ceremoniously, ostentatiously

cerrar to attack, close in upon

cerro hill, mountain

cerviz neck

cesar to cease, stop

césar emperor, Caesar

chirimía musical instrument similar to a clarinet

chiste joke

choza hut

ciegamente blindly

ciego blind

cielo sky, heaven, paradise

ciencia knowledge

ciervo deer

cierzo freezing north wind

cifra figure, number, code

cifrar combine, distill, encode

cima peak, top

cizaña weed (figuratively, dissention)

clarín bugle, horn

clavel red carnation
clima clime, region
cobarde coward
cobrado recovered
cobrar to recover, to charge
cocodrilo crocodile
codiciar to covet
codicioso greedy
col cabbage
colegir to deduce, infer
cólera rage, anger
colmillo fang
combatir to fight
compadecerse to feel sorry for
compadecido moved to pity
compás rhythm, beat
compasivo compassionate
complacer to delight, please
cómplice accomplice, guilty party
comprometerse to commit oneself
conciliar to agree to
concordar to agree, harmonize, match
condena conviction, sentence (of punishment)
condenado condemned
conforme in agreement
confrontar to cause to get along (obsolete), to confront
conjuro invocation, spell, conjuring
conmovido moved to pity
conseguir to get, obtain, achieve
consejo advice, command
conservar to preserve, store, put up
consonancia resonance
consolarse to find consolation

consuelo comfort, consolation
contar to recount, tell
contrario adversary
convecino (adj.) neighboring
convencido convicted, guilty
conveniencia agreement, coming together, tool or useful thing
convenir to agree
copa treetop, cup
copero cupbearer
copia abundance
cordura good sense, sanity
coronar to crown
coro choir
corriente current
corteza bark
corto lacking, limited
costa cost, coast
costal sack
coto designated or protected area, preserve, limit, boundary
crecer to grow
crédito belief, credit, credibility
crepúsculo twilight
crespo curly, curl
criado servant
crianza upbringing
criar raise
cría lamb or calf
crujir to creak
cuadra room
cuartel post, station
cuchilla blade
cuerda string, cord
cuerdamente wisely
cuerdo clever, savvy, sensible
cuesta slope, hillside
cuestión quarrel, fight

cuidado preoccupation, care
cuidadoso worried
culpado guilty
culpar to blame
cumbre peak, summit
cumplido completed
cumplimiento fulfillment
cumplir to do or fulfill one's duty, to comply
cuna cradle
custodia granary (for storing grain), monstrance (for displaying the Eucharist)
daño harm
danza dance
dar a entender to imply
dar a luz to give birth
dar el reloj to strike the hour (as when a clock strikes)
decoro decorum
dehesa pasture
deidad deity, god
delatar to reveal, betray
delirio delirium
delito misdeed, crime, sin
dentro offstage
denuedo boldness, courage
depender to depend on
deponer to compose, control feelings
derrotado disastrous
desabrigo exposure, lack of shelter
desagradecido ungrateful
desagrado displeasure
desagraviar to undo harm
desagravio restitution
desairado slighted, snubbed
desaire insult, snub
desaliñar to disorder, dishevel

desamarrar to untie
desamparar to abandon, forsake
desatinado foolhardy, idiotic
desatraillar to unleash
desbocado (adj.) runaway, out of control
desbocarse to bolt, run wild
descanso ease
descariño disregard
descendencia offspring
desconfianza distrust
desconfiar to mistrust, distrust
desconsuelo sorrow
desdén disdain, scorn
desdeñar to spurn, despise
desdicha misfortune, misery
desdichadamente unfortunately
desdichado unfortunate, wretched
desechar to waste
desecho waste
desembarcación disembarking
desemejado unlikely, incongruous
desempeñar to carry out, to perform (a task), to play (a role)
desempeñarse to unburden one's conscience
desempeño task
desengaño disillusion
desgracia bad luck, misfortune
deshacer to destroy, undo, to forget, get over
deshecha, hacer la deshecha to deceive
deshecho ruined, undone, destroyed
desierto desert
designios plans, designs

desigual uncertain, vague, erratic

desmandado disobedient

desmayar faint

desmentir to refute, to deny

desmenuzado crumbling

desmerecer to be unworthy, not to merit

desnudo bare, undressed

despachar to settle accounts

despavorido petrified

despedazar to tear to pieces

despedido fired, dismissed (**despedirse** to say goodbye)

despego antipathy, detachment

desperdiciar to waste

desperdicio refusal, slight, waste, loss

despertado awake

desplomado collapsed

despojo plunder

despreciar to scorn, despise

desprecio contempt

desprevenido unsuspecting

destemplado intemperate, rash

desterrar to exile, banish

destroncar to cut down, kill

destruir to destroy

desvanecer to fade, disperse, disappear, to make vain

desvanecido proud, haughty, faded

desvanecimiento fading, vanishing

desvelado tireless

desventura misfortune, misadventure

desviar to send away, divert

desvío turn, diversion

detener to detain, stop

devaneo disorientation, delirium

devorado devoured

diadema diadem, crown

dicha (n.) happiness, good fortune, **por dicha** by chance

dichoso happy, blessed, fortunate

diestro (adj.) right-hand

difunto departed, deceased

diligencia effort, diligence

discreto intelligent

disculpa defense, excuse

disculpar to forgive, pardon

discurrir to speak, to pass through, to ponder

discursivo aloud, in words

diseño design

disfraz disguise

disgustar to upset

disimular to put on an act, to disguise, to cover up

disponer to arrange, to provide

dispuesto willing

divertimiento distraction

divertir to distract

doblar to double, turn, fold, to bend, bow down, **doblar la rodilla** kneel

dolerse to take pity

dominio domain, control

don gift

dorado golden

dorar to gild, cover in gold

duelo duel, sorrow

dueño master, owner

dulce sweet

dulzura sweetness

Ea exclamation expressing resolve or determination

echar to throw, **echar (de) menos** to miss, **echarse a dormir** to take a nap

edad age

edificio building

eje axis

ejecutar to execute carry out

ejemplar (n.) model to be imitated

ejercitar to practice, exercise

elección choice, decision

elegir to choose

embajador ambassador

embarazar to present an obstacle to, impede, burden

embate onslaught

embestidura charge

embestir to attack, lunge

emboscar to ambush, to conceal, hide

embozado hidden, cloaked

embozo disguise, cloak

embustero fraud

empañar to sully

empeñar to insist

empeño effort, labor, commitment

empinado steep

empozado thrown in a well or hole

empresa undertaking, business

enajenar to overwhelm (esp. to overwhelm the senses)

encallar to come ashore, run aground

encaminado directed, channeled

encanto enchantment

encarecer to cause one to value or to care

encargar to commission, entrust

encarnado incarnate

encomendar to entrust

encubierto shrouded, hidden

encubrir to cover up

engañar to deceive

engaño trick, deception, deceit

engendrar to beget, engender

enlazarse to link, be connected with

enmendar to fix, amend, improve

enmudecer to silence

enojar to anger

enojo anger

ensangrentar to bloody

ensayo rehearsal

entendimiento understanding

enternecer to move to pity or compassion

entender to understand, to manage

entrambos both

entregar to give, present with

entretejido interwoven

entupecido clogged, choked

enviar to send

envidia envy

envolver to wrap, to envelope

envuelto wrapped up

equívoco (adj.) uncertain, equivocal

erario storehouse

errar to err, to make a mistake

escala ladder

escama fish scale

escarcha frost

escarmentado taught a lesson

esclavo slave

escoria slag, garbage

escotillón trapdoor

escrúpulo qualm, doubt, uneasiness

escrupuloso uncertain

escuadrón platoon, division

escudero squire

escudo shield, protection

escuro (oscuro) dark

esfera sphere

esgrimir to wield (a sword)

esmaltar to enamel

esmalte (n.) enamel, glaze

esmeralda emerald

esmerar to go to trouble, to dedicate effort to

espacio moment, period of time, space

espada sword

espantar to cause fear

espanto fright

esparcido spread, sprinkled

especie species, kind, image

espejo mirror

espeluzar to make one's hair stand on end

espeso thick

espesura dense woods

espiga ear or stalk of grain

espina thorn

esqueleto skeleton

esquivo unpredictable, elusive

estado country, state

estancia room, stay

estatua statue

esterilidad scarcity, sterility

estimación respect

estimar esteem

estío summer

estirpe lineage

estorbar to obstruct, hinder

estrago havoc, destruction

estrañeza (extrañeza) surprise, strangeness

estrecho close, narrow, tight

estremecer to shudder

estremecido shaken

estrépito crash

estribillo chorus (of a poem or song)

estruendo loud noise, roaring

eterno eternal

exceder to exceed

excelso magnificent, sublime, high

excusar to forego

experiencia test, experience

explorador spy

expósito abandoned, **hijo expósito** foundling, abandoned child

exprimir to crush, squeeze

éxtasis ecstasy

extraño (n.) foreigner

fábrica building, structure

facilidad gullibility

facineroso criminal

falda skirt

faltar to go missing, disappear

familiar family member, demon (familiar spirit)

fantasía imagination

fantástico unreal, imaginary

faraón pharaoh

farsa play, dramatic spectacle, farce

fatiga labor, toil

fatigado weary

fausto incredible luxury, pomp

faz face

fe faith, religion, good faith, willingness

fecundo fertile, fecund
felice (feliz) happy
felicidad happiness
feliz happy, fortunate
fértil fertile, abundant
festejo celebration
festivo festive
feudatario feudal, owing tribute to a lord
feudo respect, tribute
fiar to trust, depend, **fiarse** to entrust
fiel faithful
fiera (n.) wild beast
fiereza fierceness
fiero fierce, wild (feral)
filo sharp edge
fin goal, object
fineza action undertaken on the behalf of another
fingir to pretend, feign
fino tending toward perfection
flaco skinny
flaqueza weakness
flecha arrow
floreado finest, **pan floreado** the finest or whitest bread
florido lush, green, flowery
follaje foliage
forja (n.) forge
forzoso unwilling, inevitable, necessary
fracaso failure
franco open, unbarred
franquear to go through, to clear
fraude fraud
frenesí frenzy, delirium
freno reins, bridle
fuente fountain, platter

fuga disappearance, escape, flight, leak
fugitivo fleeting
fundamento basis, cause
fundar to deduce, surmise, to base, to found upon
funesto baleful, sad, ill-fated
furor fury, furor
galán (adj.) handsome, (n.) hero
galardón prize, award
galas finery
ganado livestock
garra claw, paw
gemido groan
gemir to moan, to groan
genio temperament
gentil pagan, gentile
gentilidad pagan or non-Christian religion
girasol sunflower
gitano Egyptian
glosa elaboration, gloss
golfo gulf
goloso gluttonous
golpe blow
gozar to enjoy
gozo joy, pleasure
gracia grace, **en gracia** in a state of grace
grandeza greatness
granizo hail
grano grain (as in grain of sand), part, drop
grieta crack
grito shout
gruta cavern, grotto
guarnecer to adorn
guiar to guide
guija pebble

hacer caso to heed, mind

hacer salva pay tribute to, honor, salute

hacienda wealth

hado fate, destiny

halago pleasure, delight, praise, compliment

halagüeño flattering

hallar to find, find out, discover

hambriento starving, hungry

harto enough, plenty, full

haz (haces) sheaf (of grain), face

hebreo Hebrew

hechizo magic spell

hecho action

helado frosted, frozen

Heliópoli Heliopolis (the city of the sun), north of Cairo

heredar to inherit

heredero heir

hereditario hereditary

herencia inheritance

herido wounded

hibierno winter

hidrópico thirsty, greedy (figuratively)

hiena hyena

hierba herb, plant, grass

hierro iron, chain

hijo natural child born out of wedlock, bastard

hinchado swollen, full

holgarse to be glad or pleased

homicida murderer

homicidio murder

honestar to honor

honesto innocent, pure

hormiga ant

hospedaje lodging, stay

huella track, footprint

huésped guest, **huésped de aposento** member of the king's household

huestes hosts (in the sense of armies)

huir to escape, flee

humanar to humble, to lower

hurtar to steal

hurto theft

idólatra idolatrous, pagan

idolatrar to worship, idolize

ignorado unheard of, novel

ignorar to be unaware or ignorant of

imán lodestone, magnet

impedir to impede, prevent

impío wicked, not pious

impura stained, impure

inadvertido unnoticed

incauto lacking prudence, unsuspecting

incendio fire

incienso incense

inconstante fickle

incruento bloodless

inculto wild, uncultivated

incurrir to take up (a subject)

indeciso uncertain, undecided

indiciado suspected

indicio charge, suspicion, sign, evidence

industria cleverness, craftiness

inescrutable indecipherable, impenetrable

infamar to defame

infamemente shamefully

infamia disgrace, infamy

infausto ill-fated, infamous

infelice de mí Woe is me!

inferir to infer

infiel unfaithful

informe (adj.) without form

infuso inspired (especially of knowledge that comes from inspiration, not study)

ingenio wit, inventiveness, acuity, wise man

ingrato ungrateful, thankless

injuria assault, affront, injury

inmoble unmoved

inobediente disobedient

inquieto restless, unsettled

instar to prompt

interceder to intercede, intervene on someone's behalf

interpolación interpolation, insertion, expansion

intrincado dense, intricate

inútil useless

invicto unbeaten

invocar summon, invoke

ira wrath, anger

irritar to enflame

ismaelita an Arab (literally, the descendants of Ishmael)

jaral thicket

jarcia rigging (of a ship)

jardín garden

jeroglífico symbol, hieroglyph, emblem

joven (adj.) young, (n.) a youth

joya jewel

juicio judgment

jumento donkey

jurar to swear an oath, pledge

juzgar to think, reason (in the sense of "judge for yourself")

laberinto maze

labrador farmer, peasant

lacayo servant in livery, footman

ladrar to bark

ladrón thief

lama silt

lamento wail

lámina sheet or plate, foil

lance dispute, incident, situation, chance

latido heartbeat, beat

latinas velas lateen (triangular) sails

latir to beat (esp. the heart)

latón brass

laurel sign of honor or victory, figuratively, a crown, crowning glory

lauro victory

lazo bond, tie, tether

leal loyal

lealtad loyalty

lecho bed

Legal Cordero Lamb of God (Christ)

légamo muck, slime

lejano distant

leño log, figuratively, a ship

letargo lethargy, stupor

letra lyrics

leva call to arms

Levante the eastern Mediterranean

leve light, insubstantial

ley law

liberal generous

liberalidad generosity

libertad freedom

libranza order of payment, draft

librar to liberate or free
librea livery, servant's uniform
licencia permission, license
licor juice, liquor
lid battle, fight
lidiar to fight or do battle
liga a metal (such as copper or silver) that is alloyed with gold
ligereza lightness, speed
ligero light
limosna alms, charity
linaje lineage
lirio iris (flower)
lisonjear to flatter
lisonjero pleasing, flattering
llano plain, plateau
llanto cry, wail
lloroso sorrowful
loable praiseworthy laudable
lóbrego gloomy, dark
lograr to achieve, win, obtain
loor praise
lozanía freshness
lozano vigorous, fresh
lucero beam or ray of light
lucido splendid
luego therefore
lumbre light
lunado horned
lustre luster, trappings
lustro five-year period
macilento gaunt, haggard
madrugar to get up early, to be sleepless
maestro (adj.) masterful, capable
mágico sorcerer
mago sorcerer
majadero dolt, fool

majestad majesty
maleza underbrush, undergrowth
malicia malice, wrongdoing, injustice
malograr to spoil
malogro failure
malquistar to take a dislike to
maltratar to mistreat, abuse
maña deviousness
manantial spring
manchar stain or spot, **manchado** spotted
mando (n.) command
manjar food, delicacy
mañoso crafty, tricky
mansión dwelling
manteca butter
maraña tangle
marañado entwined, tangled
margen riverside, edge
martingalas incredible clothes
mayor higher, greater
mayorazgo inherited estate, legacy
mayormente even more so
medio (n.) way, means, medium
medroso fearful
mendigo beggar
menester, ser menester to be necessary
mentecato fool
mentir to lie
mentira lie
menudo tiny
merced gift, mercy
merecer to merit, deserve
merecimiento worthiness, deservingness
mesías messiah
miedo fear

migaja crumb
milagro miracle
mísero lowly
modo measure, means
montaraz (n.) mountain man, (adj.) of the mountains
montería hunt
montero hunter, guide
mordaza gag or bit, such as a horse wears in its mouth
mostrar to show
motivo motive, reason
mudanza change, transformation
mudar to change, alter
mudarse to remain silent
mudo silent
muralla wall
mustia withered
nadar to swim
nado (adv. "**a nado**") swimming
navío ship
necesitado in need, needy
neciamente foolishly
necio fool, idiot
negar to deny
nevar to snow
niebla fog
Nilo Nile River
nocivo harmful
Norte North Star (Polaris), guide
nota notoriety, infamy
novedad novelty
nube cloud
nudoso knotty
nueva (n.) news
obedecer to obey
objeción objection

obscura difficult to make out or see
obscuridad darkness, obscurity
obsequio deference, respect, gift
obstar to block
ocasión opportunity
ocultar to hide
oculto hidden
ofuscar to blur
ojeo hunt, search
ola wave
opaco opaque
opimo abundant
opósito defenses, battlements
oprimir to oppress
orilla shore
osadía audacity
osado audacious, bold, daring
osar to dare
ova kelp
pacer to graze
pacto pact, agreement
padecer to suffer
paja straw
paje page (a servant)
pálido pale
palma palm tree
pámpano small bunch
panadero baker
panal honeycomb
paño cloth, **al paño** at the edge of the stage
papel dramatic role
parabién (n.) congratulations
parasismo attack, fit
parecer (n.) opinion, viewpoint
parias tribute, money paid in tribute

paridad similarity, likeness
parlero talkative
partido divided, shared
partir to divvy up, divide
parto birth
paseo promenade, walk
pasmo astonishment, shock
paso gait, step, mountain pass, stage or period
pastel cake
pasto feed, pasture
pastor shepherd
patente the meal or drink that a new arrival buys for the old timers, usually in a work or school setting
patrimonio inheritance
pautado marked
pavor terror, dread
pavoroso dreadful
paz peace
pazguato rube, simpleton
pecado sin
pecar to sin
pecho chest
pedazo piece
peinar to comb
pena pain, suffering, sorrow
penar to suffer
peña mountain, rock
pender to hang, dangle
penosamente sadly
penoso grave, serious
pepino cucumber
pérdida loss
perecer to pass away, die, perish
peregrinar to wander, make a pilgrimage
peregrino pilgrim, wanderer

pereza laziness
perezoso lazy
pernicioso destructive, evil
perturbar to disturb, disquiet
pesadez heaviness, inertia
pesar (n.) sadness, regret, bad news
pesaroso disappointed
pésimo dreadful
peso weight
pez fish
piadoso devout, merciful, pious
piedad mercy, piety, goodness, **piedades** self-righteous talk
piel skin, hide (of an animal)
pino pine
placer pleasure
plantas the soles of one's feet
plática talk
plazo term
pluma feather
poblado (n.) settlement, (adj.) inhabited
poblar to fill, populate
polvo dust
pólvora gunpowder
pompas splendor
poner en sospecha to place under suspicion
ponzoña venom
porfiar to persevere
porqué reason why
portento wonder, sign, portent
posada inn
pósito a public institution responsible for the storage and distribution of grain

postrarse to prostrate oneself, throw oneself at the feet of another

postrero last, ultimate, final

póstumo posthumous

pozo well (for water), pit

prado meadow

prato a comical mispronunciation of **plato**: plate

precepto commandment, maxim, rule

preciso necessary

predecir to foretell, prophesy, predict

premio reward, prize

prenda garment, token, offspring, child, **quedar en prendas** to hold as a deposit

prender to capture, arrest, seize

presa prey, theft

presagio omen, prophecy

preso prisoner

prestar to lend

presteza speediness

presto soon, quickly, speedy

presumir to assume, to presume, to boast

presunción presumption, something taken for granted

pretender to intend, aspire to, to request

pretensión attempt, claim

pretexto stipulation, pretext, ploy

prevenir to prepare, to prevent, to warn, to speak

priesa (prisa) hurry

primicia first fruit, novelty

principalmente above all

privilegio exclusion

procurar to endeavor, try, seek

prodigio marvel, wonder, prodigy

prolijo garrulous, wordy

prólogo prologue

promisión a promise to do something stipulated, **Tierra de Promisión** Promised Land

propensión tendency

proseguir to continue

provecho benefit

providencia preparation for the future or readiness to provide

próvido diligent

prueba evidence

publicar to make public, announce

puesto post, job

puñal dagger

puntal support that holds up a building that is falling down

punto point (of land)

pureza purity

purgar to atone, purge

quebrado broken

quebrantado disrupted

quebranto distress

queja complaint

quejarse to complain, denounce

querella grievance

quiebra chasm

quietar to quiet, calm

quietud calm, stillness, tranquility

quilate carat (of gold)

quilla keel (of a ship)

quinta residence, palace

rabia rage

racimo bunch of grapes

ráfaga blast, gust

raíz root

rama branch

rancho a place where people congregate to eat or make camp

rapaz delinquent, boy

rapto rapture

rasgo feature

rastrear to figure out, to track, to hint at, outline, trace

rastro trace, sign, trail

raudal torrent

razón reason, judgment, explanation, **razón de estado** a political philosophy that emphasizes pragmatism, **última razón** last resort

real royal

rebozado cloaked

recatado out of sight, avoiding attention

recato modesty, reserve

recelo distrust, suspicion, misgiving

recental lamb or calf

recluta growth, burgeoning

recoger to collect, harvest

recostarse to lean, lie back, lie down

recrear to delight

redentor savior, redeemer

reducido convinced

reducir to subject or reduce to, **reducirse** to be changed or restored to

referir to recount

regalo happiness, comfort

regar to irrigate, water

registrar to survey, check

registro search

regocijo joy, rejoicing

rehén hostage

rehusar to refuse

reinar to rule, govern, reign

reino kingdom

relámpago lightning

remanso pool of water

remedio remedy

remitir to refer

remo oar

rencor resentment, hatred, rancor

rendido crushed, brought low

rendimiento yielding, submission

rendir to surrender, submit, to pay or render payment

reñir to fight, quarrel

reo convict

reparado rested

reparar to observe, examine, to repair

reparo aid, remedy, assistance

repartir to distribute

representar to speak (as opposed to sing)

reprimir to control (another), repress

repugnancia disgust, repugnance

resaca undertow, surf

resguardarse to protect oneself

resguardo guarantee, deposit, protection, shelter

resolución resolve

resolver to decide or resolve to, **resolverse** resign oneself

resplandor light, brilliance

responder to answer

resquicio crack, chink

restado audacious

restaurar to restore

restituir to restore to, return

retenerse to retain, hold, or stop

retirarse to retire, move away from

retiro (n.) seclusion, secluded place, retirement

retórico (adv.) eloquently

retratar to create a portrait of, portray

retrato portrait

retroceder to go backward

revelar to reveal

reventar to burst

revestirse figuratively, to clothe or arm oneself (e.g. to arm oneself with courage or clothe oneself in righteousness), to gather oneself

revolver to stir, mix, scramble

ribazo slope, hillside

ribera shore

riesgo risk, danger

rigor harshness, severity

rincón corner

risa laughter

risco chasm, cliff

rizo curl, curly

robo robbery

rocío dew

rogar to beg, plead

rosicler rosy color of dawn

rostro face

rubí ruby

rudeza primitiveness, roughness

rudo rough

ruego plea (from **rogar**)

ruin vile

ruina destruction, ruin

ruiseñor nightingale

rústico rustic, primitive

saber (n.) knowledge

sabio wisely

sabroso tasty

sabueso hound

sacerdote priest

sacerdotisa priestess

sacrilegio sacrilege

sacro sacred

sacudir to shake

Sagrados Textos Holy Scriptures

salobre salty, brackish

salto jump, leap

salva condition, promise, salute

salvador savior

salvaje savage, wild

saña rage

sanear to restore, heal, to clean

sangre blood

sangrientamente bloodily

sangriento bloody

sano healthy

sañudamente wrathfully

sañudo furious

sarao party, soiree

sarmiento grapevine

satisfacer to keep a promise, to repay the debt

seguimiento pursuit

seguir to pursue, follow

seguro assurance

sellar to mark, brand, to seal

selva forest

semblante face, appearance

seña feature, trait, sign, hint

señal signal, sign

señalar to point, to indicate

senda path

seno bosom, declivity, hidden place

sentencia sentence, judgment

sentido sense (as in, the five senses)

sentimiento feeling, hurt, sadness

sentina sewer, bilge

sentir to notice

sepulcro grave

sepultar to entomb

sepultura tomb

sequedad dryness

séquito entourage, retinue

ser fácil to be likely

ser fuerza to be necessary

servidumbre bondage, servitude

severo harsh, severe

sien temple (of the forehead)

siervo slave

siglo age, epoch

simulacro figure, statue, idol

síncopa abridgment, abbreviation, shortening

siniestro left-hand

sinrazón injustice

sirena siren (a mythical creature that lures sailors to their doom with beautiful songs)

siríaca the Aramaic language, spoken in the Middle East

sitiar to besiege

soberano sovereign, supreme

soberbia arrogance

soberbio arrogant

sobrado exceeding, tremendous

sobrenatural supernatural

sobresaltar to startle

sobrescrito address on a letter

sobrevenir to overcome

sobrino nephew

socorrer to help, succor, rescue

socorro help, relief

soldado soldier

soler to tend to

solfa solfège, musical notes (do re mi *fa sol*)

solicitar to seek out

soltar to release, let go, drop

sombra shadow

son sound

soñador dreamer

sonoro sonorous, musical

sordo deaf

sosiego calm

sospechoso suspicious, suspect

suavidad gentleness, softness, smoothness

suavizar to soften

suceder to happen, come to pass, to follow

sucesión heir, successor

suceso (n.) event, happening, occasion

suelo (n.) ground

sueño dream, sleep

suerte luck, chance, fortune, **de suerte de** such that

sufrimiento suffering

sufrir to bear, suffer, to experience

sujeto (adj.) bound, (n.) individual, person

sumo utmost

sumptuoso (suntuoso) sumptuous, luxurious

superior upper, higher

suplicar to beg, beseech, plead

suplir to make up for

surco furrow, groove

suspender to refrain, desist
suspender to stop, halt
suspenso (adj.) awestruck, dumbstruck, silent
suspiro sigh
sustento nourishment
susto fright, scare
tablado stage
tafetán taffeta
talar (v.) to scythe or mow down (adj.) covering the entire body (of a garment)
talle appearance, figure
tardanza lateness
tardar to be slow, delay
tardo slow, tardy
temblar to tremble
temblor shiver, trembling
temer to fear
temerario bold, brash
temeroso fearful
temor fear
templado calmed, warm
templanza serenity
templar la cuerda to moderate, to tune (an instrument)
templo temple
tener la gana to feel like it
tenerse to stop, halt
término limit, border, period of time, term
terneza tenderness
ternura tenderness
terremoto earthquake
terrón lump of earth, clod
tesoro storehouse, treasure
testa head
testigo witness

tierno tender, young, inexperienced
timón helm, rudder
tinieblas darkness
tinto stained
tiranía tyranny
tirano (n.) tyrant, (adj.) tyrannical
tiro gunshot, shot
tomar estado to get married
toque sound, touch
torcer to turn, twist, turn back
torpe clumsy, awkward, lascivious, sinful
trabar to do battle, to begin the battle
tráfago traffic, coming and going
traición treachery, betrayal
traidor (n.) traitor, (adj.) traitorous, treacherous
traidoramente treacherously, falsely
traje suit
trance critical moment
tratable docile
tratarse to deal with
trato dealings, treatment
trazar to design, trace
tremolado (n.) waving (as on a flag)
triaca antidote
tribu tribe
tributo tribute
trigo wheat
Trinacria Sicily
trinado warbling of birds
tripa gut
triunfante triumphant
trocar to switch, exchange, swap
trofeo trophy

troj storehouse
tronco tree trunk
tropas troops
tropel group, mob, droves
tropezar to encounter, stumble across, to stumble
trozo piece
trueno thunder
tulipán tulip
tumba tomb
túnica tunic, coat
tunicela tunic, coat
turbado confused, embarrassed, shaken, upset
turbar to stir up, cause unrest, **turbarse** to get upset
turbio dark, cloudy
ufano proud
ultrajar to offend, outrage
umbral threshold, doorway
umbroso shadowy
uña nail, claw
undoso wavy, undulating
vago blurry, vague, confused
valer to be worth
vanidad vanity
varonil manly
vasallaje servitude
vasallo subject, vassal
vase (**se va**) actor exits the stage
vecino (adj.) nearby
vehementemente vehemently, fervently
vela sail
velo veil, disguise
veloz fast
vencedor victor, winner

vencer to overcome, conquer, figuratively, to convince or overcome objections
veneno poison
venerar to venerate, respect
venganza vengeance, revenge
vengar to avenge
vengativo vindictive
venidero future
venta sale
ventaja advantage, upper hand
ventajoso advantageous, clear, obvious
ventor hound
ventura fortune
venturoso fortunate, happy
verdor (n.) greenness
vestido (n.) clothing
vestidura garment
vestuario backstage area, dressing room
vianda food
víbora viper
vicio vice
vid vine
vidrio glass
viento wind
vil low, base, vile
villano villager
virrey viceroy (second-in-command to the king)
virtud virtue
viso sparkle, sheen, reason to suspect, **a dos visos** from two perspectives, **a viso de** within sight
volar to fly
voluntad will, desire

volver la espalda to turn one's back
volver por to defend, assist
voz word
vulgo common people
Vusted (vuestra merced) "your honor"

yacer to lie flat, recline
yermo wasteland
yerro error, mistake
yerto rigid, stiff
yugo yoke (to harness animals)
zagal young shepherd, youth

9 781589 771192